OXFORD EARLY CHRISTIAN STUDIES

THE OXFORD EARLY CHRISTIAN STUDIES series includes scholarly volumes on the thought and history of the early Christian centuries. Covering a wide range of Greek, Latin, and Oriental sources, the books are of interest to theologians, ancient historians, and specialists in the classical and Jewish worlds.

Titles in the series include:

Origen and the Life of the Stars
A History of an Idea
A. Scott (1991)

Regnum Caelorum
Patterns of Future Hope in Early Christianity
Charles E. Hill (1992)

Pelagius' Commentary on St Paul's Epistle to the Romans
Translated with introduction and commentary by
T. S. de Bruyn (1993)

Arator on the Acts of the Apostles
A Baptismal Commentary
Richard Hillier (1993)

Eunomius and the Later Arians
R. P. Vaggione (*forthcoming*)

The Christology of Theodoret of Cyrus
P. B. Clayton (*forthcoming*)

Arnobius of Sicca
Concepts of Deity in the Contemporary
Pagan–Christian Debate
M. B. Simmons (*forthcoming*)

The Desert Fathers on Monastic Community

GRAHAM GOULD

CLARENDON PRESS · OXFORD
1993

Oxford University Press, Walton Street, Oxford OX2 6DP
Oxford New York Toronto
Delhi Bombay Calcutta Madras Karachi
Kuala Lumpur Singapore Hong Kong Tokyo
Nairobi Dar es Salaam Cape Town
Melbourne Auckland Madrid
and associated companies in
Berlin Ibadan

Oxford is a trade mark of Oxford University Press

Published in the United States
by Oxford University Press Inc., New York

British Library Cataloguing in Publication Data
Data available

Library of Congress Cataloging in Publication Data
The desert fathers on monastic community/ Graham Gould.
(Oxford early Christian studies)
Revision of thesis (doctoral)—Cambridge University.
Includes bibliographical references.
1. Monastic and religious life—History—Early church, ca. 30–600. 2. Apophthegmata Patrum. 3. Egypt—Religion—Greco Roman period, 332 B.C.–640 A.D. I. Title. II. Series.
BX2465.G68 1993 271'.00932'09015—dc20 92—32203
ISBN 0–19–826345–7

Typeset by Selwood Systems, Midsomer Norton
Printed in Great Britain
on acid-free paper by
Bookcraft (Bath) Ltd.,
Midsomer Norton

PREFACE

This book is the outcome of an attempt to understand certain aspects of the teaching on the ideals and practice of the monastic life of the *Apophthegmata Patrum*, a collection of sayings, dialogues, and short narratives which preserve the words of the fourth- and fifth-century Egyptian monks known as the Desert Fathers. The widely acknowledged importance of the *Apophthegmata* as a source of our knowledge of early Christian monasticism, and as a document of considerable interest in the history of Christian spirituality, is a sufficient justification for a study of the teaching of this text. Analysis will be confined, of necessity, to the outlook of the *Apophthegmata* only on a comparatively limited range of subjects. But those which have been chosen are of central importance to the monastic life as the Desert Fathers understood it, and in some respects they dominate and inform the character of the *Apophthegmata* as a whole.

The general theme to be explored is that of monastic community, or, to use a phrase which may be applied to several of the concerns of this work, 'personal relationships' as a factor in the monastic life. This may seem an unusual theme to choose for the study of a group, the Desert Fathers, who are most often regarded as prime representatives of the desire for solitude, rather than as proponents of the value of a life of community. There are of course many discussions of the purpose of solitude in the *Apophthegmata*; but one of the things which I hope will emerge in this work is that even these sayings rarely treat solitude as an end in itself, or as a way of life which can be adopted by an individual for purely personal reasons; they are almost always more than tinged with awareness of the context of the individual in community. To show that this is the case requires a rather indirect approach beginning with some different questions. How important are relationships to the Desert Fathers? What factors disrupt the proper conduct of relationships within the community, and how are they to be overcome? What are the responsibilities of both teachers and disciples in ensuring the effectiveness of *their* relationship? The discovery of the Desert Fathers' answers to these questions occupies the earlier chapters of this work. The final two chapters address questions more directly concerned with the nature of the Desert Fathers' life considered in its totality, both in its ideals and its practical realization. Is the monastic life essentially one of solitude or of interaction, of personal goals or of openness towards others, or is it possible to combine these apparently conflicting views? How does a monk's relationship with his neighbour affect his relationship with God and his life of prayer?

Chapters 5 and 6 therefore provide the main argument of this work, supported by the prior analysis of Chapters 2 to 4. In answering the central question of 'solitude *versus* interaction', stress will be laid upon the fact that the semi-anchoritic pattern of life of the monastic communities of Nitria and Scetis was a highly flexible one. Allowing monks to live alone or with others, and to meet often, occasionally, or rarely, it demanded no *particular* life-style of any individual. There was a scope for choice and for the recognition of different goals. The *Apophthegmata*, which are the product of many different minds and reflect many different individual circumstances, are a monument to this degree of choice and flexibility; but along with the varied viewpoints which they undoubtedly contain, a general consensus on the importance of relationships does indeed emerge.

I have already alluded to my belief that this remarkable text does contain the words of the Desert Fathers themselves; although it is a late fifth-century compilation, it is not a reflection of the idealizations or the assumptions of a later generation about the past. In Chapter 1 I have attempted to justify these statements by showing that authentic recollections of fourth-century figures could have been preserved in a much later text; but this chapter is by no means a complete study of the critical problems associated with the *Apophthegmata*.

Only a commentary on the *Apophthegmata* could claim to do complete justice to the teaching of the Desert Fathers. In this work, many subjects—for instance asceticism itself, demonology, prayer, and sexuality—have been treated only briefly and in so far as they shed light on the theme of community or (in Ch. 2) on the way in which the practice of the monastic life was taught. Similarly, some of the terms used by the Desert Fathers in the identification of the goals of the monastic life, terms such as labour, stillness (*ἡσυχία*), rest (*ἀνάπαυσις*), and activity or way of life (*πολιτεία*) have been defined and analysed in a somewhat *ad hoc* way in so far as they are relevant to the main theme. This is not meant to imply that a study of these terms in their own right would not be of considerable value. None of them has a precisely fixed meaning in the *Apophthegmata* (we should not expect them to do so, given the nature of the text), but they await future work on understanding the *Apophthegmata* themselves and on their similarities to and differences from other spiritual writings.

I have tried to give an ordered and yet objective account of the teaching of the Desert Fathers; some order must be imposed on the riot of information and insight supplied by the *Apophthegmata*. But my aim throughout has been to allow the text to speak for itself and for the pattern of Christian spirituality for which it stands, without imposing on this pattern other, inappropriate ideas of spirituality drawn from different times and places. If this has meant that in detail the work is almost purely descriptive in approach, then overall at least I have tried to give it the character of an argument for the position on the nature of the Desert Fathers' concerns which I have taken up.

From my perspective, the most important problem with this work is probably the somewhat tenuous relationship which exists between it and other studies of early monasticism as a social and theological phenomenon. It would have been a much larger task to look at similar issues in the much-studied Pachomian monastic movement of upper Egypt or in contemporary or later monasticism in Syria, Palestine, or the West. For similarly realistic reasons, this work does not include a study of the complex question of the origins of monasticism in Egyptian Christianity, or an account of the history of the communities which produced the *Apophthegmata*. Again, this does not mean that I think these subjects are unimportant. Questions of monastic origins, of the social and economic significance of Egyptian monasticism, and of the relationship between the monastic movement and the Church as a whole, have been the subject of a great deal of recent work which has greatly enhanced our understanding of the monastic movement. But studies of the life and thought of the monastic communities themselves have been less common, and it is this approach to the phenomenon of monasticism which, rightly or wrongly, now seems to deserve some attention.

I am indebted, like all scholars, to the ever-expanding number of my teachers and students in Cambridge, Oxford, and London, to all of whom this work is gratefully dedicated. But in particular I would like to thank Dr Caroline Bammel, whose lectures and supervisions first introduced me to the study of the Church Fathers in general and the Desert Fathers in particular, and the Rt. Revd Dr Rowan Williams, now bishop of Monmouth, who supervised the Cambridge doctoral thesis on which this work is based with outstanding patience and perceptiveness.

G.G.

King's College London
February 1992

CONTENTS

ABBREVIATIONS

TEXTS

For details of editions, see the Bibliography.

Ch	The Coptic collection of *Apophthegmata Patrum*
Eth. Coll.	The Ethiopic collection of *Apophthegmata Patrum*
Evergetinos	*Εὐεργετινὸς ἤτοι συναγωγὴ τῶν θεοφθόγγων ῥημάτων καὶ διδασκαλιῶν τῶν θεοφόρων καὶ ἁγίων πατέρων* (4 vols.; Athens, 1957–66)
G1	The *First Greek Life* of Pachomius
GSC	The Greek systematic collection of *Apophthegmata Patrum*
HL	Palladius, *Historia Lausiaca*
HM	*Historia Monachorum in Aegypto*
N	The Greek anonymous series of *Apophthegmata Patrum*
Pa	Paschasius's Latin collection of *Apophthegmata Patrum*
PJ	Pelagius and John. The Latin systematic collection of *Apophthegmata Patrum*
S	Supplement: indicates a saying of the alphabetical collection not included in the text in PG, lxv, but edited by J.-C. Guy
VA	Athanasius, *Vita Antonii*

SERIES, JOURNALS, AND INDIVIDUAL WORKS

CSCO	Corpus Scriptorum Christianorum Orientalium
CSS	Cistercian Studies Series
ECR	*Eastern Churches Review*
JAC	*Jahrbuch für Antike und Christentum*
JTS n.s.	*Journal of Theological Studies*, new series
OCA	Orientalia Christiana Analecta
OCP	*Orientalia Christiana Periodica*
PG	Patrologia Graeca, ed. J.-P. Migne
PGL	*A Patristic Greek Lexicon*, ed. G. W. H. Lampe
PL	Patrologia Latina, ed. J.-P. Migne
RAM	*Revue d'ascétique et de mystique*
SCH	Studies in Church History
SP	*Studia Patristica*
TU	Texte und Untersuchungen zur Geschichte der altchristlichen Literatur

I

Introduction: The Community and the Text

1. Introduction

The phenomenon of asceticism as an expression of Christian spirituality is a much older one than the monastic movement of which asceticism is one necessary element.[1] But it is only in the fourth century AD that we begin to see the emergence into clear light of relatively organized and well-defined ascetic or monastic communities in upper and lower Egypt. In the Thebaid in upper Egypt, Pachomius (*c.*292–346) was responsible for founding a community which grew into the first organized monastic order in Christian history, and which was no doubt able to absorb into its ranks many practitioners of an older form of ascetic life including perhaps some who held heterodox or even gnostic views.[2] In lower Egypt there were many centres of the monastic life. Antony the Great (*c.*252–356), the founder of desert monasticism according to the historical tradition started by his biographer, was active on the east bank of the Nile where he established and visited communities.[3] Later sources, the *Lausiac History* of Palladius, and the *History of the Monks in Egypt*,

[1] R. Murray, 'The Features of the Earliest Christian Asceticism', in P. N. Brooks (ed.), *Christian Spirituality: Essays in Honour of Gordon Rupp* (London, 1975), 65–77; J. C. O'Neill. 'The Origins of Monasticism', in R. Williams (ed.), *The Making of Orthodoxy: Essays in Honour of Henry Chadwick* (Cambridge, 1989), 270–87; and A. Hamman, 'Les Origines du monachisme chrétien au cours des deux premiers siècles', in C. Mayer (ed.), *Homo Spiritalis: Festgabe für Luc Verheijen, OSA zu seinem 70. Geburtstag* (Würzburg, 1987), 311–26.

[2] P. Rousseau, *Pachomius: The Making of a Community in Fourth-Century Egypt* (Los Angeles, 1985) is the fullest study. For the possible presence of heterodox elements in monasticism, see F. Wisse, 'Gnosticism and Early Monasticism in Egypt', in B. Aland (ed.), *Gnosis: Festschrift für Hans Jonas* (Göttingen, 1978), 431–40; and J. E. Goehring, 'New Frontiers in Pachomian Studies', in B. A. Pearson and J. E. Goehring (eds.), *The Roots of Egyptian Christianity* (Philadelphia, 1986), 236–57; in G. E. Gould, 'Early Egyptian Monasticism and the Church', in J. Loades (ed.), *Monastic Studies: The Continuity of Tradition* (Bangor, 1990), 1–10, I have criticized extreme forms of this view.

[3] Athanasius, *Life of Antony* (hereafter *VA*), PG xxvi. 835–976, chs. 14–15, 54–5. See F. van der Meer and C. Mohrmann, *Atlas of the Early Christian World* (London, 1958), map 17, for the most complete available map of the Egyptian monastic centres.

witness to the development of monasticism in Nitria after the foundation of this centre by Amoun, probably in the 330s.[4] Nitria was about fifty kilometres south-east of Alexandria in the diocese of Hermopolis Parva or Damanhur.[5] Further away from the cultivated land to the south-west was the desert of Scetis, the home of many of the Desert Fathers referred to in the *Apophthegmata Patrum*. This text contains an account, cast remarkably in the form of a narrative in the first person, of the foundation of Scetis by Macarius of Egypt, again around the year 330.[6] Between Nitria and Scetis was a third community, Kellia (the cells), some of whose archaeological remains have been excavated and provide an indication (besides that which can be gained from the literary sources) of the physical context of the Desert Fathers' lives.[7]

The monastic movement has been variously regarded by scholars. Church historians have often seen it as a movement of protest against the gradual creation of a state Church in the fourth century following the conversion of Constantine, or as a biblically motivated call for a return to the values of primitive Christianity and to the era of the martyrs.[8] E. R. Dodds, on the other hand, treated monasticism as one element in a pattern of intellectual and religious history which was

[4] Palladius, *Lausiac History* (hereafter *HL*), ed. E. C. Butler, *The Lausiac History of Palladius* (Texts and Studies, 6: 1–2; Cambridge, 1898, 1904), chs 7–8; *History of the Monks in Egypt* (hereafter *HM*), ed. A.-J. Festugière, *Historia Monachorum in Aegypto* (Subsidia Hagiographica, 34; Brussels, 1961), ch. 20.

[5] F. Daumas and A. Guillaumont, *Kellia I: Kom 219: Fouilles exécutées en 1964 et 1965* (Cairo, 1969), p. vii.

[6] *Apophthegmata Patrum*, alphabetical collection, PG lxv. 72–440, Macarius 1.

[7] For the archaeological evidence, see Daumas and Guillaumont, *Kellia I;* also C. C. Walters, *Monastic Archaeology in Egypt* (Warminster, 1974). For the history of Nitria, Scetis, and Kellia, see D. J. Chitty, *The Desert a City: An Introduction to the Study of Egyptian and Palestinian Monasticism under the Christian Empire* (Oxford, 1966), 1–81; H. G. Evelyn-White, *The History of the Monasteries of Nitria and Scetis*, vol. ii of *The Monasteries of the Wadi'n Natrun* (Metropolitan Museum of Art Egyptian Expedition Publications, 7; New York, 1932); J.-C. Guy, 'Le Centre monastique de Scete dans la littérature du Ve siècle' *OCP* 30 (1974), 129–47; and A. Guillaumont, 'Histoire des moines aux Kellia', *Orientalia Lovanensia Periodica*, 8 (1977), 187–203.

[8] See e.g. S. G. Hall, 'The Sects under Constantine', in W. J. Sheils and D. Wood (eds.), *Voluntary Religion* (SCH 23; Oxford, 1986), 4; and W. H. C. Frend, 'Town and Countryside in Early Christianity', in D. Baker (ed.), *The Church in Town and Countryside* (SCH 16; Oxford, 1979), 27–8. Frend does not however believe that early monasticism advocated social revolution against the empire: see 'Early Christianity and Society: A Jewish Legacy in the Pre-Constantinian Era', *Harvard Theological Review*, 76 (1983), 68–9; and 'The Monks and the Survival of the East Roman Empire in the Fifth Century', *Past and Present*, no. 54 (1972) 3–24, esp. 10–12. The most detailed study of the associations in Christian thought between martyrdom and asceticism is E. E. Malone, *The Monk and the Martyr* (Studies in Christian Antiquity, 12; Washington, DC, 1950).

common to Christians and pagans, and saw it as part of an ascetic reaction to an 'age of anxiety'.[9] A sociological, rather than ecclesiastical or Dodds's psychological, approach to monasticism has been persuasively and influentially advocated by Peter Brown, who argues that monasticism offered a Christian response to the deep-seated religious and social needs of late-antique Syria and Egypt.[10] Brown's view is both more sophisticated and more convincing than older theories, which saw the growth of Egyptian monasticism as a resurgence of Coptic nationalism or as a simple response to the economic hardship of the fourth century, and has been developed in a number of directions by more recent work.[11]

These interpretations of early Egyptian monasticism need not be seen as mutually exclusive, and in any case it is not necessary to decide between them in this context, for they do not preclude or undervalue attempts to assess the teaching of the Desert Fathers on the monastic life as a subject of interest in its own right, quite apart from the light it may shed on the social and religious context of the monastic movement. The ancient sources already mentioned illuminate not only the historical and sociological context of early monasticism but also the ideals of the monks and their realization. Other early monastic writers share this concern, notably Evagrius of Pontus and John Cassian, who drew on their experiences of the monastic life of the desert to produce reflective or systematic works on the monastic life which use the stories and

[9] E. R. Dodds, *Pagan and Christian in an Age of Anxiety: Some Aspects of Religious Experience from Marcus Aurelius to Constantine* (Cambridge, 1965), 31–6. See the comments of P. Brown, *Religion and Society in the Age of Saint Augustine* (London, 1972), 74–80.

[10] P. Brown, 'The Rise and Function of the Holy Man in Late Antiquity', *Journal of Roman Studies*, 61 (1971), 80–101, reprinted in *Society and the Holy in Late Antiquity* (London, 1982), 103–52; and *The Making of Late Antiquity* (Cambridge, Mass., 1978), 81–101. The former of these works deals mainly with Syria, the latter with Egypt.

[11] For the older view, see H. I. Bell, *Egypt from Alexander the Great to the Arab Conquest* (Oxford, 1948), 108–14; and W. H. MacKean *Christian Monasticism in Egypt to the Close of the Fourth Century* (London, 1920), 14–66; and for a critique of traditional views of monastic origins, see the introduction to *Theodoret of Cyrrhus: A History of the Monks of Syria*, trans. R. M. Price (CSS 88; Kalamazoo, Mich., 1985), pp. xxiii-xxvii. The questions of nationalism and of the influence of pagan Egyptian religion on monasticism (referred to by Bell and MacKean) are discussed by J. G. Griffiths, 'A Note on Monasticism and Nationalism in the Egypt of Athanasius', *SP* 16 (TU 129; Berlin, 1985), 24–8. Important studies of the socio-economic context of monasticism more recent than Brown include Rousseau, *Pachomius*, 1–36; J. R. Binns, 'The Early Monasteries', *Medieval History*, 1: 2 (1991), 12–22; and J. E. Goehring, 'The World Engaged: The Social and Economic World of Early Egyptian Monasticism', in J. E. Goehring, C. H. Hedrick, J. T. Sanders (eds.), with H. D. Betz, *Gnosticism and the Early Christian World: In Honor of James M. Robinson* (Sonoma, Calif., 1990), 134–44.

sayings of the Desert Fathers as authoritative sources of their own teaching.[12]

The *Life of Antony*, the *Lausiac History*, the *History of the Monks*, Evagrius, and Cassian are all among our primary sources for the life and teaching of the Desert Fathers; but despite the importance of these early works, there can be no doubt—especially when it is the teaching of the monks themselves which we wish to consider—that the most important single source for our knowledge of the monasticism of fourth- and fifty-century lower Egypt is the *Apophthegmata Patrum*. This collection of sayings and stories contains many hundreds of individual pieces dealing with every aspect of the monastic life and draws on the words and experiences of many different speakers. The variety of different attitudes to the problems and possibilities of the monastic life embodied in the collection is responsible, in fact, for much of its interest and value. In the words of Owen Chadwick, it bears no trace of the 'unifying interest' of an individual author; it is rather the 'raw material' from which an account of the teaching of the Desert Fathers can be built.[13] The *Apophthegmata Patrum* has exercised a profound influence on the history of Christian monasticism and spirituality, and the persistence of its influence today is illustrated by the continued use of its sayings in recent works of spiritual theology.[14] In order to begin to understand the outlook of this influential source and prepare the ground for an examination of its teaching on the theme of personal relationships, it will first be necessary to say something about the origins of the text in the monastic communities which it portrays. This will help to illustrate the extent to which, despite the characteristics to which Chadwick rightly refers, the *Apophthegmata* does display an overall unity

[12] Evagrius, *On Prayer*, 106–9 (illustrating the instruction of 105); *Praktikos*, 91–9; Cassian, *Institutions*, 5. 24–32. Evagrius writes, 'It is necessary to enquire carefully into the ways of the monks who have gone before, and to conform ourselves to them. For many things are to be found which were both said and done well by them' (*Praktikos*, 91). For details of the editions of these works, see the Bibliography.

[13] O. Chadwick, *Western Asceticism* (London, 1958), 34, 33. Cf. J.-C. Guy, 'Les *Apophthegmata Patrum*', in G. Lemaître (ed.), *Théologie de la vie monastique: Études sur la tradition patristique* (Collection Théologie: Études publiées sous la direction de la faculté de théologie s. j. de Lyon-Fouvière, 49; Paris, 1961), 78–80, 82–3. Guy comments that the *Apophthegmata* 'representent ce qu'on pourrait appeler le "material brut" à partir duquel c'est constituée la spiritualité monastique postérieure, ce qu'une expression anglaise rend fort exactement: *the monasticism in the making*[*sic*]' (p. 82).

[14] e.g. R. C. Bondi, *To Love as God Loves: Conversations with the Early Church* (Philadelphia, 1987); A. Jones, *Soul Making: The Desert Way of Spirituality* (London, 1986); K. Leech, *True God: An Exploration in Spiritual Theology* (London, 1985), 127–62.

of concern arising from its particular place and time of composition and from its distinctive attitude to the past life of the community. It is also necessary to address the problem of the reliability of the *Apophthegmata* as a historical source for the life and teaching of the Desert Fathers.

2. The Text

The history of the text of the *Apophthegmata Patrum*, and of the translation of the original Greek texts into the other languages of Eastern and Western Christianity is an extremely complicated one, but a brief account of the different collections which are to be used in this work and of their relation to one another must now be given.[15]

The most familiar of the extant texts of the *Apophthegmata* is the Greek alphabetical collection, in which the individual units are arranged in alphabetical order according to the name of the principal speaker or figure in each story, or of the monk who transmitted it.[16] The author of the preface to the collection states that in compiling it he has made use of written sources,[17] and some of these sources can be identified with certainty. Evagrius, Cassian, the *History of the Monks*, and the *Lausiac History* are all quoted, and quotations from other lesser texts can be identified.[18] But it is the case that the vast majority of the stories

[15] The major studies of the text and versions of the *Apophthegmata* are W. Bousset, *Apophthegmata: Studien zur Geschichte des ältesten Mönchtums* (Tübingen, 1923), 1–208; and J.-C. Guy, *Recherches sur la tradition grecque des Apophthegmata Patrum* (Subsidia Hagiographica, 36; Brussels, 1962; reprinted with additional comments, 1984).

[16] See above, n. 6. From now on this text will be referred to by the appropriate name in the alphabetical series followed by the number which identifies the individual unit; for example 'Poemen 36', not 'alphabetical collection, Poemen 36'. Names for which only one piece is printed are not followed by a number. A number of additional pieces (identified by the prefix 'S') have been published in Guy, *Recherches*, 19–36. To refer to one or more individual units of the text I have spoken of 'sayings' or 'stories'; to refer to the text as a whole I have used the expressions 'the Sayings' or 'the *Apophthegmata*'.

[17] PG, lxv. 73.

[18] Cassian and Evagrius are quoted under their own names, and Evagrius's *On Prayer* also in Nilus 1–8 (the work came to be attributed to the fifth-century Nilus of Ancyra). For the sources of the quotations, see *Les Sentences des Pères du désert: Troisième Recueil et tables*, trans. and ed. L. Regnault (Solesmes, 1976), 212–13, 220–1, 226–7. *HM*, 15, is quoted under Pityrion in the alphabetical collection and elsewhere; *HL*, 10.6–7, in Pambo 5, 8, 9. The bulk of the remaining quotations consists of extracts from the *Sentences* of Hyperechius (PG, lxxix. 1473–89) and the *Life of Syncletica* (PG, xxviii. 1487–1558). For a fuller list, see *Les Sentences ... troisième recueil*, 290; and for a wider discussion M. Starowieyski, 'Remarques sur les sources de quelques Apophtegmes des Pères du désert', *SP* 18: 2 (Leuven, 1989), 293–8.

in the alphabetical collection are not derived from any written source which survives today.

The alphabetical collection alone was not meant to be a complete collection of sayings. According to the preface,[19] the alphabetical compilation was followed by a series of anonymous sayings, arranged in chapters according to their subject. This Greek anonymous series is preserved in several manuscripts, and the work of editing it was begun by F. Nau.[20] Though this work was not completed, the manuscript used by Nau was examined further by Guy,[21] and a complete French translation of the anonymous series, including material from different manuscripts, has been published.[22] Guy's analysis showed that the collection of sayings in the manuscript used by Nau consists of several identifiable blocks of material, and that the chapters on different subjects referred to by the writer of the preface to the alphabetical collection form not the first but the fourth section of the manuscript, containing the sayings numbered N 133–369. This original core of the anonymous series is, in the present form of the text, preceded by three shorter collections of sayings (N 1–88, 89–132, 132A-E), and followed by more than 300 other pieces which must have been added to it at a time subsequent to its original compilation as an appendix to the alphabetical collection. In this work extensive use will be made of the fourth section of the anonymous series, but without excluding from consideration some material from the other sections of the text which in origin may well be little, if at all, later in date.

These conclusions about the formation of the anonymous series seem

[19] PG, lxv. 73.

[20] F. Nau, 'Histoires des solitaires égyptiens', *Revue d'orient chrétien*, 12 (1907), 48–68, 171–81, 393–404; 13 (1908), 47–57, 266–83; 14 (1909), 357–79; 17 (1912), 204–11, 294–301; 18 (1913), 137–46. These pages contain the Greek text of sayings 1–392. Nau had already published in *Revue d'orient chrétien*, 10 (1905), 409–14, the text of four sayings which fall between 132 and 133, now usually numbered 132A-D. A fifth saying which occurs in this position in manuscripts of the anonymous series, 132E, has not been published in Greek.

[21] Guy, *Recherches*, 63–88.

[22] *Les Sentences des Pères du désert: Série des anonymyes*, trans. L. Regnault (Solesmes, 1985), which replaces the earlier partial translation in *Les Sentences des Pères du désert: Nouveau Recueil*, ed. L. Regnault (Solesmes, 1970; 2nd edn. 1977), 13–162. For a review of the earlier work and some comments on the text of the anonymous series, see J.-M. Sauget, 'Paul Evergetinos et la collection alphabético-anonyme des *Apophthegmata Patrum*', *OCP*, 37 (1971), 223–35. Sayings from the manuscript used by Nau—whether edited by him or available only in translation—are referred to by the prefix 'N' plus a number.

to be generally accepted today.[23] The same agreement cannot quite be said to exist on the subject of the relationship between the combined alphabetical–anonymous collection of sayings and the other major form in which the *Apophthegmata* exist, the systematic collection. In this collection, all of the material is arranged in chapters dealing with particular subjects. The systematic collection exists in different forms including a Latin version, translated from Greek in the sixth century,[24] and a considerably larger Greek version, which is so far unpublished.[25] Guy argued that the Greek texts of the alphabetical–anonymous and systematic series were not directly dependent on one another;[26] but as Chitty showed, this argument will not apply to the Latin version, PJ, which must represent an earlier text of the systematic collection than the Greek. The correspondence—extending both to which units are present and to the order in which sayings taken from the alphabetical–anonymous collection occur within each chapter of the systematic—between the contents of PJ and that of the alphabetical collection plus the sayings N 133–369 is very close, and strongly suggests that the first systematic collection was dependent on an early text of the alphabetical–anonymous series.[27] It may also be noted at this point that the claim of PJ to primitive status as a representative of the systematic type of collection is supported by the close parallels between it and the partly surviving Coptic collection of *Apophthegmata*.[28]

[23] Cf. D. J. Chitty, 'The Books of the Old Men', *ECR*, 6 (1974), 15–21, esp. 17–18. For an older analysis of the anonymous series, see Bousset, *Apophthegmata*, 10–15.

[24] PL, lxxiii. 855–1022. This text is referred to as 'PJ' (for Pelagius and John, the translators) followed by a chapter number and a saying number, e.g. PJ 12.4. Chadwick, *Western Asceticism*, 338–60, includes as an appendix to his translation of chapters 1–17 of PJ a list of variant manuscript readings which is very useful in the absence of a proper critical edition of the text.

[25] An edition of the Greek systematic collection (hereafter GSC) is forthcoming in *Sources Chrétiennes*. See Guy, *Recherches*, 117–200, for a discussion of the manuscripts. Most of the unpublished material is translated in *Les Sentences ... troisième recueil*, 65–121.

[26] Guy, *Recherches*, 190–200. On the relation of the Greek and Latin texts, see also A. Wilmart, 'Le Recueil Latin des *Apophthegmata Patrum*', *Revue Bénédictine*, 34 (1922), 185–98; and Bousset, *Apophthegmata*, 6–10.

[27] Chitty, 'The Books of the Old Men', 18–19; there is a summary of critical discussion in F. M. Young, *From Nicaea to Chalcedon: A Guide to the Literature and its Background* (London, 1983), 44–6. For another textual study of the alphabetical collection, see R. Draguet, 'Le Patérikon de l'Add. 22508 du British Museum', *Le Muséon*, 63 (1950), 25–46. The tables in *Les Sentences ... troisième recueil* are the best guide to the interrelation of the collections.

[28] *Le Manuscrit de la version copte en dialecte sahidique des 'Apophthegmata Patrum'*, ed. M. Chaine (Bibliothèque des études coptes, 6; Cairo, 1960) (Coptic text and French

Chitty's conclusions again seem convincing, but in a more recent work, Samuel Rubenson has taken a somewhat different approach to the relationship between the alphabetical–anonymous and systematic collections which must be noted briefly.[29] He argues that, rather than the systematic collection having been formed by a rearrangement of the sayings of the alphabetical–anonymous, as Chitty thought, these two major collections evolved separately. The existence (in various languages) of 'alphabetical collections without signs of any systematical principle, and systematical collections without any alphabetical order' proves that 'both types must be original creations' (p. 148). Rubenson's assessment of the evidence of the Armenian and Syriac systematic collections to which he refers leads him to conclude that the earliest systematic collections were not (as PJ is) arranged alphabetically within each chapter, and that they only came to be rearranged in this way at a later date under the influence of knowledge of the alphabetical collection and of an impulse to improve the organization of the texts (p. 149).

The proposition that alphabetical and systematic forms of the *Apophthegmata* were originally independent is certainly an interesting one; it raises the possibility that some of the different versions of the *Apophthegmata* may be *independent* witnesses to many of the individual sayings which they have in common. From the point of view of the teaching of the *Apophthegmata*, it is the reliability of the contents of the collections, rather than their form or the relationship between them, which matters; and as Rubenson himself points out, the arrangement of the collections may differ, but the individual saying usually remains 'strikingly constant' (p. 150). It does not however seem possible to apply Rubenson's theory to the relationship between the Greek alphabetical–anonymous series and PJ, which seems far too close (as Chitty argued) to be accounted for by anything other than direct dependence (with the qualification, to be referred to again below, that the absence from PJ of many sayings found in the alphabetical collection suggests that it may be based on an even earlier version of that text than that which is now extant). There is still the problem of the Armenian and Syriac systematic texts, which are certainly not related to the alphabetical–anonymous collection in such a simple way (though more work would

translation); the tables on pp. 155–9 of the edition illustrate the remarkable closeness of most of the Coptic collection (hereafter Ch) to PJ.

[29] S. Rubenson, *The Letters of St Antony: Origenist Theology, Monastic Tradition and the Making of a Saint* (Bibliotheca Historico-Ecclesiastica Lundensis, 24; Lund, 1990), 145–52.

be needed before it could be held that they were not orginally related to it at all).[30] But whatever the origin of these, it does not seem likely that they will ever be proved (as Rubenson implies they may) to be *more* primitive, as regards the date of their contents, than the alphabetical–anonymous collection. The internal evidence for the early date of this collection and for its situation at a primitive stage in the codification of the tradition of the Sayings in the major collections will be considered in the next section.[31]

3. The Text and the Community

What can we learn, from an examination of the alphabetical–anonymous collection of *Apophthegmata* as a whole, about the nature of the monastic community which the text portrays, and about the likely origins of the text itself? Both Lucien Regnault[32] and Derwas Chitty[33] have suggested that the text originated, not in the Egyptian monastic centre of Scetis itself, but at the time of what Chitty refers to as the *diaspora*, the period in the early fifth century when many renowned figures left Scetis, partly as a result of barbarian raids on the monasteries there.[34] The *Apophthegmata*, he points out,[35] are particularly concerned with recording the sayings of monks who lived at the time of the *diaspora* and who ended their careers outside Scetis. Renault goes further, and argues that the text originated in Palestine.[36] The evidence which he puts forward

[30] Rubenson's attempts on 148–9 to prove that this is the case are not entirely successful. The material from the Syriac and Armenian collections which is not paralleled in the published texts of the Greek and PJ is translated in *Les Sentences ... nouveau recueil*, 219–75. Ch also has a number of pieces not found in any other collection.

[31] Rubenson, 149, refers to the sayings quoted by Cassian and Evagrius (see above, n. 12) as evidence that systematic arrangements of the sayings in fact preceded alphabetical ones; but there is no definite evidence that Cassian and Evagrius did have written collections (as opposed to depending on personal knowledge and oral tradition), nor that they were systematically arranged. Even if they did exist, they would have been small personal collections which can shed no direct light on the form of the earliest major compilations, whether alphabetical or systematic.

[32] L. Regnault, 'La Transmission des Apophtegmes', in *Les Pères du désert à travers leurs Apophtegmes* (Solesmes, 1987), 65–72, esp. 69–70.

[33] Chitty, 'The Books of the Old Men', 16–17; *The Desert a City*, 67–8.

[34] Ibid. 60–1, 66–71. On the barbarian assaults on Scetis, see also Evelyn-White, *The History of the Monasteries of Nitria and Scetis*, 150–67.

[35] 'The Books of the Old Men', 19.

[36] L. Regnault, 'Les Apophtegmes en Palestine aux Ve-VIe siècles', *Irénikon*, 54 (1981), 320–30, reprinted in *Les Pères du désert à travers leurs Apophtegmes*, 73–83.

is persuasive: first, a number of Palestinian works of the fifth and sixth centuries show acquaintance with stories of the Desert Fathers, many of which can be identified with sayings now preserved in the alphabetical collection. Secondly, a number of sayings in the alphabetical collection refer to a group of monks headed by Silvanus, who migrated from Scetis to Sinai and then to Palestine.[37] Another exile from Scetis was Abba Isaiah or Esaias, who died in Palestine in the late fifth century.[38] Among his works is a collection of sayings which, there can be no doubt, was among the sources used by the compiler of the alphabetical collection, and which can therefore be considered one of the oldest extant collections.[39] The importance of Isaiah's collection as a check on the reliability of the text of the alphabetical–anonymous series will become clear below.

Though Regnault's arguments for the Palestinian origin of the earliest collections of *Apophthegmata* are convincing, it must still be borne in mind that the alphabetical and anonymous collections are primarily and overwhelmingly concerned with the sayings and doings of Egyptian monks, whether those who stayed in Egypt or those who, like Silvanus, went elsewhere. Basil of Caesarea, Ephrem Syrus, Epiphanius of Salamis, and Gregory of Nazianzus stand out in the alphabetical collection as non-Egyptian figures, but they are of course well-known writers and controversialists who might be expected to find a place in almost any collection of material like the *Apophthegmata*, whatever its precise origin.[40] The number of Palestinian monks who figure in the sayings is again quite small: Gelasius, Theodore of Eleutheropolis, Hilarion, Milesius (who was from or lived for a while in Persia, if Milesius 2 is historically trustworthy), and Philagrius. No one from these two groups of non-Egyptians is the subject of a large number of individual pieces. Epiphanius is an exception to this generalization, but of the seventeen pieces attributed to him in the alphabetical collection, only two are included in PJ, and the absence of the other texts even from the Greek

[37] Cf. Chitty, *The Desert a City*, 71–3.

[38] Ibid. 73–7; and his 'Abba Isaiah', *JTS* n.s. 22 (1971), 47–72.

[39] Chitty, *The Desert a City*, 74, 80 n. 117, and 'Abba Isaiah', *passim*; Regnault, 'La Transmission des Apophtegmes', 66–9. The Greek text of Isaiah's collection is in *Les Cinq Recensions de l'Ascéticon syriaque d'Abba Isaïe, i. Introduction au problème isaïen. Versions des logoi I-XIII avec des parallèles grecs et latins*, ed. R. Draguet (CSCO, 293; Scriptores Syri, 122; Louvain, 1968), *Logos* 6, pp. 27–81.

[40] Regnault, 'Les Apophtegmes en Palestine', 328 (reprint 81) refers to the saying of Basil as especially indicative of a Palestinian milieu for the compilation of the alphabetical collection, as Basil was greatly respected there as a monastic legislator.

systematic collection (which is longer than PJ) strongly suggests that most of the Epiphanius material is a later addition to the original alphabetical series.[41] Scetis and the *diaspora* certainly seem to be at the centre of the text's attention.

The time-span covered by the Sayings is also limited. Antony and Macarius, the pioneers of desert monasticism in the early fourth century, are quoted extensively, but so are Arsenius and Poemen, who lived until the mid-fifth century.[42] Yet there are very few sayings in the collection which can certainly be dated later than this. Only a few stories reflect the situation in Palestine or in Egypt following the Council of Chalcedon. Poemen 183 refers to a monk exiled by the Emperor Marcian; Gelasius 4 refers explicitly to the time of Chalcedon, while Phocas 1 is a story set at a time when rival Chalcedonian and anti-Chalcedonian congregations had been established in Kellia.[43] But these two narratives too are absent from the Latin and Greek systematic collections and may not be part of the original text of the alphabetical series.

This 'correction' of the alphabetical collection by reference to PJ should not however be taken too far. As already noted, it may be the case that PJ is based on an earlier and smaller version of the alphabetical collection than that which now exists. For example, many of the sayings of John Kolobos, Macarius, Poemen, and Sisoes, four of the most important figures in the alphabetical collection, are not found in PJ, and there is a general tendency (not of course an invariable rule) for the earlier sayings of each monk to be present in, and the later ones to be absent from, PJ. Thus forty-one sayings are attributed to Macarius in the alphabetical collection: of the first twenty of these, only three are not found in some form in PJ; of the last twenty-one, only four are in PJ. And similar proportions apply to the other names.[44] This suggests

[41] See *Les Sentences ... troisième recueil*, 210, for parallels to Epiphanius' sayings.

[42] For the date of Arsenius' death, see Chitty, 'Abba Isaiah', 57; and Evelyn-White, *The History of the Monasteries of Nitria and Scetis*, 162–3. Poemen outlived Arsenius (Arsenius 41) and survived Chalcedon (Poemen 183: the phrase which refers this to after Chalcedon is relegated to a footnote in PG, but the version of PJ 18.16 supports its inclusion; cf. Bousset, *Apophthegmata*, 67). Chitty suggests that Poemen died in the 450s in 'Abba Isaiah', 59, and outlines a possible chronology of his life in *The Desert a City*, 69–70.

[43] The sayings of Longinus also suggest some anti-Chalcedonian influence (Chitty, *The Desert a City*, 74). On the effects of Chalcedon on the monasteries, see Evelyn-White, *The History of the Monasteries of Nitria and Scetis*, 219–24; Chitty, *The Desert a City*, 88–122; and more generally E. R. Hardy, *Christian Egypt: Church and People* (New York, 1952), 111–43.

[44] *Les Sentences ... troisième recueil*, 216, 222–4, 228–36, 238–40.

that additions were made to each name in the alphabetical collection as it was recopied. But even if the alphabetical collection was revised in this way after its original compilation (and if it was an earlier version which was used as the archetype of PJ), no suspicion need be cast on the authenticity of most of the additional pieces. In fact, the collection's retention of its Scetiote and pre-Chalcedonian character appears even more remarkable, extra material about established figures having apparently been added to it (drawn either from written sources or from oral tradition) without significantly widening its range. The scarcity of its references to monks in Egypt or Palestine in the period after Chalcedon strongly suggests that whatever the precise history of its compilation and expansion, the alphabetical collection had attained stability not just in the form which lies behind PJ, but in more or less its *present* form relatively early in the half century after 451. It is difficult to date the collection later than the end of the century, for by then most of the bearers of an exclusively Scetiote and pre-Chalcedonian oral tradition would have been dead, and wider concerns would surely have begun to intrude (as they did into sayings N 370 and following of the anonymous series). But the exact date of the alphabetical collection cannot be determined, even with the aid of a probable source like Isaiah's collection.[45]

Sayings in the anonymous series are of course much harder to date or locate geographically than sayings of named figures; but in the original core (N 133–369) of the anonymous series there is nothing which can be clearly attributed to the period after the *diaspora*. This does not apply to the remainder of the anonymous text, which includes a number of stories located in Palestine, and, despite the fact that it is conventionally referred to as anonymous, a number of stories about named individuals.[46] It does not in fact retain the overwhelmingly

[45] Chitty, 'Abba Isaiah', 51–60, argues that Isaiah probably 'gathered his information not earlier than the 450s' (p. 60), but we do not know exactly when, nor how long it was before the alphabetical compiler used Isaiah's work. On the date of the alphabetical series, see also Bousset, *Apophthegmata*, 66–8.

[46] Palestinian locations occur in N 450, 527, 528, 587, and others; for sayings of named figures see N 391 (Poemen), N 490 (Antony), N 509–10 (Zeno), N 596 (Daniel of Scetis, sixth century, on whom, see Chitty, *The Desert a City*, 145–7), etc. The group N 1–88 was possibly once an independent compilation; it includes texts which are attributed to the late sixth-century author John Moschus in other manuscripts (Guy, *Recherches*, 75–6), which suggests a late date for its present form. It also includes stories about named figures: N 1, 2, 3 (= Gregory the Theologian 1), 9, 11 (also found under the name Theodotus in some alphabetical manuscripts and printed by Guy, *Recherches*, 22), 14, 15, 16 (related to Macarius the Citizen 3), 33, 69, 70.

Scetiote outlook of the alphabetical collection plus the chapters of N 133–369.[47] The fact that material about named figures was added to the expanded 'anonymous' series rather than being incorporated into the alphabetical collection reinforces the contention that the latter did not continue to expand indefinitely, but quickly attained stability and, with the exception of texts like Phocas 1, retained its primitive, pre-Chalcedonian and Scetiote character.

The exclusion from the early collections of most material not concerned with Egyptian monasticism as it was known before the mid-fifth century gives the impression of deliberateness. Whatever its precise origins, the alphabetical–anonymous series was originally compiled by individuals or communities who wished to preserve a clear view of Scetiote monasticism as it had existed before the *diaspora*. It is not that the period embraced by the *Apophthegmata* (approximately one hundred and fifty years) was short, or that the text deals with a single monastery, for the locations mentioned in the text are scattered over a wide area of lower Egypt. It is rather that between several centres and over a few generations communications and memories are maintained in such a way as to suggest that the Sayings are the product of a tradition of monastic life which was conscious of its own identity and concerned to preserve evidence of the ties which held it together and connected later generations with the founders of the tradition.

The interdependence of some of the founders of monasticism is particularly carefully indicated. We learn that Amoun, the founder of Nitria, was visited by Antony, and that together they decided the location of a new, more remote settlement, probably Kellia.[48] The connections of the founder of Scetis, Macarius, with Pambo, an early Nitrian, and Antony are also noted—one of these texts explicitly stating, and another implying, that in the early days of Scetis the monastery possessed no 'offering', that is eucharist, of its own, and was dependent on Nitria.[49] As already noted, Macarius' initial move from his village to Scetis is also recorded in a story told by him.[50] The early and later

[47] N 370 and following also include a number of quotations from various works; N 133–369 only one possible quotation, from Moschus (*Les Sentences . . . troisième recueil*, 290). This fact too reinforces belief in the primitive character of N 133–369.

[48] Antony 34.

[49] Macarius 2, 4, 26.

[50] Macarius 1. Like Amoun (*HL*, 8) and Antony (*VA*, 3–4), Macarius began his ascetic career living in or near his own village rather than in the desert. Cf. G. E. Gould, 'The *Life of Antony* and the Origins of Christian Monasticism in Fourth-Century Egypt', *Medieval History*, 1:2 (1991), 3–11, for a discussion of this phenomenon in early monastic sources.

generations are linked by such sayings as Sisoes 28, in which he is asked why (seventy-two years before) he had left Scetis to live on Antony's mountain, and Poemen 75, in which he recounts a saying of Antony about Pambo, both figures of the first generation. Pambo is cited as a model in other sayings of Sisoes and Poemen,[51] and the earliest and latest generations of the period covered by the *Apophthegmata* are brought together by three sayings which link Poemen directly with Macarius.[52] The movements and dwelling-places of the *diaspora* figures are also recorded: Anoub and Poemen, Arsenius, Theodore of Pherme, and of course the Silvanus-group.[53]

Several other factors also suggest that the Sayings are the product of a community which was conscious of its own identity. The relative scarcity of sayings about the relations between monks and lay people or monks and the Church suggests a preoccupation with the monastic community in itself rather than with its wider contacts and influence, though this is not of course to say that all such wider concerns were excluded completely.[54] Similarly, the almost total absence from the Sayings of references to Pachomian monasticism in upper Egypt seems significant, and perhaps suggests that the transmitters and compilers of the Sayings were aware that their own monastic community had an identity distinct from that of the Pachomian system.[55] The distinction between the monasticism of the Sayings and of the Pachomian community, customarily referred to by the terms 'semi-anchoritic' and 'cenobitic' respectively, can easily be exaggerated, for the two forms of monastic life had a common origin in the ascetic traditions of fourth-

[51] Poemen 150; Sisoes S 1 (Guy, *Recherches*, 33).

[52] Macarius 25; Ethiopic collection (Eth. Coll.) 13.49, 72. The Ethiopic collection of Sayings forms chs. 13–14 of the Ethiopic *Collectio Monastica*, ed. V. Arras (CSCO 238–9; Series Ethiopici, 45–6; Louvain, 1963), vol. 238, pp. 83–126 (text), and vol. 239, pp. 62–93 (Latin translation).

[53] Anoub 1, Poemen 4; Agathon 28, Arsenius 32, 34, 42 (transmitted by Arsenius' disciple Daniel); Theodore of Pherme 26, Zeno 3, 5, 6, Mark 1–5, Silvanus 4, 5. See Sozomen, *Historia Ecclesiastica*, 6.32, for a brief statement of Silvanus' movements.

[54] See G. E. Gould, 'Lay Christians, Bishops, and Clergy in the *Apophthegmata Patrum*', forthcoming in *SP*; P. Rousseau, *Ascetics, Authority, and the Church in the Age of Jerome and Cassian* (Oxford, 1978), 60, is more inclined to see in the Sayings a strict segregation of ascetic and secular concerns. N 1–88 include a larger number of stories about laity than N 133–369 (N 37–9, 47–9, 52, 67, 84), suggesting that the concern of the monastic community with its own identity may have faded as time went on.

[55] Orsisius and Psenthaisius are the only Pachomian monks quoted in the alphabetical collection. These three sayings are taken from the *First Greek Life* of Pachomius (G1), 126, 118, and 25 respectively. For details of the editions of this and other Pachomian works, see the Bibliography.

century Egypt, as is illustrated by the fact that Pachomius was himself the disciple of a hermit.[56] But this makes it even more striking that in the *Apophthegmata* the independence of the two movements is maintained. On the Pachomian side, one passage at least forcibly inculcates an awareness of the difference between the two styles of monastic life.[57]

The community's awareness of its own unity and continuity with its past is illustrated, rather negatively, by a number of sayings which maintain the inferiority of the speaker's contemporaries to earlier monks. 'If we keep the commandments of our fathers,' Moses said, 'I pledge to you before God, that the barbarians will not come here. But if we do not keep them, this place must be laid waste.'[58] Poemen, in the next generation, commented that 'Since the third generation in Scetis and Abba Moses, the brothers no longer make progress'.[59] Declining standards were attacked by Felix and Megethius, who criticized the inadequate obedience or worldliness of their contemporaries compared with the monks of the past, and by Theodore of Pherme, who compared the high standards 'when we were in Scetis' with the lower standards prevailing 'now', that is, presumably, in the period of the *diaspora* and devastations.[60] Abba Elias spoke 'in Egypt' about Agathon (presumably they were contemporaries in the *diaspora*): 'he is good for his generation; as for the ancients [*ἀρχαῖοι*], I saw a man in Scetis who could make the sun stand still.'[61] Isidore fought against the temptation to pride by

[56] G1, 6; cf. Rousseau, *Ascetics, Authority, and the Church*, 34–5, and Gould, 'Early Egyptian Monasticism and the Church'. Pachomius is now regarded not merely as an organizer and legislator, but as a charismatic teacher like the monks portrayed in the Sayings: Rousseau, *Ascetics, Authority, and the Church*, 22, and M. S. Burrows, 'On the Visibility of God in the Holy Man: A Reconsideration of the Role of the Apa in the Pachomian *Vitae*', *Vigiliae Christianae*, 41 (1987), 11–33.

[57] G1, 120. Macarius the Citizen 2 is the only saying which describes an encounter between Pachomius and a representative of the semi-anchoritic tradition. *HL*, 18.12–16, also has a story of an encounter between Macarius and Pachomius. For an account of some contacts between the Pachomian community and Nitria, see the *Letter of Ammon*, 30–32. J. E. Goehring, *The Letter of Ammon and Pachomian Monasticism* (Patristische Texte und Studien, 27; Berlin, 1986) is a critical study of this work.

[58] Moses 9. On pessimism, see Regnault, 'La Transmission des Apophtegmes', 69–70; and Chitty, *The Desert a City*, 66.

[59] Poemen 166.

[60] Felix; Megethius 4; Theodore of Pherme 10.

[61] Elias 2 (cf. the story in Bessarion 3). Elias 8 (also a pessimistic saying) speaks of an Elias at the monastery of Abba Saba in Palestine. If the Scetiote Elias made his way there from Egypt it would not have been before *c.*478: see O. F. A. Meinardus, 'Historical Notes on the Lavra of Mar Saba', ECR, 2 (1968–9), 392–401; and Chitty, *The Desert a City*, 94–118. Elias 8 is however a quotation from John Moschus, *Pratum Spirituale*, 52 (PG, lxxxvii. 2908A-B) and need not refer to the same person as Elias 2.

asking himself if he was really worthy to be compared with Antony and Pambo, monks that is of the first generation.[62] Even Macarius could make a pessimistic comment about the achievements of the present compared with the past.[63] An anonymous monk compared the actions of the present generation adversely with those of 'our fathers' who put into practice what the prophets wrote.[64] The Ethiopic collection of Sayings contains a remarkable number of comments on the declining fervour and austerity of the monks.[65]

Particularly interesting are a number of sayings in which this pessimism about the present state (or future) of the community is expressed in visionary experiences. Silvanus wept after seeing a vision of the final judgement in which many monks were consigned to hell, while lay people were going to heaven.[66] Other old men saw visions symbolizing the weakness of the present generation, or the destruction of the monasteries in Scetis.[67] It appears that maintaining a critical attitude towards the quality of the community's monastic life was one of the functions of visionary experiences and was recognized as such. The chapter on visions in PJ includes not only the last two sayings referred to, but also a number of sayings which do not involve explicitly visionary experiences, but which show the same interest in the future of the community and adopt the same pessimistic view.[68]

It is easy to see how monks who were both conscious of the links which bound their monastic community to its past history, and yet also aware that leading figures of the community had expressed a deep pessimism about its ability to live up to the standards set by earlier generations, could be led by the experiences of decline associated with the barbarian devastations and the *diaspora* to begin the task of writing down the words and deeds of the Egyptian monks whose memory and whose words they treasured. Whether he worked in Egypt or in Palestine, the alphabetical compiler's perspective is that of a Scetiote of the

[62] Isidore 6.
[63] Macarius 25.
[64] N 228.
[65] Eth. Coll. 13.16, 22, 23, 27, 38, 47, 70; 14.37, 59.
[66] Silvanus 2.
[67] John Kolobos 14 (PJ 18.8); N 361 (PJ 18.25).
[68] Ischyridon (PJ 18.34); Macarius 5 (PJ 18.11); Moses 9 (PJ 18.13). Note that PJ 18 is divided into two parts in the PL text. PJ 18.1–20 (cols. 978–88) form *Vitae Patrum*, bk. 5, sect. 18; *Vitae Patrum*, bk. 6, sect. 1, begins with PJ 18.21 (col. 993). For a vision of Pachomius concerning the future of his community, see G1, 71.

diaspora.[69] He certainly wanted first and foremost to edify and instruct his readers in the virtues of the monastic life,[70] but his achievement, and, it may be maintained, his purpose also, was to provide a permanent record of the historical development of a monastic community.

4. The Transmission of the Text: Personal Relationships

The concern of the *Apophthegmata* to establish the identity of the community which it represents—by exclusion of non-Egyptian material and by recording the connections between different localities and different generations—is mirrored at the individual as opposed to the community level by a far-reaching interest in the pattern of personal relationships within the monastic community. Many of the stories which record the history of the community are in fact sayings about the relationships of individuals—Antony and Macarius for example, or the *diaspora* figures and their disciples; though some of the 'pessimistic' sayings refer to the community in general and not to specific persons. In fact the transmission of texts which speak either about the life of the community or about individual relationships may itself be said to depend on one particular form of individual relationship, the personal contact between teacher and disciple in the context of which a story or a saying was first told or was subsequently passed on in oral tradition. André Louf comments that 'we can almost say that the literature of the desert identifies itself with the exercise of spiritual direction',[71] meaning that the texts as we read them have come into being, at a stage before the compilation of the major collections, in the form of orally transmitted recollections of the answers which different spiritual fathers or abbas gave to the questions which they were asked by their disciples. Similarly, Regnault believes that 'la source principale des apophtegmes est assuré-

[69] Bousset, *Apophthegmata*, 68–71, suggested that the sayings transmitted by Poemen and his contacts are the nucleus (or were the principal source) of the present alphabetical collection; cf. Rubenson, *The Letters of St Antony*, 152 n. 1. This view is compatible with that taken here—that whatever his precise sources, the compiler chose to preserve the self-awareness of the Scetiote *diaspora*. Cf. again Bousset, *Apophthegmata*, 78–9.

[70] Preface, 72–3.

[71] A. Louf, 'Spiritual Fatherhood in the Literature of the Desert', in J. R. Sommerfeldt (ed.), *Abba: Guides to Wholeness and Holiness East and West* (CSS 28; Kalamazoo, Mich., 1982), 37.

ment les relations des jeunes moines avec les anciens'.[72] The following investigation into the historical reliability of the *Apophthegmata* will take the form of an examination of this view of the origins of the text.

The problem of the historicity of the *Apophthegmata* arises from the question, how can we be sure that the sayings, dialogues, and narratives which are preserved in the text, which appear to tell of the history and nature of the community and of the individual relationships of monks with one another, really are a record of words spoken and events which took place in the desert of Scetis? The simple answer to this question is to claim that the Sayings depend on an oral tradition which was capable of preserving information about Scetiote monks even over a considerable period of time before the units of tradition were committed to writing; but this answer requires justification. How can we be sure that the oral tradition worked in this reliable way? Even if the oral tradition was reliable, does the extant text of the Sayings accurately represent it? Is it possible to trace a path back from the late fifth-century text, to the ideas of the fourth and early fifth-century community?

The work of Guy on the *Apophthegmata* was notable for its scepticism about the origins of narratives and dialogues in oral tradition; he tended to regard these units of the text as a literary rather than an oral phenomenon.[73] A similar view has been taken by Peter Nagel, who treats it as impossible to prove that any of the narratives of the particular type which he discusses are actually historical.[74] But this scepticism about narratives can be answered. Regnault has referred to the evidence for the important phenomenon of the reuse of a previous saying, dialogue, or narrative in order to answer a question.[75] He speaks of the transformation of a *rhêma*, the instructive word of an abba to his disciple, into a saying, that is a unit of the oral tradition or the written text, by

[72] Regnault, 'Aux origines des Apophthegmes', in *Les Pères du désert à travers leurs Apophtegmes*, 61; cf. 'Qui sont les Pères du désert?', *La Vie spirtuelle*, 140 (1986), 196, reprinted in *Les Pères du désert à travers leurs Apophtegmes*, 34.

[73] J.-C. Guy, 'Remarques sur le texte des *Apophthegmata Patrum*', *Recherches de science religieuse*, 43 (1955), 252–8; cf. my criticisms of this article in G.E. Gould, 'A Note on the *Apophthegmata Patrum*', *JTS* n.s. 37 (1986), 133–8.

[74] P. Nagel, 'Action-parables in Earliest Christian Monasticism: A Examination of the *Apophthegmata Patrum*', *Hallel*, 5 (1977–8), 251–61, esp. 260–1; the sayings discussed include Anoub 1, John Kolobos 2, 18, Macarius 23, Moses 2, Pior 3, and Silvanus 5, all of which he regards as literary constructions fabricated to illustrate a particular point of teaching.

[75] Regnault, 'La Transmission des Apophtegmes', 65–6.

this reuse.[76] Poemen 46, a saying in which Poemen answers a question by quoting John Kolobos, is a clear example of such a reuse of a *rhêma*, but by no means the only one. Dioscorus 2, Nisterus 2, and Poemen 144, all referred to by Regnault, supply clear examples of the reuse, not simply of the words of another abba (as in Poemen 46), but of the story of an encounter between an abba and a disciple or brother in which the dialogue or narrative form is preserved and passed on by the second speaker. In Dioscorus 2, Poemen, in telling a story of Dioscorus and his disciple, says far more about the relationship between the two than would be necessary simply to answer his questioner's enquiry. He is interested, in fact, in using the relationship between Dioscorus and his disciple to establish a proper narrative context for the words of Dioscorus which he reuses in his own teaching.[77] Such sayings seem to provide good grounds for belief that the oral tradition could accurately pass on recollections, including narratives, about earlier figures.

It is of course the case that not all of the individual units which make up the *Apophthegmata* show signs of this process of oral transmission. Many lack any narrative context, and others give no indication of how or by whom they were transmitted. But this fact is no proof that the sayings or narratives concerned are literary inventions or are not faithful to the oral tradition. Many sayings must once have possessed what Chitty calls the 'pedigree' element: 'Abba A said that Abba B said' or 'Abba A told this story of Abba B',[78] but have lost it in the course of first being written down, or in being transferred from an early written collection to the alphabetical–anonymous series. That this is the case can be clearly demonstrated with reference to the collection of sayings made by Abba Isaiah, referred to above as a source of the alphabetical collection.

Isaiah begins his account with a short introduction: 'Brothers, those things which I heard and saw of the old men, these I recount to you, neither omitting anything from them nor making any additions.'[79] Each

[76] Ibid. cf. id., 'Aux origines des Apophtegmes', 62–3; and also F. von Lilienfeld, 'Die Christliche Unterweisung der *Apophthegmata Patrum*', *Bulletin de la Société d'Archélogie Copte*, 20 (1971), 85–110, reprinted in *Spiritualität des frühen Wüstenmönchtums: Gesammelte Aufsätze 1962 bis 1971* (Erlangen, 1983), 86–113, on pp. 91–2 of the reprint, for comments on the reuse of sayings.

[77] See Gould, 'A Note on the *Apophthegmata Patrum*', 137–8, for other examples.

[78] Chitty, *The Desert a City*, 67–8; cf. Rousseau, *Ascetics, Authority, and the Church*, 24.

[79] Isaiah, *Logos* 6, la (p. 28). Future references will be given by means of the sections and paragraphs provided by the editor.

section begins with a phrase such as, 'Abba John said to me' (2a), or, 'Abba Amoun said to me' (4Aa), and some end with, 'These things were told to me by Abba Abraham, who dwelt with him [Agathon]' (5Ga), or, 'These things were told me by the brother who heard them from Abba Sisoes' (6C). There seems to be no reason to doubt this evidence that Isaiah is recording in writing an oral tradition which included the transmission of some long narratives and dialogues, and which valued the information which the tradition supplied about the named figures which it mentions, not just the teaching on different points which it contains.[80] When we look at these sayings as they occur in the alphabetical collection we see that they have lost the indications of personal reminiscence that they have in Isaiah's text and show fewer signs of transmission through one or more generations of oral tradition. For instance, one of Isaiah's informants is Amoun, who had been a disciple of Poemen: 'Abba Amoun said to me, "I said to the old man Abba Poemen"' (4Aa); further on, Amoun begins another story: 'I said to Abba Peter the disciple of Abba Lot' (4Ba). In the alphabetical collection the first of these stories is combined with another saying about an Amoun, and the connection with Isaiah and the signs of oral transmission disappear,[81] while the second story begins simply, 'A brother said to Abba Peter',[82] and the saying thus gives no indication that it has been passed on from that brother (Amoun) to Isaiah and thus to the written source.

There is another text which sheds light on the problem of the relation of the alphabetical collection to oral tradition—the Ethiopic collection of Sayings already referred to.[83] This is a collection of 166 sayings, most of which were unknown before the publication of the Ethiopic text. Like Isaiah's collection, this series is marked by the prevalence of a first-person style of reporting, and by several striking examples of oral transmission of a story over several stages.[84] It has therefore a good claim to be as primitive as Isaiah's collection. In addition, it notably confirms the characteristics of the alphabetical collection which have

[80] Rubenson, *The Letters of St Antony*, 149, argues that an arrangement of sayings by subject-matter is more natural than an alphabetical one (cf. above, n. 31). Isaiah's interest in stories of individuals as well as in teaching shows that this is not the case.

[81] Amoun of Nitria 2.

[82] Peter the Pionite 2.

[83] See above, n. 52, and the studies of J.-M. Sauget, 'Une nouvelle collection éthiopienne *d'Apophthegmata Patrum*', *OCP*, 31 (1965), 177–82, and esp. L. Regnault, 'Aux origines des collections d'Apophtegmes', *SP* 18:2 (Leuven, 1989), 61–74.

[84] Ibid. 63–4; Eth. Coll. 13.6, 24, 36, 75, 14.32, 44.

already been cited as evidence of an early date: the absence of sayings referring to non-Egyptian figures, and the signs that the compiler was a figure of the *diaspora*, but that he knew many monks, including Poemen (who figures as largely in this collection as in the alphabetical), who had been in Scetis.[85]

The Ethiopic collection is important, in contrast to the collection of Isaiah, not because it is a source of the alphabetical–anonymous series, but because it is not. Most of the sayings in the Ethiopic collection have no parallel in the alphabetical–anonymous, which probably therefore did not have access to the Ethiopic as a source (no reason can be suggested why the alphabetical compiler, if he had known them, would have omitted these sayings). The units in the Ethiopic collection which do have alphabetical–anonymous parallels are therefore of special significance: they are a check on the sort of changes that occurred to units in oral tradition, and therefore on the reliability of that tradition and the fidelity with which the alphabetical collection reproduces it.

An analysis of the parallels between the two collections has been undertaken by Regnault,[86] but the importance of the question demands that a summary of their relationship be given here. The total number of sayings in the Ethiopic collection which are paralleled more or less closely in the alphabetical–anonymous is about twenty-four, depending on exactly how parallels are defined. In several cases, a story which in the alphabetical collection has no clear signs of oral transmission appears in the Ethiopic as part of a first-person narrative.[87] These units confirm, in the same way as the collection of Isaiah, the dependence of the text of the *Apophthegmata* as a whole on oral tradition, even where no explicit signs of this appear in the alphabetical collection. Elsewhere, a narrative in the Ethiopic collection has been reduced to a simple saying without narrative context in the alphabetical, though without any serious distortion of the message of the text.[88] In other cases the relationship between the two texts is more complex: for example the long narrative of Eth. Coll. 13.80 (beginning 'I knew a brother who', so probably again a primitive text) has apparently been simplified in different ways to produce two shorter stories in N 7 and N 339; or again, Eth. Coll. 14.34 emerges split into two sayings in the alphabetical collection

[85] Regnault, 'Aux origines des collections d'Apophtegmes', 65–7; Poemen is recalled in Eth. Coll. 13.48, 57, 79.

[86] Regnault, 'Aux origines des collections d'Apophtegmes', 68–72.

[87] Notably Eth. Coll 14.27 (N 173), 14.33 (N 4), and 14.44 (Poemen 62).

[88] e.g Eth. Coll 13.51 (N 196), 13.83 (Ammoes 4), and 14.38 (Isidore 2).

(Zacharias 3 and 1), but again without any serious distortion of its message. Other examples show a much closer correspondence between the two texts;[89] in yet other cases, the similarity extends only to a resemblance in the teaching of the saying or in the incident involved, and the texts may not be true parallels.[90]

By comparing it with one of its sources, and with another text to which it is related less closely, we can thus see that in dealing with the alphabetical–anonymous collection, we are at least one remove, and probably two, away from the oral tradition. Almost all of the parallels between Isaiah and the Ethiopic collection on the one hand, and the alphabetical–anonymous series on the other, show that the texts of the former are more primitive and should be preferred, where available, to that of the larger collection.[91] But in the majority of cases it is not the content or message of the sayings or narratives which has been seriously deformed by the process of their incorporation into the larger collection. This is true even in the cases of Eth. Coll. 13.80, or of Isaiah 5A (Agathon 1), an important example of the transmission of a lengthy narrative in oral form,[92] but one which has suffered more deformation at the hands of the alphabetical compiler than most of Isaiah's text. What has been lost is the explicit indication of the stages by which a saying was passed down from the original speakers and actors to the point where it entered the written tradition, along with some of the personal and circumstantial detail of the more primitive version. In the case of Isaiah's collection, his own comments on the material he is recording have also been lost (2h, 5Gb, 7).

The problem of changes in the attribution of a saying to one or other named figure must also be mentioned. Though between the different major collections of sayings the vast majority of attributions are stable, some variation does occur.[93] In the parallels between the Ethiopic and

[89] Eth. Coll 13.12 (N 355), 13.29 (N 518), 13.30 (Poemen 111), 13.50 (N 391), 13.84 (Poemen 21), 13.89 (Poemen 54), 14.21 (Pambo 2), 14.35 (Zacharias 5)

[90] Eth. Coll. 13.55 (Achilles 5), 13.92 (Alonius 3), 14.29 (Bessarion 8), 14.45 (Agathon 18), 14.46 (Poemen 120, Elias 3), 14.47 (Poemen 20), 14.64 (Macarius 20). Again it should be noted that different judgements about the extent and nature of these parallels are possible

[91] In just one case, Eth. Coll 14.11 (Poemen 52), the alphabetical text has a more concrete indication of oral transmission than the Ethiopic

[92] Cf. Gould, 'A Note on the *Apophthegmata Patrum*', 136

[93] For example, the parallel to Dioscorus 2 in the Latin Sayings collection of Paschasius (Pa), 15.5 (PL lxxiii. 1039A), has the name Isidore instead of Dioscorus. This could be due to a transcription error in the Greek source, or to a tendency to attribute sayings about little-known figures to more famous names.

alphabetical–anonymous collections, there are a number of changes in attribution which Regnault regards as problematic for the reliability of the alphabetical collection.[94] But in four of these, a saying which in Ethiopic is attributed to a named figure has become anonymous in the larger collection.[95] (These texts are among those which demonstrate the superiority of the oral tradition of the Ethiopic collection.) Other apparent changes are in fact simply instances of a resemblance in the teaching involved rather than being true parallels.[96] In only three cases is there a change which suggests that there has been an actual falsification, deliberate or accidental, of the attribution.[97] Changes of this type must be borne in mind if any attempt is made to build up a picture of an individual monk from the *Apophthegmata*, but it is again the case that the change does not necessarily distort the contents of the saying or mean that it is not faithful to the oral tradition.[98]

Though these comparisons do reveal distortions in the alphabetical–anonymous text, we may safely conclude that in general they are of minor significance; they are of less importance than the evidence which Isaiah and the Ethiopic text supply of the phenomenon of oral tradition as the means by which the Sayings were formed and preserved.[99] The surviving indications of oral transmission of material in the Isaiah text,

[94] Regnault, 'Aux origines des collections d'Apophtegmes', 68.

[95] Eth. Coll. 13.51 (N 196), 13.80 (N 7 and 339), 14.27 (N 173), 14.33 (N 4). Rubenson, *The Letters of St Antony*, 151 n. 3, believes that attributions are on the whole stable, and that sayings were more likely to become anonymous than to gain a false attribution (cf. Chadwick, *Western Asceticism*, 33), a judgement which these examples from Eth. Coll. seem to confirm.

[96] Eth. Coll. 13.92 (Alonius 3), 14.29 (Bessarion 8), 14.46 (Poemen 120, Elias 3), 14.64 (Macarius 20).

[97] Eth. Coll 13.29 (N 518), 13.83 (Ammoes 4), 14.21 (Pambo 2).

[98] Isaiah's collection (3B) supplies another interesting example. It appears as N 363, and in a slightly longer form as Cronius 1. 'No reason has yet been found', comments Chitty ('Abba Isaiah', 54), 'for the attribution to Cronius'. The most likely answer however is that the alphabetical compiler had a different source (oral or written) which attributed the saying to Cronius. This saying was also discussed by J.-C. Guy, 'Note sur l'évolution du genre apophtégmatique', *RAM* 32 (1956), 63–8 (cf. Gould, 'A Note on the *Apophthegmata Patrum*', 138 n. 22).

[99] Regnault, 'Aux origines des collections d'Apophtegmes', 72–3: 'Ce qui est remarquable, c'est que les altérations voulues et intentionelles semblent très rares'; cf. 'La Transmission des Apophtegmes', 71. Butler, *The Lausiac History of Palladius*, i. 208–15, also believed the Sayings to be a reliable source. It is interesting to observe the views of a New Testament form critic on the transmission of the text: see M. Dibelius, *From Tradition to Gospel* (London, 1934), 172–7. He too is convinced of its reliability (175–6), but sceptical about the transmission of some narratives (174: 'the real tradition of logia is independent of any context, very often without any occasion').

the Ethiopic collection, and the alphabetical collection itself,[100] are sufficiently common to make it reasonably certain that many more sayings must once have been the subject of oral transmission, and that the simple forms of introduction such as 'he also said' or 'the old men used to say' which are common in the alphabetical and anonymous series in fact replace original, more concrete indications of the process of transmission.

The view that the text of the *Apophthegmata* originated in an oral tradition arising from the reuse of sayings and stories in the context of the teaching relationship between abba and disciple is thus justified by the evidence of Isaiah, the Ethiopic text, and the alphabetical collection. The oral tradition intentionally preserved material both of an anecdotal and a doctrinal character, and its reduction to writing was relatively conservative even though losses and changes undoubtedly occurred.[101] Scepticism about the historical value of the Sayings is thus not well founded on a consideration of the evidence which is currently available.[102]

The arguments of this chaper form a preliminary to the observations of the rest of this work. The *Apophthegmata Patrum* has been shown to be a text marked by a distinctive conception of the history of the monastic community and a notable concern with the relationships of the individuals who founded it and represented its ideals over several generations. But this concern extends from the phenomena noted in this chapter to relationships in general—to the nature of the relationships between individuals which, in a semi-anchoritic society not governed by the more formal rules and structures of a cenobitic community like the Pachomian one, were the basic data of community life. It will be the task of the rest of this work to substantiate the claim that teaching on personal relationships figures largely in the *Apophthegmata*, and to

[100] e.g Bessarion 1–4, reported in the first person by his disciple Doulas, Poemen 79 (another story about Bessarion), Poemen 87.

[101] The fact that the oral transmission (or its commission to writing) must have involved translation from Coptic to Greek in the case of many sayings certainly complicates any picture of the process, but it is difficult to pinpoint any generally harmful effect on the accuracy of the tradition which resulted. Comparison of the Ethiopic, Latin, and Greek collections does not suggest that translation necessarily leads to distortion. Cf. Bousset, *Apophthegmata*, 89–91.

[102] Rubenson, *The Letters of St Antony*, 151–2, 188, bases his scepticism on doubt about the possibility of any oral tradition (but he ignores the evidence of Isaiah and Eth. Coll.) and on the belief that after the Origenist controversy of 399 deliberate falsification of the tradition took place to eliminate evidence for the literate and sophisticated theological character of early monasticism. For criticism of this thesis in general, see G. E. Gould, 'Recent Work on Monastic Origins: A Consideration of the Questions Raised by Samuel Rubenson's *The Letters of St Antony*', forthcoming in *SP*.

show that individual viewpoints are set within the general context of a shared belief that relationships within the community were important and had to be conducted properly. But it is not only with the teaching of the *Apophthegmata* as a text with which we are concerned: it is the probability that narratives of the Desert Fathers' actions and encounters with one another were accurately transmitted by the tradition which serves to confirm the belief that in looking at the *Apophthegmata* we are looking not only at the literary expression of an ideal constructed at a later date, but to an extent at least, at a treasured record of the reality, in word and deed, of the life of the monastic communities of Scetis and lower Egypt.

Among the relationships which the Sayings describe, that between a teacher and disciple is of special importance; though, as this chapter has shown, it was a means of the handing down of information which helped to preserve the community's own memories and sense of identity, the teaching relationship was also far more than this. It was a personal relationship which made great demands on the abba and his disciple alike, as the next chapter will attempt to show.

2

The Abba and his Disciple

The nature of the relationship between a teacher of the monastic life and his disciples is a subject which, for the reason given in Chapter 1, may be illuminated by a very high proportion of the individual sayings and stories contained in the *Apophthegmata Patrum*. The importance of the theme of spiritual direction in the *Apophthegmata* has in fact been widely recognized and has been studied both in itself and for its place in the development of a tradition of spiritual direction in Christian monasticism in general.[1] In this chapter an attempt will be made to describe and illustrate the nature of the teaching relationship as the Desert Fathers understood it, drawing both on explicit discussions of the importance of teaching and on some of the many illustrations of how it worked in practice. Teaching takes place in the context of a personal relationship, which makes great demands on both parties involved. The primary responsibility of the abba[2] or 'old man' (*γέρων*)

[1] For a general study of spiritual direction in ancient monasticism, see I. Hausherr, *Spiritual Direction in the Early Christian East* (CSS 116; Kalamazoo, Mich., 1990). On the *Apophthegmata*, see H. Dörries, 'The Place of Confession in Ancient Monasticism', *SP* 5 (TU 80; Berlin, 1962), 287–90; J.-C. Guy, 'Educational Innovation in the Desert Fathers', ECR 6 (1974), 44–51; A. Hamilton, 'Spiritual Direction in the Apophthegmata', *Colloquium*, 15 (1983), 31–8; Louf, 'Spiritual Fatherhood in the Literature of the Desert'; T. Merton, 'The Spiritual Father in the Desert Tradition', in *Contemplation in a World of Action* (London, 1971), 269–93; L. Regnault, 'Obéissance et liberté dans les Apophtegmes des Pères', *Studia Anselmiana* 70 (Rome, 1977), 47–72, reprinted in *Les Pères du désert à travers leurs Apophtegmes*, 87–111; 'Qui sont les Pères du désert?', 28–34; and *La Vie quotidienne des Pères du désert en Égypte au IVe siècle* (Paris, 1990), 139–51; Rousseau, *Ascetics, Authority, and the Church*, 19–32; C. Stewart, 'Radical Honesty about the Self: The Practice of the Desert Fathers', *Sobornost*, 12 (1990), 25–39; F. von Lilienfeld, 'Anthropos Pneumatikos—Pater Pneumatophoros: neues Testament und *Apophthegmata Patrum*', *SP* 5 (TU 80; Berlin, 1962), 382–92, reprinted in *Spiritualität des frühen Wüstenmönchtums*, 1–13; B. Ward, 'Spiritual Direction in the Desert Fathers', *The Way*, 24 (1984), 61–70; K. Ware, 'The Spiritual Father in Orthodox Christianity', in J. Garvey (ed.), *Modern Spirituality: An Anthology* (London, 1986), 39–58.

[2] The title and form of address 'Abba', suggesting the regard of a disciple for an experienced and authoritative father and teacher, is itself indicative of the importance of spiritual direction in the Sayings: cf. L. Regnault (trans.), *Abba, dis-moi une parole* (Solesmes, 1984), 7–8; B. Ward (trans.), *The Wisdom of the Desert Fathers* (Oxford, 1975), p. xiii.

is to teach his disciple how to live the monastic life and to face up to the problems and temptations to which any monk is exposed. For the disciple the process of learning requires self-disclosure, endurance, and obedience. But these attitudes are also required, if in a different form, of the abba, if he is to teach with the integrity and efficiency which the Desert Fathers demanded as an ideal.

1. The Aim of the Teaching Relationship

What was the essential purpose which the Desert Fathers ascribed to the relationship which was formed between an abba and a disciple? It is clear that for a new disciple, the first aim of living with or near an abba would be to learn, from an older and more experienced monk, the basic practices of the monastic life, such as how to fast and to spend his time alone in his cell,[3] and how to do his manual work.[4] That this was the case is taken for granted in the *Apophthegmata*, and sayings which discuss the importance for a disciple of his relationship with his abba almost always refer to something more than these purely practical aspects of teaching. The relationship is seen as a form of training through obedience on which a disciple's attainment of the virtues and qualities which are the aim of the monastic life was directly dependent—and which directly affects his standing before God as well. Thus:

> The old men used to say that if someone has faith in someone else, and makes himself subject to him, he does not need to apply himself to the commandments of God, but only to give up his will to his father, and he will not suffer reproach from God; for God requires nothing more from beginners [ἀρχάριοι] than the labour which comes through obedience.[5]

'Will not suffer reproach' and 'God requires' are to be taken seriously as pointers to the Desert Fathers' understanding of the teaching relationship: it is not a matter of practical convenience but a divinely guaranteed

[3] N 291: *πῶς δεῖ καθίσαι ἐν τῷ κελλίῳ*. Cf. Poemen 168.

[4] Theodore of Pherme 21. Cf. the long narrative in *HL*, 22.1–9, showing how (in Palladius' reconstruction) Antony taught a new disciple how a monk should work and eat. On these practical matters, see esp. Regnault, *La Vie quotidienne*, 75–124.

[5] N 290. The conclusion is repeated in N 292. See also the text, *On How to Live in the Cell and on Contemplation*, ed. J.-C. Guy, 'Un Entretien monastique sur la contemplation', *Recherches de science religieuse*, 50 (1962), 230–41, qu. 8: 'He who has a spiritual father hands over to his father every care he has, and does not worry about anything, and is no longer judged by God.'

means by which a monk grows, by obedience and trust[6] in what his abba tells him to do, in his acceptability to God.

This saying is one of the most explicit in attributing a disciple's progress in virtue to his dependence on his abba, but others illustrate the same ideas:

Abba Poemen said that someone once asked Abba Paisius, 'What shall I do for my soul, because it is without feeling and does not fear God?' He said to him, 'Go and adhere to someone who fears God, and by your staying close to him, he will teach you too to fear God.'[7]

Abba Poemen said, 'Do not assess yourself, but adhere to someone who lives well.'[8]

A brother came to Abba Poemen and said to him, 'What shall I do?' The old man said to him, 'Go and live with someone who says, "What do I want?" and you will have rest.'[9]

In each of these three sayings of or reported by Poemen the emphasis lies on a particular quality of life possessed by the abba. This quality is either something which the disciple hopes to learn, or it is a mark of the abba's own experience and self-knowledge—a sign of his ability to supply guidance which will relieve others with less self-awareness and experience of the worrying desire to measure or assess their own progress and achievements.[10] Thus in the last saying quoted the brother is in a state of distress, unsure of what kind of life he ought to adopt;[11] Poemen's response to his question means that the brother should live with someone who has learnt to cope with these doubts or frustrations by a careful assessment of his own needs or wishes. The way to peace and freedom from these worries about himself, and to virtues like fear of God, lies in the disciple's submission to the authority and teaching of a wiser and more experienced figure, who practises the kind of relationship with God which the disciple desires but from which his

[6] Cf. Rousseau, *Ascetics, Authority, and the Church*, 19–21.

[7] Poemen 65. On fear of God, see Ch. 3, n. 14.

[8] Poemen 73. For 'assess' (*μετρεῖ*), cf. Poemen 36 (quoted below) and 79, and Paphnutius 3 (which has *μὴ μετρεῖ* instead of the *γενοῦ ἀψήφιστος* found in the parallel and probable source in Isaiah, *Logos* 6, 3a. For the latter word, cf. also *Logos* 6, 6Ba).

[9] Poemen 143. On rest (*ἀνάπαυσις*), see Sisoes 43 and N 245 (to be quoted further on in this section), and Ch. 4, n. 8.

[10] Cf. P. Rousseau, 'The Desert Fathers, Antony and Pachomius', in C. Jones, G. Wainwright, and E. Yarnold (eds.), *The Study of Spirituality* (London, 1986), 124, who refers to avoidance of 'a sterile estimation of yourself' apropos of Poemen 65.

[11] See Sisoes S 3 (Guy, *Recherches*, 33) for an expression of frustration with one's way of life: 'I am wasting my days, Father.'

own inabilities or sins separate him: 'An old man said, "Be like a camel, bearing your sins and following, bridled, someone who knows the way of God."'[12]

These sayings generally take for granted, I think, that it is the new monk, the *ἀρχάριος*, who needs to submit himself in this way in order to learn what the monastic life involves: 'He [Isaiah] said to those who were making a good beginning [*καλῶς ἀρχομένους*] and submitting to the holy Fathers, "The first dyeing does not fade, as in the case of purple cloth", and, "As tender shoots are easily twisted and bent, so are beginners who live in submission."'[13] In submission to his abba the life of the disciple acquires the form and colouring which will characterize the rest of his time as a monk.

The converse of this emphasis on the necessity of teaching for beginners is a warning, expressed strongly in two anonymous stories, against those who believe that they can manage without the help of the old men:

A certain brother, having withdrawn from the world and taken the habit, immediately shut himself up, saying, 'I am an anchorite.' When the old men heard they came and threw him out [of his cell], and made him go round to the cells of the brothers, doing penance and saying, 'Forgive me, for I am not an anchorite but a beginner.'[14]

The old men said, 'If you see a young man climbing up to heaven by his own will, grab his foot and pull him down, for this is good for him.'[15]

The message of both of these stories is fairly clear: in the first case, the brother ought to realize that he needs help in order to become a monk

[12] N 436. Nau's edition of the Greek text stops at N 392, although he added a few sayings from later in the manuscript, of which this is one (numbered by him 399). For texts from later in the N series, which Nau did not publish, Regnault's translation, *Les Sentences des Pères du désert: Série des anonymes* may be consulted, but some of the texts were included in the eleventh-century anthology of Paul Evergetinos, *Εὐεργετινὸς ἤτοι συναγωγὴ τῶν θεοφθόγγων ῥημάτων καὶ διδασκαλιῶν τῶν θεοφόρων καὶ ἁγίων πατέρων* (4 vols.; Athens, 1957–66). N 436 = Evergetinos vol. i, ch. 19, sub-sect. 7, no. 2. Future references will be of the form Evergetinos 1.19.7.2. The method of numbering individual units within each chapter varies from edition to edition (and from reprint to reprint of the Athens edition); strictly, a four-figure reference is necessary, though the French translation uses a three-figure reference for vols. i and ii (by counting the units continuously from the beginning of each chapter rather than from the start of each sub-section—e.g. for N 436, Evergetinos 1.19.7.2 = 1.19.17), and sometimes for vols. iii and iv as well. When doubt arises, it may be assumed that the correct reference is to be found within a section of each chapter entitled *ἐν τῷ γεροντικῷ*.

[13] Esaias 2. Cf. 1 for his views on what is good for beginners.

[14] N 243.

[15] N 244 (= N 111).

and cannot learn and understand everything he needs to know on his own. He needs, in fact, to submit himself to instruction in the same way as the monks who received Poemen's advice to live with people able to guide them through the dangers of worrying pointlessly about themselves. His failure to do this requires an apology to those brothers who (we may assume) have been more realistic about their own limitations. In the second case, the problem lies in the brother's straightforward, probably quite unmalicious, reliance on himself, on his own will, and not on others.[16]

The fundamental problem here is, obviously, that a brother who relies on his own knowledge and judgement rather than on his abba may be deceived about his life and fall into error or sin, or even just achieve nothing. This is expressed clearly in a story about a disciple who found a 'withdrawn and quiet place' in the desert where he wanted to live, and asked his abba to allow him to go there; 'and I hope in God and in your prayers that I will be able to work hard there'.[17] The old man however would not let him go:

> I know well that you will work hard, but because you do not have an old man, you will come to be confident that your work is pleasing to God, and because of this confidence that you have done all the work of a monk, you will lose your labour and your wits [φρένας].

The problem is not that the brother will be negligent in his labours, but that he will come to believe that he has already made good progress in the monastic life and that he has nothing further to achieve or to learn. His ability to think objectively (is this what is meant by φρένας?) about his life will be impaired by his lack of either experience or guidance. The company of an 'old man' would show him where, perhaps to his surprise, he still fell short of the virtues of fear of God and self-knowledge to which Poemen's sayings refer. Antony makes a closely related point about the necessity of teaching, using similar terms: 'I know of monks who have fallen after many labours and gone out of their wits [φρενῶν] through trusting in their works and disobeying the commandment which says, "Ask your father, and he will tell you."'[18] To 'fall after many labours' and to 'lose your labour' both express the

[16] Cf. Eth. Coll. 13.8 for someone's own will not allowing him to listen to others, and Ch 246: even Adam in paradise should have asked the advice of the angels.

[17] N 370. See Guy, *Recherches*, 19, for its presence in some manuscripts of the sayings of Antony.

[18] Antony 37; Deut. 32: 7.

fruitlessness of a monastic life which is lived with no proper awareness of your own real needs. Similarly, 'He who wishes to live in the desert needs to be capable of teaching, not to be in need of teaching, lest he suffer loss [*ζημιοῦται*].'[19] This allows that a monk may make sufficient progress to allow him to live without supervision, though warning against the dangers of taking this step prematurely—obviously every abba was once a beginner and has travelled the path to maturity along which life together with one of the old men is the first step, but which the various brothers who wished to live alone have tried to follow before they were ready.

The importance for a disciple of submitting himself to the care of an abba is underlined by sayings which insist on the necessity of disclosure of 'thoughts'.[20] A brother was tempted by fornication and went to see an old man to tell him about this thought (*λογισμός*). The old man comforted him and sent him away, and when the brother continued to come to see him, still tempted, the old man told him to keep on coming whenever he was tempted by a demon: 'You will defeat him ... for nothing distresses the demon of fornication as much as revealing his works, and nothing makes him as happy as hiding his thoughts.'[21] It is not surprising that some disciples seem to have found this potentially shaming counsel difficult to put into practice. A brother asked Poemen why he was not able to 'be free with the old men in my thoughts'—that is, why he found it difficult to speak about them.[22] Poemen replied with what was, it seems, a common teaching, but one which in this context only warns the brother of his danger, and does not really answer his question: 'The enemy rejoices over nothing as much as over those who do not reveal their thoughts.'

Some brothers once asked an abba whether someone who is afflicted with a *λογισμός*, and who has read what the fathers taught on the subject should 'be zealous in himself to make use of what he has read, and to be satisfied in his own conscience', or whether he should reveal the

[19] N 221. Cf. N 668 (Evergetinos, 1.38.4.5) and 669 (Evergetinos, 4.38.7.2) for related teaching (Regnault numbers these pieces J 700 and 701, since he prefers to follow a manuscript other than that used by Nau for this part of the anonymous series). In *VA*, 3–4, Antony is portrayed as learning the practices of the monastic life from local recluses before venturing out into the desert.

[20] Cf. Guy, 'Educational Innovation in the Desert Fathers', 49–50.

[21] N 164.

[22] Poemen 101.

thought to a father.[23] The abba replies that the thought must be revealed, 'for no one can help himself, especially when he is fought against by the passions'. To obtain advice and help in the fight against temptation, that is, is the main purpose of disclosing thoughts. But the abba goes on to tell of his own experience of the demonic temptation not to reveal his thoughts. He went to see Abba Zeno to tell him of a thought from which he was suffering, 'But Satan prevented me, suggesting "Because you know what you ought to do, behave in the way you have read: why go and bother the old man?"' Not until some time later did he decide to disclose the thought to Zeno, and even then he could not bring himself to do so until the abba realized that something was wrong:

> He, turning and seeing me tormented by my thoughts, tapped me on the chest and said to me, 'What is the matter? I too am a man.' When he said this, I thought that my heart was open to him. I fell on my face at his feet, beseeching him with tears and saying, 'Have mercy on me.' But the old man said to me, 'What is the matter?' I answered, 'Don't you know what the matter is?' He said, 'You must say it.' Then, with great shame, I told him of my passion. He said to me, 'Why were you ashamed to tell me before? Am I not a man too? But do you want me to tell you what I know? Have you not been coming here for three years already with these thoughts, and not revealing them?'

The brother's disclosure of his passion marks a turning-point. We are not told what the passion was, and the advice given by Zeno is not very specific ('Go, do not be careless about your prayers, and do not slander anyone'); but after he finally succeeds in telling Zeno what is wrong, then, 'by the grace of Christ and the prayers of the old man, I was no longer disturbed by that passion'. Clearly the fact that demonic temptation to remain silent is overcome and the passion disclosed to an abba who can pray for the brother[24] is, in itself, the most important reason

[23] N 509 (Evergetinos, 1.20.3.1). This is a story from the later expansion of the anonymous series and belongs to a period when written accounts of the teachings of the fathers were already available. But it shows that some material in this part of the anonymous series is not much later than the alphabetical collection, for the old man who tells this story about Zeno must have encountered him before 450 (and therefore recounted the story *c.*500 at the latest), as Zeno died one year before Chalcedon according to John Rufus of Maiuma, *Plerophories*, 8, ed. F. Nau (Patrologia Orientalis, 8: 1; Paris, 1912), 21.

[24] On an abba's prayer for his disciple as, normally, a means by which he is delivered from temptation, see the striking examples in Antony 14 (ambiguous—is the brother saved or not?), Amoun 3, Sisoes 12, N 169 (below, n. 57), 293; in N 82 a brother dies when his abba prays for his deliverance from fornication—a shocking story but perhaps a warning against an old man coming to believe that his prayers control what God does.

for his recovery. This is consistent with the teaching of N 164.[25]

The brother in this story is not deceived about the nature of his life: he knows that he is a sinner, but finds it difficult to bring himself to do what he needs to in order to be helped. In a saying attributed to Antony, disclosure is not limited to thoughts or passions which require healing, but extends to the smallest practical detail of a monk's life: 'If possible, a monk ought to confide in the old men about how many steps he takes or how many drops he drinks in his cell, so that he does not make a mistake in these matters.'[26]

To summarize then, a disciple must submit himself to an abba and disclose his thoughts to him in order to avoid error and confidence in his own works, or on the other hand, worry and uncertainty about his progress in the monastic life. Renunciation of his own will is the keystone of true progress in the monastic life; a disciple should give up his will to the commands of his father, even to the extent of ceasing to worry about his own obedience to the commandments of God;[27] and a brother should be restrained who, contrary to this teaching, wishes to climb up to heaven by his own will.[28]

Many sayings confirm or elaborate these basic positions, including some which show that teaching on the need to overcome one's own will is a general feature of the Desert Fathers' outlook, not something confined to the teaching relationship or to the behaviour of beginners. These sayings on the will also deserve a brief discussion, and three

[25] Zeno's advice is, in fact, hardly more specific than the teaching on 'the salvation of the soul and how someone is cleansed from defiling thoughts' which he is reported as giving to the speaker 'according to custom' *before* he realizes that his visitor has something specific to disclose. Later, after a year free of the passion, the brother begins to wonder whether 'God had mercy on you, and it was not because of the old man'. He goes to see Zeno, to test him, and asks him to pray about the passion. 'But he left me lying at his feet, and after being silent for a short time said, "Get up, have faith." When I heard this, through shame I wanted the earth to swallow me. I got up, unable to look at the old man, and returned to my cell, amazed and frightened.' The old man's words are perhaps meant to show that he is aware of the brother's new temptation to doubt the value of the old man's help; or he may mean merely that the brother should have faith in his freedom from the old passion.

[26] Antony 38. Cf. N 176 for an example of disclosure of a trivial incident by a disciple. Cf. Eth. Coll 14.67: the labour of a monk is vain if he does not visit a 'man of the Lord' and disclose his thoughts to him; and N 592/50 (Evergetinos, 1.20.3.8, has the first half only): not to disclose thoughts is a sign of lack of humility; when thoughts are disclosed to someone and he replies, it is God who speaks through him. N 215 considers the case of someone who has no one in whom to confide his problem: if he sincerely asks God, he will receive an answer.

[27] N 290.

[28] N 244.

sayings of Poemen again supply a convenient illustration:

To throw himself before God, not to assess himself, and to cast his own will behind him: these are the tools of the soul.[29]

The will of a man is a wall of bronze between himself and God, and a rock which blocks his path. When a man renounces it he will say, 'With God's help I will leap over the wall'. If what is right agrees with his will, then a man works hard.[30]

Do not fulfil your own will; rather, you must humble yourself before your brother.[31]

Two of these sayings refer to the monk's relationship of dependence on and submission to God, and to the separation from God which following his own will causes. The third saying refers quite generally to the need for renunciation of one's own will in the context of relationships with others (not in the specific context of the teaching relationship). Closely parallel to these in wording and message is a saying of Sisoes, which implies a similar attitude of self-renunciation in dealings with others: 'Be despised, cast your will behind you, and do not worry, and you will have rest.'[32] To 'be despised' is to allow others to treat you badly, or at least perhaps to imagine that you deserve to be so treated—a more expressive phrase than Poemen's 'humble yourself'; while 'do not worry' probably implies the same viewpoint as Poemen's 'do not assess yourself'.

These general sayings on the necessity of renouncing all self-will reinforce the point made earlier in discussing the other instance of 'do not assess yourself' in Poemen 73, where the context is the relationship between disciple and abba. By submitting to his spiritual father, or to God (as in Poemen 36), a monk may avoid the temptation continually to assess his own progress in the monastic life as if he alone, rather

29. Poemen 36. On the problem of the will, see above, n. 16; and Regnault, 'Obéissance et liberté', 96–7.

30 Poemen 54. Ps. 18: 39. For another biblical interpretation concerning renunciation of your own will, see Ammonas 11 (= N 249). N 248 makes a distinction between someone who 'does something following his own will, and is not in agreement with God, but is ignorant' and someone who 'grasps his own will, not in accord with God, and does not want to listen to others, but thinks he knows his own good'. The former, 'will certainly come into the way of God', while the latter, 'comes into the way of God [only] with labour'. An offence through ignorance (i.e. through failure to realize the dangers of following your own will) is more easily corrected than that of someone who deliberately chooses to follow his own will and disobeys others. See also Isidore 9 and Moses 17.

31 Poemen 158.

32 Sisoes 43; the issues raised by the 'be despised' of this saying will be explored in Ch. 4 on anger and praise.

than God or his abba, was responsible for it. As Poemen said elsewhere, conveying the necessity of this freedom from care about oneself to a brother worried about 'what I should do': 'When God is watching over us, what have we to be concerned about?'[33]

Elsewhere again the problem of the will, which these sayings identify in general terms, is more directly linked to the necessity of submission to a teacher in the monastic life: 'We must govern our souls with discernment [*διακρίσει*], and if we live in a cenobium, not seek our own good, nor serve our own will, but obey our father in the faith.'[34] Although this saying refers to a 'cenobium', which implies a community of a different type from the semi-anchoritic monasticism of Nitria and Scetis, its comments on the will and on submission to an elder are fully in line with those of Poemen. Finally, two other sayings about the will deserve to be quoted as further, more complex, illustrations of this and other points which have been made in this section:

> A brother said to an old man, 'I do everything that is necessary in my cell, yet I do not find comfort from God.' The old man answered him, 'This happens to you because you live with someone who is idle, and want to impose your own will.' The brother said to the old man, 'What do you command me to do, Father?' The old man said, 'Go, and adhere to someone who fears God, and humble yourself before him, surrendering your own will. And then you will find comfort from God.'[35]

As in N 370—the story of the brother whose abba will not allow him to live alone—the problem is not that the brother is negligent, nor even that he believes he is making good progress. He knows that there is something wrong, that he has no 'comfort from God', and the answer is that he has not learnt the important lesson of renunciation of his own will which living in submission to an abba is meant to teach. In the other instance, the brother is initially less aware that something is wrong:

> A brother said to a great old man, 'Abba, I wish to find an old man who suits my wishes, and die with him.'[36] The old man said to him, 'You are looking for something good, my Lord.' But he was convinced in his mind to do this, and did not consider what the old man had meant. When the old man saw that he

[33] Poemen 162. 'Our sins', the brother replies to Poemen's question. Of course Poemen did not mean that a monk need not worry about his sins, and answers, 'Let us go into our cells and remember our sins, and the Lord will be with us in everything.' Remembrance of sin is itself a means of submission to and trust in God. Cf. Antony 4.

[34] Syncletica 17.

[35] N 484 (Evergetinos, 1.19.7.3). Note the parallel to Poemen 65 on fear of God.

[36] That is, to live with him until death.

thought that what he wanted was good, he said to him, 'If you find an old man who suits your wishes, do you want to stay with him?' He said, 'Yes, especially if I find what I want.' The old man said to him, 'Isn't it in fact that case that you want to find rest not by conforming to the will of an old man, but by his conforming to your will?' The brother realized what he had said, stood up and made a prostration, saying, 'Forgive me, I boasted a great deal, thinking I had spoken well, when I understood nothing.'[37]

The abba's sarcasm ('My Lord') is meant to draw attention to the brother's error of wanting to find someone congenial to him, or even to impose his own will on someone else, rather than considering what an experienced abba would be capable of teaching him. The abba implies that the brother will not find rest by this search for satisfaction of his own self-defined needs but (as taught consistently by Poemen, Sisoes, and Syncletica) by giving up these worries and conforming to the will of someone else, someone, in Poemen's words, who really knows 'what I want'.[38] To find rest or 'comfort from God' when worried about his own spiritual condition, and to overcome his own will, emerge here again as the primary reasons for which a disciple should submit himself to the instruction of an abba.[39]

[37] N 245.

[38] Poemen 143.

[39] Although the submission of a disciple to *one* abba as his *principal* teacher was probably the norm, it should not be thought that this pattern of relationships was rigidly adhered to, or that a disciple's consultation of other abbas when appropriate was precluded. Cf. Regnault, 'Obéissance et liberté', 99–101, for this point, and 97–108 for the flexibility that was possible in the form of the teaching relationship. Rousseau, *Ascetics, Authority, and the Church*, 36 n. 15, suggests that some disciples tried out several abbas, rejecting one or more before settling on one to their taste. The evidence he cites includes N 245 (which as we have seen, rejects the idea), and sayings in which a disciple questions first one abba and then another on the same subject: Poemen 88–9, 97–8 (cf. Sisoes 35–6), N 216, 217. But there is no reason to think that these questions are an attempt to establish a permanent relationship with an abba; rather, they represent the consultation of more than one abba as a perfectly normal practice. In N 182–3 a brother questions three abbas, but is not trying to decide with whom to form a permanent bond. Similarly Agathon 28 (cited by Rousseau) does not mean that his disciples found him unsatisfactory and moved to Arsenius, but simply that occasional changes in the pattern of relationships were accepted. Antony 27 and Paphnutius 3 (Isaiah, *Logos* 6, 3a) may also refer to occasional consultation, not to the exclusive adherence of a disciple to one abba. N 351 shows that a group of old men could share jointly in the task of looking after brothers, who lived alone rather than with one old man. (*HM*, 20.10–11, perhaps suggests a similar corporate concern for the well-being of new monks.) Ward, 'Spiritual Direction in the Desert Fathers', 66, is thus not strictly correct to state that 'in the desert there could only be one father to a disciple'. Ares, Dioscorus 2, Macarius 33, Eth. Coll. 13.79, and N 291 also show that an abba could supervise someone who lived apart rather than in the same cell. (In Macarius 33, the supervision is rather lax, as he leaves two brothers on their own for three years, but he regarded this as exceptional.) The problem in N 243 thus seems

2. The Word of the Abba

The teaching relationship is established by the disciple's submission of his will to the teaching of an abba; but what account is given by the Desert Fathers of the nature of this teaching? The evidence suggests that the abba's words enjoy a special authority which compels respect, attention, and obedience, both from an abba's immediate disciples and from visitors and others who consulted him on one occasion or another. This is perhaps best illustrated by the persistence with which, in different circumstances, disciples would seek a word from an abba. Some brothers waited for four days to hear a word from Pambo when he was unwilling to speak.[40] Another visiting group of brothers came to see Antony and asked him to 'Speak a word to us; how may we be saved?'[41] 'Have you attended to scripture? It is good for you,' Antony replied, but the brothers persisted in their request for a word: 'We want to hear something from you too, father.' He answered their wish, but only repeated the words of scripture. An abba's own concern that someone should be persistent in seeking advice is illustrated by a saying about John. An old man who was 'very hard-working in bodily things, but not accurate in his thoughts' came to see him about forgetfulness, but forgot what John had told him, and continued to do so despite several visits. Eventually he stopped consulting him, but John told him not to be doubtful about coming, and used an illustration to show him that the old men do not lose anything by being consulted so often.[42]

to be not the fact that the brother wishes to live alone, but that he considers himself to need no instruction. Two other sayings on adherence to an abba may be noted: Esaias 3 criticizes beginners who move from one monastery to another; but Poemen S 14 (Guy, *Recherches*, 30) stresses the necessity of trust in the person to whom you commit yourself: 'Do not entrust your conscience to a man in whom your heart is not fully confident.' Some discretion on the disciple's behalf is perhaps legitimate.

[40] Pambo 2.

[41] Antony 19. The question 'How may I be saved?' (cf. e.g. Euprepius 7, Macarius 25, N 387) has been seen as appropriate to a new monk attempting to establish a permanent relationship with a teacher (cf. Gould, 'A Note on the *Apophthegmata Patrum*', 134). But Antony 19 shows that like the questions referred to above, n. 39, it too could be a means of occasional consultation of different abbas. Stories of how permanent relationships were established do occur in, e.g. N 17, 46, 190, 291, 346, and Ch 270, some of which will be noted in Sec. 4 of this chapter, but they are quite different in form; see Regnault, *La Vie quotidienne*, 142–4, for other examples.

[42] John Kolobos 18. Clearly the old man was not a beginner, but someone who still needed teaching in certain respects. N 223 supplies another instance of a disciple being made to act out a parable concerning forgetfulness: here however the point is to illustrate the effect of repeated consultation of an abba on the disciple, rather than on the abba. Cf. Eth. Coll. 13.72 for a related point: repeated hearing and recalling of the words of the old men is good, even if the hearer cannot put them into practice.

The old man's response to the 'acted parable'[43] which John uses to show that he is not harmed by repeated visits itself supplies an illustration of the high regard in which a disciple or questioner could hold the words of an abba. John tells the old man to light a lamp, and to use it to light some more in turn, then points out to him that the lamp has not been harmed by being used to light others. (Similarly, the old men are not harmed by sharing their wisdom with others.) The parable is a simple one, but the old man's willingness to obey John's curious instructions illustrates the Desert Fathers' concern for exact obedience (the value of which will be the subject of Sect. 4 of this chapter) to the words of an abba. A story about Macarius provides another example: he tells a brother to 'go to the cemetery, and abuse the dead'.[44] The brother obeys this bizarre command punctiliously, being made, like the old man to whom John spoke, to act out a parable which taught him an important lesson about the nature of the monastic life.

The story about Pambo quoted above contains an explanation, given to the visitors by *οἱ κληρικοί* (presumably the priests or minor clergy who assisted Pambo as senior priest in Nitria), of the old man's silence: 'Do not be troubled, brother ... for this is the old man's custom. He does not readily speak, unless God gives him confidence.'[45] This comment implies that the abba's word to a disciple could be seen as possessing an inspired or charismatic quality, an authority derived directly from God, and dependent on God's will for its exercise.[46] Such a definite view of the inspired nature of the word of an abba is not developed very far in the *Apophthegmata*,[47] but it is important to give

[43] Cf. Nagel, 'Action-Parables in Earliest Christian Monasticism', 258–9, who does not of course regard the story as historical.

[44] Macarius 23; cf. Nagel, 'Action—Parables in Earliest Christian Monasticism', 253–4, for this and other 'death' parables.

[45] The reference to the priests and the motif of Pambo's unwillingness to speak without divine assurance are not found in the parallel in Eth. Coll. 14.21 (attributed to Ammoes). But *HL*, 10.7, helps to confirm that the story in its Greek form is appropriate to Pambo, and perhaps explains how it came to be attributed to him in a tradition different from that known to Eth. Coll.

[46] Rousseau, *Ascetics, Authority, and the Church*, 29, regards 'supposed inspiration by God' as 'the essential basis of trust in the teaching of the fathers'. But this is a generalization only from Pambo 2, 7, and the stories about Pambo in *HL*, 10.7, and 14.6. On the charismatic quality of the abba's words, see also Guy, 'Educational Innovation in the Desert Fathers', 45–6, and on his spiritual authority in broader terms (mainly with reference to the *VA*), P. Henry, 'From Apostle to Abbot: The Legitimation of Spiritual Authority in the Early Church', *SP* 17 (Oxford, 1982), 491–505.

[47] The Pachomian sources supply a passage in which the role and authority of an abba is explained and justified more fully than anywhere in the *Apophthegmata*. See the fragment

some attention to those sayings which do portray the word of the abba in this way. The most explicit of these is a story about Ephrem. 'One of the saints' saw a vision in which a group of angels discussed who was worthy to receive a *κεφαλίδα* (defined as 'a book written on both sides') which they had brought with them from heaven, concluding that only Ephrem was able to be entrusted with it: 'Then the old man saw them give the scroll to Ephrem. Rising early, he heard Ephrem teaching, as if a spring was flowing from his mouth, and knew that what comes from the lips of Ephrem is of the Holy Spirit.'[48] This saying has a fairly secure place in the early texts of the *Apophthegmata* and was obviously felt by the compiler to be of significance and value. But it would be a mistake to treat it as a definitive illustration of the Desert Fathers' belief in the inspiration of teaching, for it is certainly far more definite than most other texts dealing with the subject. The story also occurs in traditions about the Syrian Ephrem and should probably be regarded as an importation into the *Apophthegmata* from an outside source, rather than as stemming, ultimately, from the oral tradition of the Egyptian desert.[49] Nevertheless, the existence of a belief in inspiration in a less definite form is illustrated by three other main stories besides that about Pambo, which will be examined in the rest of this section.[50]

They used to say that if anyone came to Abba Poemen, he sent them to Abba Anoub first, because he was older in years. But Abba Anoub used to say to them, 'Go to my brother Poemen, because he has the gift of the word [*τοῦ*

of the *First Sahidic Life* of Pachomius in *Sancti Pachomii Vitae Sahidice scripta*, ed. L. Th. Lefort, (CSCO 99–100; Scriptores Coptici, 9–10; Louvain, 1933–4), vol. 99, 253–4, trans. A. Veilleux, *Pachomian Koinonia* (3 vols., CSS 45–7; Kalamazoo, Mich., 1980–82), i, 425–7. Here the author first explains why referring to someone as father is legitimate despite Christ's injunction in Matt. 23:9, and then speaks in explicit terms of the indwelling of the Trinity in those who are (spiritual) fathers. G1 17 is another biblically-based comment on the community's attitude to its fathers, Pachomius and his immediate companions and successors. Antony 37 (quoted above) is the only saying attempting a similar biblical vindication of the role of the spiritual father.

[48] Ephrem 2; 1 also comments on his quality as a teacher, but without an explicit reference to inspiration.

[49] Ephrem 1 and 2 occur in PJ 18.5, 6, which is evidence of their presence in early texts of the Sayings. They are also found in the Latin *Life of Ephrem* (PL, lxxiii. 321–4). For some comments on their occurrence in Syriac sources and possible provenance, see A. Vööbus, *Literary Critical and Historical Studies in Ephrem the Syrian* (Papers of the Estonian Theological Society in Exile, 10; Stockholm, 1958), 14, 26 (n. 6), 32–3, 44.

[50] Besides these, see also Ch 249, where an Abba Abraham is described as 'the prophet of the region'.

λόγου τὸ χάρισμα].' And if Abba Anoub was sitting with Abba Poemen, Abba Poemen used not to speak in his presence.[51]

Anoub recognizes in Poemen a gift of teaching. The saying leaves unanswered, however, the question of whether inspiration was seen as a common possession of all or many abbas, or as the special gift of certain individuals. Anoub's words do not absolutely imply the latter, for his comment may be seen simply as intended to reciprocate Poemen's humility towards him by disclaiming any special gift of teaching for himself.[52]

A brother came to ask Abba Ares, 'Tell me what I should do to be saved.'[53] The abba sent him away to spend a year eating bread and salt in the evenings, and when the brother came back at the end of the year, imposed an even harsher ascetic regime on him. When the brother had gone away, Abba Abraham asked Ares why he imposed such a heavier burden on this brother than on others.

The old man said to him, 'Whatever the brothers come to seek, they leave having got it. This one comes to hear a word for God's sake, for he is a hard worker. Whatever I tell him, he will do with zeal. Therefore I speak the word of God to him.'

The story does not explicitly assert the inspiration of the abba's words, only that he teaches something that is in accord with God's will and fitted for a brother who wants to obey and live 'for God's sake'. Less reticent in claiming inspiration for the words of an abba is Felix:

Some brothers came to Abba Felix, bringing some seculars with them, and they

[51] Poemen 108. For a saying which gives greater honour to the older of two natural brothers rather than to the more experienced in the monastic life, see N 246.

[52] Some sayings which refer to different *χαρίσματα* certainly imply that they are special gifts: N 40 speaks of a *χάρισμα τῆς ἐλεημοσύνης*; N 287 of a *χάρισμα τῆς διακονίας*: both mean that the brother concerned is specially gifted, or assisted by God, in performing a duty to which all are in some way bound. The same may apply to the abba's charism of speech. In N 380 an old man prays to receive a charism (we are not told what) and is told by another that he ought to pray to have it taken away again: clearly a special gift which distinguishes him from others, and which therefore tempts him to pride, is meant. See also N 34 and N 398 (Evergetinos, 4.5.2.21–2). Mention of charisms is frequent in *HL* (12.1, 24.1, 35.2, 49.1) and *HM* (2.6, 5.7). For some comments on charisms in the *Apophthegmata*, see A.M. Ritter, 'Statt einer Zusammenfassung: Die Theologie des Basileios im Kontext der Reichskirche am Beispiel seines Charisma-verständnisses', in P.J. Fedwick (ed.), *Basil of Caesarea: Christian, Humanist, Ascetic* (2 vols.; Toronto, 1981), i. 414–17. Also (referring mainly to the *VA*) K. Holl, *Enthusiasmus und Bussgewalt beim griechischen Mönchtum* (Leipzig, 1898), 138–55, esp. 148–53.

[53] Ares.

besought him to say a word to them. But the old man was silent. After they had besought him many times he said to them, 'Do you want to hear a word?' They said to him, 'Yes, Abba'. The old man said, 'There are no words now. When the brothers used to question the old men, and do what they said to them, God would show them how to speak. But now, since they ask, but do not do what they hear, God has taken the grace of the word [*τὴν χάριν τοῦ λόγου*] away from the old men, and they do not find anything to say, because there is no one who works.' When they heard these things the brothers wept and said, 'Pray for us, Abba.'[54]

Two important things should be noted about these sayings on inspiration. First, three of them (Ares is the exception) relate to incidents in which the abba's gift of teaching was not exercised, or in which he was reluctant to teach. This phenomenon is one to which we shall return in the last section of this chapter.[55] Secondly, two of the sayings explicitly relate the exercise of the abba's gift to the attitude of his questioners. Ares does so specifically: the brother's hard work calls forth the word of God from the abba; Felix is more general: God has taken away the abbas' words because disciples are not as obedient and diligent as they ought to be. Inspiration was not, in fact, an isolated phenomenon, but a response (of God through the abba) to the disciple or disciples with their individual needs, capacities, and attitudes.[56]

Like the acted parables of John and Macarius, these sayings draw attention to the Desert Fathers' insistence on a disciple's obedience to the abba's words, on his renunciation of his own will, and on a patient search for advice about his own needs (even the brothers in the saying about Pambo were eventually rewarded for their long wait by an answer to their question). These virtues of obedience and submission were, as we have already seen, regarded as good in themselves in determining the disciple's capacity to make progress in the monastic life; their importance was no doubt reinforced by belief in the inspiration of the abba's words, even though this belief emerges at comparatively few points, and even with some reticence, in the texts of the Sayings.

[54] Felix.

[55] See below, Sect. 8. Reluctance to answer questions is a feature of Zacharias 1 and 3 (Eth. Coll. 14.34) which, together with 2, imply a gift of speech. In 3 Moses tells him, 'I have seen the Holy Spirit descending on you, and so I am compelled to question you.'

[56] Cf. N 592/50 (above, n. 26): God responds through an abba to a disciple's disclosure of his thoughts.

3. The Practice of Teaching: Visions and Discernment

The belief that the words of an abba were inspired is a very general expression of the belief that in the practice of teaching, which was his duty towards the disciples or visitors who submitted themselves to his care, an abba received divine assistance and guidance. A more specific form of divine guidance in teaching, easier to illustrate than the belief in inspiration which is seldom referred to explicitly, are the visionary experiences with which many abbas were visited and which helped them to discover the hidden causes of the particular problems of their disciples. This divine assistance to the abba is best illustrated by two clear examples. A brother came to see an abba to ask him to pray for him because he was tempted by fornication. After a while the abba seems to have become worried that the brother was not finding peace and asked God to show him how the brother was living in his cell:

> And God showed him what the brother was doing. He saw him sitting down, and the spirit of fornication was near him. An angel stood by, sent to help him, and was angry with the brother because he did not throw himself upon God, but took pleasure in the thoughts, and devoted his whole mind to this activity.[57]

As a result of this revelation the abba confronts the brother, tells him that his problem arises from his own consent to the thoughts, and teaches him how to resist them, so that the brother finds peace 'through the prayer and teaching of the old man'.

Of course this saying is designed mainly to serve as a warning to those who heard it repeated or read it, reminding them that the persistence of their temptations was often a result of their own willingness to entertain them rather than the severity of the temptation itself; however, there is no reason to think that the visionary element in the story would not be taken seriously as an indication of how an abba might gain the information about his disciple which he needed to teach him effectively. A lengthy story about Macarius supplies another example. Macarius lives alone in the desert, but near to an area where there are many brothers, over whom he clearly exercises some form of supervision.[58] Once 'the old man was surveying the road, and saw Satan coming in the form of a man, as if to pass by him.' Macarius responds to this vision by asking the enemy what he is doing, and he tells him that he is going to offer evil suggestions to (ὑπομιμνῄσκειν) the brothers:

[57] N 169. Cf. N 532 (Evergetinos, 1.21.6.5) for a somewhat similar incident.
[58] Macarius 3.

he carries many different kinds of food (that is, temptation or thought) for them, hoping that each brother will accept at least one. After a while Macarius sees him coming back and asks him how he has got on. Satan tells him that one brother only is friendly towards him, 'and when he sees me, he changes like the wind'. Macarius asks the brother's name, and when the visitor has gone he goes to see the brother concerned. Because of his vision he knows that the brother is suffering from temptation and persists in asking him about his temptations even though the brother, being ashamed, initially replies that everything is well. When the brother has admitted to his thoughts, Macarius tells him how to resist them: 'Fast until late, struggle, meditate on the gospel and the other scriptures, and if a thought comes to you, never look down, but up, and immediately the Lord will help you.'[59] Finally, we learn that the brother is no longer open to Satan's attacks but has become his most determined opponent.

This story says a great deal about the Desert Fathers' understanding of the activity of demons, and how their various temptations may be resisted;[60] but again the visionary element should be taken seriously, however disturbing it may seem. An ability to see demons or to understand their ways was an important aspect, for the Desert Fathers, of their visionary experience. An old man might pray to be allowed to see the activity of the demons,[61] or, having received the ability to see 'what was happening', might report that he had seen a demon unable to enter a brother's cell and fight against him as long as the brother continued to meditate (probably, as in Macarius' advice, on the scriptures).[62] In Macarius' case his vision of the enemy serves the cause of effective teaching.

[59] *Μηδέποτε πρόσχῃς κάτω ἀλλὰ πάντοτε ἄνω* is rather cryptic, although it presumably implies attention to God rather than the thought. A more detailed teaching is found in the text cited above, n. 5, which after the comment about the role of the spiritual father adds: 'Someone who has surrendered himself to God should not worry about a thought, or fight against it, or allow it any room to come in. If it comes in, lift it up to your Father and say, "I have nothing to do with it; behold, my Father knows".' Attention to God drives the thought away, for a thought 'cannot come with you to your God and Father'. For surrender to God (expressed in various ways), cf. Agathon 21, Poemen 146, N 174, and Eth.Coll. 13.52. In Eth. Coll. 14.6 someone who surrenders to God has his heart opened by God to the words of all—a useful quality for an abba.

[60] Learning how to combat particular demons is the subject of Evagrius, *Praktikos*, esp. 43, 50, 58–9. Comparatively little has been written on the demonology of the *Apophthegmata*, but see Regnault, *La Vie quotidienne*, 196–207.

[61] N 369. An element of caution is injected when God tells the monk, 'You have no need to see them.'

[62] N 366. N 359–69 are headed *περὶ διορατικῶν*, and all illustrate in various ways the

Like N 169, several sayings involve the visionary experience of an abba in perceiving the spiritual state of a brother for the purpose of teaching him more effectively.[63] As was pointed out in Chapter 1, one other important function of visions is to assess and criticize the quality of the monastic life of the community as a whole. Not all visions serve either of these two purposes,[64] but in some cases, as has been illustrated here, visions do assist the abba in the specific and personal task of teaching.[65]

Although examples of the use of visionary experiences in the practice of spiritual direction are quite numerous, they are nevertheless a relatively small proportion of all the examples of teaching which the *Apophthegmata* contain. Many examples of teaching presuppose the same sensitivity to a disciple's needs and insight into the ways of the demons which, in the sayings which have been referred to, are the product of visions and revelations, but without any reference to these experiences. N 509, a saying which has been referred to as teaching the necessity of disclosure of thoughts, is also a good example of this sensitivity.[66] Here

Desert Fathers' understanding of the nature and purpose of visionary experiences. H. Waddell, *The Desert Fathers* (London, 1936), 26, commenting on the relevant chapter (18) of PJ, was however disappointed: 'it is the dullest and least rewarding ... a patchwork of minor prophecies and commonplace materialisations of angelic and demonic powers'.

[63] In N 454 (Evergetinos, 2.28.7.8) an old man encourages a brother to resist temptation after seeing in a vision that God is rewarding him. In N 521 (Evergetinos, 2.32.7.22) an old man discovers in a vision that the gift of tears and compunction comes easily to one brother, whereas another finds it difficult to shake off his sins and repent. He is therefore able to exhort the latter to greater efforts. N 85 and N 359 also involve visions which reveal the spiritual state of monks. The saying about Paul the Simple claims that he 'saw the state of the soul of everyone', and shows him using this gift (*χάρις*) to discover that a brother has repented of his sins, and summoning the others to give thanks to God for the brother. An abba's ability to understand what was in the heart of a monk is a theme of *HM*, 2.12; 8.52; 12.10; 13.10; 16.1; also the *Letter of Ammon*, 16–17.

[64] In Ammonas 7 and Zeno 5 visions serve a purely private function. In N 368 a revelation explains a puzzling and worrying fact, why a good monk had been eaten by a hyena, to his servant: this too serves no immediate teaching function, though obviously addressing an important general problem (cf. Antony 2 for this problem, and N 74 for another example of private revelation).

[65] As pointed out in Gould, 'A Note on the *Apophthegmata Patrum*', 135, interpretation of Scripture could also be seen as a manifestation of a visionary ability: N 360, 362, 363. In N 314 an angel reveals the meaning of a text to a brother; in Antony 26 God sends Moses to him to interpret a passage of Scripture; and in Ch 250 Jeremiah reveals the meaning of one of his prophecies to a monk. Cf. the comment of H. Dörries, 'Die Bibel in ältesten Mönchtum', in *Wort und Stunde I: Gesammelte Studien zur Kirchengeschichte des vierten Jahrhunderts* (Göttingen, 1966), 271. This use of visionary experience obviously serves as a powerful support to the practice of teaching. *HM*, 2.7, and *HL*, 47.3, see interpretation of Scripture as a charism.

[66] See above, n. 23.

Abba Zeno sees that the brother is suffering from his thoughts and knows that the brother's problem is such that a personal disclosure to the abba is necessary to heal it; he then discloses in turn the fact that he knows the brother to have been suffering for a long time, and that he has been waiting for him to explain what is the matter. Here, clearly, the abba is exercising a personal judgment on how the brother must be treated, but he does not seem to know exactly what the problem is.

Perhaps the sensitivity which an abba ought to show towards his disciple's spiritual condition is best illustrated by two stories which contrast an abba who possesses it with one who does not. A brother came to Poemen to tell him that he was tempted by fornication, and that another abba had said to him, 'You should not let it stay with you.'[67] The reply is obviously no help to the brother, who precisely cannot get rid of the thought. Poemen responds by excusing the other old man and by establishing a bond of common experience between himself and the disciple. 'Abba Ibistion's deeds are on high with the angels, and it escapes him that you and I are subject to fornication.' He then offers the brother a description of the ascetic life which is more concrete and achievable than Ibistion's advice, and therefore more suited to the brother's needs: 'If a monk controls his belly and his tongue, and becomes a stranger, be confident that he will not die.'[68] In the other example a brother asks an old man whether someone who has a particular thought will be saved. The old man says no.[69] In fact the brother has himself committed the sin, but does not tell the old man. It is left to a different abba, Silvanus, to convince him that salvation is possible for someone who repents, and to point out to the first abba that he had made a mistake. The first abba has failed to realize that the disciple is talking about himself, and then fails again to answer the question itself

[67] Poemen 62 (Eth. Coll. 14.44). N 183 is a contrast: here a brother is scandalized by what an abba says about freedom from warfare, but another encourages him to go back and find out what the old man *really* meant. N 174 concerns another conflict of advice. Paphnutius 5 is another case of seeking a 'second opinion', but here the first abba's advice is confirmed by the others consulted. Stewart, 'Radical Honesty about the Self', 37, is wrong to characterize a normal process (cf. above, n. 39) pejoratively as 'playing off' one abba against another.

[68] The closing advice is not found in Eth. Coll. 14.44, but may be authentic, for it could have been omitted by the brother who witnessed the incident and reported the saying to the Eth. Coll. compiler, but included by him (or Poemen) when transmitting the saying by a different route to the alphabetical compiler's source. On the meaning of 'exile' (*ξενιτεία*), see Ch. 5, Sect. 5. A link between eating and fornication appears often, in Daniel 2, John Kolobos 4, N 94, N 532 (Evergetinos, 1.21.6.5), Eth. Coll. 13.33, 38, 14.24, 26, 27 (= N 173), 48, 49.

[69] N 217.

properly. His error is a very serious one, contradicting the important principle that repentance and a chance to begin again are always available to a sinner.[70]

In this text the first abba is described as 'inexperienced in discernment' (*ἄπειρος ὢν διακρίσεως*), and the conclusion of the saying is that it is dangerous to reveal thoughts or sins to the *ἀδιακρίτοις*, to the undiscerning. The saying establishes, in other words, a close relationship between the practice of good teaching and the possession of the virtue of discernment.

The importance of discernment in the *Apophthegmata* is illustrated by several short sayings which explicitly emphasize its necessity. It can be referred to as 'greater than all the virtues',[71] or as a key principle of the monastic life, without which a monk will not be able to live properly. Antony said, 'There are many who have worn out their bodies through asceticism, and yet who through not having discernment, are far from God.'[72] Sayings of this type do not offer a definition of what the possession of discernment is characteristically thought to involve for a monk. For this we must turn to other sayings like N 217, which mention discernment in the context of a narrative or story. The importance of the possession of discernment for an abba is clear from this text, and also from the many sayings which, though they do not mention *διάκρισις* explicitly, were included in the chapter of PJ on the subject and the corresponding section of the anonymous series N 133–369.[73]

Discernment at its most general involves knowing how to act for the best in any particular situation—which can sometimes involve acting in a way contrary to general expectations. John Kolobos saw that it was right to allow himself to be served by an elder, when all present expected him, because he was the youngest, to refuse.[74] This decision is explicitly attributed to his discernment.

A more complicated case concerns Poemen, who with some old men

[70] See e.g. Poemen 86, 99, Sisoes 38, N 208, and (implicitly) N 187.

[71] N 106.

[72] Antony 8 (cf. Poemen 106). See also Poemen 35, 52 (Eth. Coll. 14.11 is parallel but emphasizes a different virtue), 60, N 93, Eth. Coll. 13.18, 14.56; Syncletica 17 links discernment to renunciation of the will.

[73] See PJ 10 (with 115 pieces, the longest chapter), and N 216–53 (corresponding, in general, to PJ 10.78–114).

[74] John Kolobos 7, quoted Ch. 3, p. 94. For a comment on discernment as knowing 'exactly what is going on at any given moment', see S. Tugwell, *Ways of Imperfection: An Exploration of Christian Spirituality* (London, 1984), 15. Antony 35 is another excellent example of the exercise of discernment: a monk must be clear about his aims (cf. again Poemen 143); unfocused activity is pointless.

visited the house of a certain 'friend of Christ', who offered them meat to eat.[75] Poemen refused to eat it:

The old men were astonished that he had not eaten, because they knew of his discernment. When they got up they said to him, 'You are Poemen, and yet you have done this?' The old man answered them, 'Forgive me, fathers. You have eaten, and no one will be shocked; but if I had eaten, then since many brothers come to me, they would have suffered harm through saying, "If Poemen has eaten meat, why shouldn't we eat it?"'. And they were astonished at his discernment.

Here the old men initially expect Poemen to eat the meat which is offered. Two sayings may be noted which shed light on this. One of these is a simple warning by an old man to a brother that if he wishes to maintain his own ascetic practice he should stay at home; if he visits someone else he should fall in with the host's regime and not 'reveal your own way of life'.[76] The other is about a priest who similarly refused to break his own ascetic regime when visiting someone else, and who during a visit heard his hosts neither singing psalms nor praying, 'for their work was hidden'—that is they continued with their own normal pattern of life in secret.[77] The point of the story is the visitor's misunderstanding of his hosts' way of life, which he takes to be ascetically lax.[78] Eventually he discovers his error, and his host, 'Taught him discernment of thoughts, and cut off from him everything human. He became more accommodating, and used to eat everything that was set before him, and he too learnt to work in secret.'

To return to the saying about Poemen: it can be seen from the examples just given why the old men would expect him, as an abba well-known for his discernment, to eat the meat set before him in order to avoid making a show of his own asceticism or (the implication of a refusal) appearing to criticize his host's regime. But Poemen's answer shows the flexibility of response to different circumstances of which an abba must be capable if he is to be an effective teacher. He is aware of the bad impression that might be made on his disciples, and therefore

[75] Poemen 170.

[76] N 257; cf. N 256. But see Serinus 1.

[77] Eulogius the Priest; cf. Poemen 138 and Eth. Coll. 13.7 for other comments on a monk keeping his 'work' (asceticism or penance) secret from others. In Eth. Coll. 13.2 Poemen rejects the idea (suggested to him by a brother) of making his virtuous way of life a subject of his teaching.

[78] Cf. N 229, 242, which also discuss the attitudes of visitors (who, it is implied, lack discernment) to the regime of their hosts.

goes against normal practice and refuses to share what his host offers.

In another saying which mentions discernment explicitly an old man praises a brother who, having committed a sin, responds to the ensuing demonic temptation to give up the monastic life by saying to his thoughts, 'Why do you come in and trouble me in order to make me give up hope. I have not sinned. I say again, I have not sinned.[79] Of course the brother is not literally denying that he has fallen, but simply finding the most effective way of combating the temptation to despair. Discernment always includes this element of response to a particular need or situation.

We must now look briefly at the use which an abba makes of discernment in the practice of teaching, though it is impossible to cite in this context more than a few of the many sayings relevant to this theme contained in the chapters on discernment in PJ and the anonymous series. One important use of discernment, parallel to the use made of visions, lies in teaching brothers how best to understand and respond to the temptations which they experience; this can involve disabusing brothers of damaging or erroneous ideas. Someone asked Poemen how the demons fight against him. He replied:

> Do the demons fight you? They do not fight against us while we do our own will. For our own wishes have become demons, and it is these which trouble us, in order for us to gratify them. If you want to see whom the demons fight, it is against Moses and those like him.[80]

Here the brother is dissuaded from concentrating too much on what demons are doing to him. His attempt to overcome his own will is more important.[81]

The combat against thoughts, which has already been discussed at a number of points in this chapter, is a subject of intense interest to the Sayings. Discernment undoubtedly includes the ability of an abba to

[79] N 50 (another instance of an old man being granted a vision of a brother's spiritual condition which enables him to advise him correctly).

[80] Poemen 67 (PJ 10.62). Perhaps related is Poemen S 12 (Guy, *Recherches*, 30): 'No one can know those [passions, demons] which are from without, but when they rise up from within, if someone fights them, he expels them.' For a view of temptation as something which arises from within, an encounter with one's own personality which is voluntarily entered into, see Brown, *The Making of Late Antiquity*, 89–91.

[81] Cf. N 383 (PJ 10.66), where Pambo tells a brother not to say that demons prevent him from doing good, but to accuse himself of not really wanting to do it. If he accuses the demons he 'calls God a liar', for God said, 'I give you authority to tread snakes and scorpions under foot, and over all the power of the enemy.' God promises victory over the demons, and it is our own fault if we do not achieve it.

distinguish between the different spiritual capacities of different people and deal with their temptations appropriately. This is implicit in Poemen's response to the brother who had been worried by Abba Ibistion's teaching on the possibility of freedom from the thought of fornication. A report of a discussion included in the anonymous series on discernment deals with the different capacities of monks quite generally. It begins when a brother asks whether someone who simply has an evil thought is 'defiled' or not. Some say yes, but others say no, what matters is not the experience of temptation, but not to commit the sinful deed which the thought encourages.[82] The brother who began the discussion is confused and goes to ask an old man about it. He supports the second answer, explaining that 'It is demanded from each according to his measure [*μέτρον*]'; someone who has reached a high *μέτρον*, a high level of achievement in the monastic life, when he is tempted by a desire to take something forbidden, will not even allow the thought to remain but will cut it off and will therefore not be defiled. But even someone who has not reached this level need not be defiled: he will desire the object and even dwell upon the thought, but he will not take it.

This is not of course intended to allow that it is not wrong willingly to entertain wicked or pleasurable thoughts of various kinds; it is directed at those who, it is recognized, are simply unable to 'cut off' thoughts, that is, to free their minds entirely from temptations. They fall victim to thoughts which they cannot control, but survive the experience without finally consenting to the sin. The experience of temptation and successful resistance to it can in fact be turned into a virtue: 'It is not the fact that thoughts enter which subjects us to judgement, but the bad use of thoughts. For through our thoughts we can suffer shipwreck and through our thoughts we can be crowned.'[83]

[82] N 216; cf. N 454 (above, n. 63) and Evagrius, *Praktikos*, 74–5.

[83] N 218. Sayings which distinguish in various ways between the presence of temptations and the way we respond to them are frequent: N 167 maintains that it is not possible to get rid of the passions, only to resist them. Cf. Antony 4 (= Poemen 125) and Poemen 28 (PJ 10.55). Poemen 15, 20 (Eth. Coll. 14.47), 21 (Eth. Coll. 13.84, though with a slightly different message) maintain that passions are ineffectual if ignored or patiently endured; they present themselves but can be rejected (N 185). But N 220 demands that ceasing to act sinfully must be followed by ceasing to desire sin; cf. N 83 and N 429 (Evergetinos, 2.28.7.3). Whether we are prepared for temptation is a measure of what profit we have gained from our life: Eth. Coll. 13.44. For a further discussion of combat against thoughts, see L. Regnault, 'The Beatitudes in the *Apophthegmata Patrum*', *ECR* 6 (1974), 36–9; also T. Špidlík, *The Spirituality of the Christian East: A Systematic Handbook* (CSS 79; Kalamazoo, Mich., 1986), 233–66.

The 'crowning' which a monk may expect as a result of temptation is the reward of his successful combat against it. In a specific case, a brother tells his abba not to pray for temptation to be taken away from him: 'I know, Abba, that I am labouring, but I see that my labour bears fruit for me; so beseech God that he may give me endurance to bear it.'[84]

Even in giving out teaching like this, it is dangerous for an abba to generalize; he must respond with discernment to the different needs of his disciples. Abba Joseph told Poemen (a young man, obviously, in this saying) that he should, 'Let the passions enter [your mind], and fight against them', but to another disciple he gave the opposite advice, 'Do not let the passions enter, but cut them off immediately.' 'If the passions come in', he tells Poemen when the latter asks him for an explanation of the differing pieces of advice, 'and you battle to and fro with them, they make you stronger'; but there are others who will not gain from this and who must cut off their thoughts immediately.[85]

The problem of sexual temptation is obviously an important subject for the exercise of discernment, and no doubt the views and experiences of abbas differed. Cyrus believed that warring against fornication in thought was necessary, a defence against falling into the actual act without offering any resistance.[86] Poemen believed however that it was wrong to think about the *λογισμὸς* of fornication or to try to understand (*διακρῖναι*) it.[87] Cyrus' view is in accord with the spirit of Joseph's advice to Poemen to do battle consciously against the passions in order to learn how to defeat them. Poemen's own saying seems to contradict this position, but perhaps he was not really warning against fighting the temptation in order to gain strength and experience, but simply against interest in it or a desire to discuss it for its own sake.[88]

[84] N 170; on the effectiveness of an abba's prayer for delivering a brother from temptation, see above, n. 24. For the necessity of warfare and its reward, see Antony 5, John Kolobos 13, Sarah 1, and N 210. Successful warfare is rewarded by relief, granted by God, from temptation: Olympius 2, N 188.

[85] Joseph of Panephysis 3 (PJ 10.29). N 219 claims that it is possible to fight against only one passion at a time, not against them all; Poemen 126 that passions should be fought one *day* at a time, without worrying about becoming too weak to fight in the future. Sisoes 22 (like N 218 in fact) advocates that passions should be cut of immediately if possible, not fought in the manner Joseph allows. Evagrius, *Praktikos*, 42, gives advice on *how* passions may be 'cut off'. For views on being able to control all the passions, see Poemen 88, 89, Eth. Coll. 13.25, 31, 90, 93.

[86] Cyrus.

[87] Poemen 154 (which also refers to the thought of slander).

[88] On the temptation of fornication, see also N 181, 183, 186, all of which, in different ways, involve the abba who deals with them in the exercise of discernment.

It was the duty of an abba always to encourage his disciples in the fight against temptation and to watch out for signs of slackness or complacency. 'Wherever I go,' a brother said to Poemen, 'I find support'.[89] The abba answers in terms which seem meant to encourage the brother to undertake combat rather than seek release from it: 'Even those who hold a sword in their hand have God to have mercy on them in the coming age. If we then are courageous, he will have mercy on us.' Similarly, someone who does not 'perceive any warfare in my heart' may be shown that he is subject to deception: all he has to do is to put up some resistance and then he will realize that the thoughts are fighting against him.[90] An old man who has completed fifty years of asceticism thinks that he has 'killed fornication, covetousness, and vain-glory'.[91] In this case an abba shows him his error of believing that an ability to overcome temptation is the same as freedom from it. 'The passions live, but they are bound by the saints.'

Helping someone to fight against various demonic temptations and thoughts was not of course the only use of discernment in the practice of teaching, but it is probably the most important. An abba also had to offer teaching on the proper extent and value of certain ascetic practices. Poemen and Sisoes are both found discouraging a brother from an excessive length of time spent in penance after a sin.[92] Poemen again encouraged moderation in fasting.[93] Antony, as we have seen, thought that asceticism was of little value without the practice of discernment itself, and the same view is adopted by a saying which, though by no means discounting the value of ascetic practices, sees them as valueless if not accompanied by humility and charity.[94] Agathon too saw bodily labour as like foliage, playing a secondary role to the fruit, the aim of the ascetic life, which is inner.[95] Antony maintained the necessity of

[89] Poemen 94. Cf. Poemen 102 (he encourages a brother not to lose heart in the face of suffering), and N 25 (God helps those who fight against the passions).

[90] N 270.

[91] Abraham 1 (PJ 10.15); cf. N 266.

[92] Poemen 12 (PJ 10.40), Sisoes 20.

[93] Poemen 31 (PJ 10.44); cf. Megethius 2 and Eth. Coll. 14.63 (adopting a less severe fast with discernment enables a brother to obtain victory). N 231 introduces a note of accommodation to the needs of the individual into teaching on fasting. For John Cassian, *Conferences*, 2.17–26, moderation in fasting was an essential part of the practice of discernment.

[94] N 222. One of the ascetic practices mentioned is memorization of books of the Bible: for comments on this practice, cf. N 228, 385.

[95] Agathon 8 (PJ 10.11).

occasional relaxations in asceticism, to avoid stretching anyone beyond his capacity for work.[96]

The value of discernment in the teaching relationship is, finally, illustrated by a story about a brother who suffers from visions provoked by demons. An old man tells the brother that the apparitions are demonic and sends him away with instructions on how to fight them. But the demons appear to the brother again and tell him that the old man is a liar, and they cite as evidence the fact that the old man once sent away a brother who wanted to borrow some money, even though he had some that he could have lent. The brother tells the old man of his vision, and the old man admits that he did act as the demons allege, 'For I knew that if I gave it to him, we would both suffer loss to our souls. I thought it was better to break one commandment, than to break ten and come into tribulation. As for you, do not listen to the demons, who want to lead you astray.'[97] The aim of the demons is to break up the relationship between abba and disciple, and therefore to leave the disciple undefended against their attacks. But the abba shows discernment both in his treatment of the one brother, and in the explanation he gives to the other. He is open and sensitive to the spiritual condition and needs of both—in one case realizing (although we are not told how, from what signs in the brother's behaviour or from what experiences of his own) that the brother intends to use the money for something wrong, or that the loan will be a source of future rancour; in the other case seeing that he will satisfy the brother by answering the accusation honestly and sending him back to fight against the demons who have made it. This kind of awareness is the essence of discernment as far as an abba is concerned, and the abba provides a text-book example of the practice of effective teaching.

4. Obedience and Trial

It was suggested in the first section of this chapter that sayings on obedience and submission apply principally to the beginner, to the disciple who needs to learn how to live as a monk. It should be noted however that several sayings present obedience as a permanent way of

[96] Antony 13 (PJ 10.2b).

[97] N 224. For another example of an abba showing some brothers that their visions are demonic, see Antony 12 (PJ 10.2a).

life which is superior to other ascetic or spiritual practices. Submission of one's own will to another is seen as something of value in itself, and not only a means to an end which can be set aside once formation in the monastic life has been completed. For example, four monks who pursued different ways of life spoke on one occasion to Pambo about their different virtues. The four were, respectively, someone who fasted a great deal, one who was poor, one who had acquired great charity, and one who had lived in obedience to an old man for twenty-two years.[98] Pambo replied that the virtue of the last one was the greatest: 'For each of you has attained whichever virtue you wanted to by your own will, but he has abandoned his own will to do the will of another. Such men are confessors [ὁμολογηταί], if they endure to the end.' Here there does not seem to be any doubt that obedience figures as a special way of life alongside other virtues which a monk may wish to cultivate or practice according to where his particular gifts or energies lie.[99] A saying of Hyperechius probably points in the same direction: 'Obedience is the treasure of the monk. He who has attained it will be heard by God, and will stand before the crucified with confidence, for the crucified Lord was obedient unto death.'[100] Despite these sayings, which present obedience in general terms as a way of life in its own right, and some others which refer to it as a virtue which is specially necessary in a cenobium,[101] most of the sayings about obedience which are found in the *Apophthegmata* refer specifically to the obligation of an individual disciple in the context of his relationship with his teacher. The practice of obedience in this context is obviously related to themes which have been discussed in the earlier sections of this chapter, a corollary of the submission of his will and the willingness to be taught which is required of a beginner, and a response to the discerning teaching which the Abba

[98] Pambo 3.

[99] Renault, 'Obéissance et liberté', 105. See also Joseph the Theban (quoted ch. 3, p. 90). N 296 reads simply, 'He who lives in obedience to a spiritual father has a greater reward than he who withdraws alone into the desert'. This is repeated and illustrated in Rufus 2, where four ways of life are referred to: giving thanks to God when ill, serving others by hospitality, living alone in the desert, and living in obedience to a father.

[100] Hyperechius 8 (the two halves are separate in Hyperechius, *Sentences* 59, 139). On 'will be heard by God', see also Mius 1: 'If someone obeys God, God obeys him'. N 388 is a general saying on the necessity of obedience to the Scriptures and to one's fathers.

[101] Poemen 103, Syncletica 16. Both refer explicitly to life in a *κοινόβιον*. The latter rates obedience above asceticism: on this cf. N 294 (also an explicitly cenobitic saying) where an ascetic brother puts an obedient brother to the test and miracles take place in response to his obedience. On cenobitism in the *Apophthegmata*, cf. Syncletica 17 (above, n. 34), and Ch. 1, nn.55–7; Ch. 2, n. 135; Ch. 5, Sect. 1.

provides. It is the aim of this section to look further at some sayings which illustrate the obedience of the disciple.

The exactness of a disciple's obedience, his willingness to do just what his abba has told him without offering judgements of his own, is praised in a number of sayings. Mark left his cell as soon as Abba Silvanus called him, breaking off in the middle of writing the letter omega.[102] Arsenius was surprised by the exactness of his disciple Alexander, who did not come to eat with him until late in the evening, because he was obeying Arsenius' instructions to finish his manual work first.[103]

In these examples, the purpose of obedience is not stated explicitly, but clearly what is under consideration is the extent of the disciple's commitment to renunciation of his own will and acceptance of his abba's authority as a teacher of the monastic life. A willingness to obey is an indication of a disciple's readiness and ability to learn how he should live. This may be illustrated by a story about a brother who came to see an abba to ask him how he should behave when working at the harvest.[104] The old man does not answer the question immediately, but instead enquires into the brother's willingness to obey him: 'If I tell you something will you trust me?' The brother says that he will, and the old man tells him to give up harvesting and come to be taught by him. (We are probably supposed to believe that the old man has a reason for not allowing the brother to go harvesting, but we are not told what it is.) The brother does so, and the old man tells him to spend fifty days in his cell eating bread and salt. The old man has now in effect tested the brother's obedience three times—by asking him to obey, by telling him to do something unexpected, and by imposing a harsh ascetic regime on him. When the brother has finished the fifty days the old man realizes that he is a hard worker,[105] and proceeds to tell him 'how to live in his cell', which in this saying appears to mean how to fight against the demons, since in the remainder of the text it is shown how the brother overcomes the opposite temptations of pride in his achievements and despair. By renouncing his own will and accepting

[102] Mark 1.

[103] Arsenius 24. Arsenius responds by telling Alexander not to fast too late but to 'say your prayers and have some water, or your body will soon become weak'. Cf. Agathon 28 for another reference to Alexander's obedience and slow rate of manual work.

[104] N 291.

[105] *ἐργάτης*, as in Ares.

the abba's authority the brother makes good progress in the monastic life.[106]

Another story about Mark and Silvanus illustrates the extent of the required renunciation and acceptance:

They said about Abba Silvanus that he was once walking in Scetis with the old men, and wished to show them the obedience of his disciple Mark, because of which he loved him. He saw a little wild boar, and said to Mark, 'Do you see that little antelope, my child?' He said to him, 'Yes, Abba'. 'And his horns, how beautiful they are?' He said, 'Yes, Abba'. The old men were astonished at his reply, and were edified by his obedience.[107]

Incidents like this do not in fact appear particularly edifying. Arsenius' genuine surprise at Alexander's self-discipline and devotion to his work seems preferable to Silvanus' concoction of a pretext to display the obedience of Mark. But we must accept the fact that the Desert Fathers did value this sort of deliberate trial of a disciple's obedience. In one saying an abba tests the obedience of a would-be disciple by telling him to place his hand in a flame; he does so, and, the disciple recalls, 'if he had not removed it, I would no longer have it'.[108] Sayings about John and Sisoes also illustrate this kind of deliberate test. John is told by his abba to water a dry stick until after three years it bears fruit.[109] Sisoes is the subject of one of two stories in which in order to test someone's obedience an old man tells him to kill his son: a shocking and dangerous procedure, although neither story actually ends with the death of the child.[110] Besides the simple test of obedience, what is at issue here is

[106] In N 17 a new brother is less successful in obeying his abba: he keeps some money after being told to renounce the world and is consequently prey to materialistic thoughts. Finally he succeeds in getting rid of everything, but is disturbed by the thought of being eaten by a lion. His abba tells him how to combat this and sends him away to pray. In N 46 an old man imposes on a new monk a five-year vow of silence; he sends him away to a cenobium without lifting the ban, and in obedience the brother remains mute for the rest of his life.

[107] Mark 2. The motif of Silvanus loving Mark for his obedience is also found in 1.

[108] Ch 270.

[109] John Kolobos 1. Cassian, *Institutions*, 4.24, has the story without a miraculous ending and brings out the fact that the command was a trial of the genuineness of the disciple's obedience in other matters.

[110] Sisoes (10) countermands his order, while in the other story, N 295, a miracle saves the child from harm, and the father is compared to the patriarch Abraham because of his willingness to sacrifice his son. In Saius an old man tells his disciple to steal from the brothers. He does so, 'because of his obedience, giving thanks to the Lord in everything'. Here though, a doubt is perhaps cast on whether the brother should have obeyed the command, for as well as being obedient, 'he was very rigid [*σκληρὸς δὲ ἦν πάνυ*]'.

the disciple's willingness to renounce all connections with his former secular life and family.[111]

A somewhat more acceptable example of testing, which incidentally also illustrates the Desert Fathers' capacity for humour, concerns an abba who sees some dung near a hyena's lair and tells his disciple to go and collect it. The brother asks him what to do about the hyena.

The old man said frivolously, 'If it comes after you, bind it and bring it here.' In the evening the brother went there. The hyena came after him and he, in accord with the word of the old man, tried to catch it. The hyena ran away, and he chased it saying, 'My Abba said that I should bind you', and caught it and bound it. The old man was worried, and sat waiting. Then the brother came with the bound hyena, and the old man was amazed. But he wished to humble him, so he hit him and said, 'Fool, have you brought me a silly dog?' Then he let the hyena go and sent it away.[112]

Here the abba probably does not initially intend the command to be a test, but when he has discovered the extent of the disciple's obedience he goes on to make sure that the incident also serves to prove the disciple's humility and endurance in the face of criticism and ill-treatment.

Other examples of apparently capricious behaviour by an abba serve the same purpose and should not be seen as evidence of the existence of bad relationships. An abba wished to test (*δοκιμάσαι*) a brother, so when he arrived at his dwelling he began to beat his vegetables with his stick.

When he saw what the abba was doing the brother hid. When only one stalk was left he said to the old man, 'Abba, if you wish, leave it so that I can cook it, and we will eat together.' The old man made a prostration before the brother, saying, 'Because of your endurance of evil the Holy Spirit rests upon you, brother.'[113]

[111] Cf. N 72, where an abba tells a monk who is living in the same monastery as his son that he must treat him as a stranger (*ξένος*). When the son is dying the abba allows the father to speak to him, but he refuses saying, 'If you commanded, shall we not keep the command until the end?' On the necessity of separation from relatives, see Ch. 5, n. 85.

[112] John the disciple of Abba Paul. The dung was presumably used as fuel. 'Frivolously' (*χαριεντιζόμενος*) occurs also in Antony 13. It implies relaxation of customary ascetic discipline or spiritual vigilance. Cf. *HL*, 35.8, 10.

[113] N 343. The monks grew vegetables for their own use (cf. Arsenius 22 for a discussion). The propriety of growing things for wider charitable purposes is questioned by Poemen 22 (although this is a saying in which Poemen displays well the ability of an abba to speak to the personal needs of a brother, rather than simply stating a general principle).

A trial of this type appears to have been an accepted part of the teaching relationship, to which the brother knows how he ought to respond. Endurance in the face of temptation, hardship, and ill-treatment are among the most essential of virtues and are tested out by the abba in incidents like these.[114] In another example, Antony kept Macarius waiting outside his cell until he had seen his endurance, and when he had eventually let him in and spent the night with him weaving ropes and speaking of the 'salvation of souls', praised him for how much work he had done: 'Great power comes out of these hands.'[115] Macarius' behaviour has proved to Antony that he is capable of bearing every hardship of the monastic life.

Sometimes an abba did not so much deliberately test his disciple as simply recognize his virtue in a particular incident. When he was young, Poemen went to see an old man about three thoughts, but forgot one of them. He remembered what it was as he was arriving home and went back to the old man immediately.[116] 'Now it was a very long way. So the old man said to him, "Shepherd of the flock, your name will be spoken in all Egypt." ' In another story, a disciple's obedience is proved by his unwillingness to leave his abba without being dismissed, the abba having fallen asleep while speaking to him.[117]

In conclusion to this and the preceding sections we may therefore say that the abba must ensure that the self-disclosure and obedience which are the duty of the disciple in the teaching relationship bear fruit in his development of his ability to resist temptation, and of the necessary virtues of the monastic life. Rousseau speaks of the 'docile faith' of the true disciple,[118] but this is not the air of the texts which have been quoted; these see obedience and self-disclosure as heroic activities directed to the end of personal development in the virtues of the monastic life, not as something supine, passive, or signifying immaturity or lack of individuality. Whether through a deliberate test or by watching his disciple's response to an ordinary or chance incident,

[114] See Antony 15 and Esaias 1 for the importance of being able to bear insults. In Agathon 28 his humiliation of Alexander is explained as serving to prove to the others that Alexander is truly obedient, when they are grumbling about him. In N 192 a brother's endurance of ill-treatment is tested not by his abba but by his community in general who cold-shoulder him.

[115] Macarius 4.

[116] Poemen 1.

[117] N 211. The abba has a vision in which he sees seven crowns prepared for his disciple. The message is that God rewards even minor struggles against our thoughts, so it is good to 'do violence' to ourselves for the sake of God.

[118] *Ascetics, Authority, and the Church*, 59.

the abba gauges his disciple's progress in virtues like humility and endurance, and instructs him in their practice, even by criticism (in the case of the hyena) or apparent mistreatment (in the case of the vegetables).

5. The Response of the Abba: Teaching by Example

How should an abba teach his disciple? From what has been observed so far, by sensitivity to his needs and by offering appropriate and authoritative teaching and advice. But the Desert Fathers' analysis of the teaching relationship does not stop here. They were concerned with the questions of what (apart from direct divine assistance) makes teaching authoritative, and how an abba can teach effectively while at the same time maintaining his own integrity, his own practice of virtues like humility and endurance and, above all, the surrender of his own will—which was required not only of a disciple but of all as an essential component of the monastic life.[119]

As with some other issues which have been discussed in this chapter, the response of the Desert Fathers to these questions of authority and integrity is best introduced by some sayings of Poemen:

Someone who teaches, but who does not himself do what he teaches, is like a spring which gives drink to all and cleanses all, but cannot purify itself.[120]

A brother asked Abba Poemen, 'What is a hypocrite?' The old man said to him, 'A hypocrite is someone who teaches his neighbour something which he himself has not previously done. For it is written, "How can you see the speck in your brother's eye, when you have a beam in your own eye", and what follows.'[121]

How can someone who has seen something and not mastered it for himself teach it to his neighbour?[122]

In slightly different ways, all of these sayings convey the simple message that an abba's teaching must be a product of his own experience in the monastic life.[123] Implicit in Poemen's words is the view both that an

[119] Cf. above, p. 34.

[120] Poemen 25.

[121] Poemen 117. Matt. 7: 3–4.

[122] Poemen S 10 (Guy, *Recherches*, 30). 'Mastered' or 'retained' (ἐφύλαξεν) implies attentive learning of and adherence to a practice.

[123] Cf. Theodore of Pherme 9, which warns a brother against talking about things he has not actually done. In *VA*, 39–41, Antony is portrayed as teaching about the behaviour of demons exclusively from his own experience.

abba who teaches something which he has not done is harming, or doing no good to, himself—the question of integrity—and (less clearly) that teaching of this sort brings little benefit to its recipient—the question of authority or efficiency. The first saying quoted does not seem to consider this latter possibility, but the others suggest that an abba's own inability to do what he teaches impairs his ability to teach or to correct others. 'How can you see the speck?' requires the answer that it is impossible to do so. The difficulty, if not impossibility, of teaching with authority without personal experience of what is taught is referred to by an anonymous saying: 'Spiritual work is necessary—that is why we came [to the desert]. For it requires great labour to teach with the mouth, without having done the work of the body.'[124] It is not entirely clear here whether the 'spiritual' activity which is required of a monk and the 'work of the body' without which teaching is difficult are the same or different (in which case the saying makes a rather awkward transition). But perhaps the two terms are to be interpreted as parallel to those adopted in the previous piece in the anonymous series, attributed to the same old man, which makes a distinction not between 'spiritual' and 'bodily' work but between inward attitude and outward behaviour: 'If our inner man is vigilant, we can guard [*φυλάξαι*] the outer too—and if not, let us guard our tongue as far as we can.'[125] Ideally, that is, three things—what a monk thinks, how he behaves, and what he says—should be in accord with one another;[126] guarding the 'outer man' should follow the vigilance of the 'inner man' as its natural outcome. Except in so far as the tongue must be guarded 'as far as we can' even though the inner man may *not* be vigilant, what is essential here is the fact that a connection is made between a monk's inward attitude and his outward behaviour, or between what is said and what is present in the heart; the connection may be put either way round without a significant change of emphasis: 'Teach your heart', said Poemen, 'to guard [*τηρεῖν*] what your tongue teaches,'[127] or alternatively, 'Teach your mouth to say what you have in your heart.'[128] These and other sayings on this theme refer to situations and problems other than the conduct of the abba in the teaching relationship,[129] but they do have

[124] N 240.

[125] N 239; cf. Arsenius 9, N 272.

[126] Cf. N 122: 'God seeks these things from a man: thought, word, and action.'

[127] Poemen S 1 (Guy, *Recherches*, 29).

[128] Poemen 63 (= 164).

[129] For instance to the problem of how to respond to insult or ill-treatment (cf. above, n. 114): John Kolobos S 6 (Guy, *Recherches*, 24) is a model example of the condition

a particular application there, emphasizing the lack of integrity, as Poemen says the hypocrisy, of an inexperienced teacher: 'An old man said, "If the soul possesses speech, but not action, it is like a tree which has leaves but no fruit. For as a tree which has fruit also has flourishing leaves, thus speech is appropriate to a soul which has a good activity." '[130]

The other problem that has been noted, that of the inefficiency of inexperienced teaching as a guide for the disciple, is considered further by a saying of Syncletica which makes a careful distinction between the effect of an abba's words, which may be good, and of his behaviour, which may be evil:

> It is dangerous for someone who has not been trained in the practical life to teach. For just as if someone who owns a house which is falling down harms any strangers he has received when his house collapses, so it is with those who destroy those who come to them, because they have not first built themselves up. For by their words they call them to salvation, but by their evil behaviour they really injure those who follow them.[131]

From both points of view therefore, that of the abba and his disciple, the Desert Fathers maintain that teaching should spring from an abba's example, and from his personal experience of the monastic life, and not consist of advice or instructions ungrounded in the abba's own willingness and ability to do the necessary work for himself. 'Go and do whatever you see me doing,' Abba Or was able to say with confidence to Sisoes when the latter had asked him for a word—although in order to make the message clear he was, even then, forced to tell Sisoes what he was supposed to be looking for.[132] A brother came to tell Poemen that some others lived with him; did the old man want him to tell them what to do?[133] 'No,' said Poemen, 'do the work first, and if they want to live, they will see to themselves.' But the brother persisted with his enquiry, perhaps thinking that the old man had misunderstood and was

recommended in N 239: he is no more troubled inwardly by being insulted than his calm outward response suggests. But in Moses 3, as N 239 also demands, control of the tongue is required even when you cannot prevent yourself from being inwardly grieved in the face of an insult (in this case a deliberate test). See Poemen 51 and N 345 (Ch. 3, pp. 97–8) for more comments on the relationship between inward attitude and outward behaviour or speech; also Ch. 4, nn. 28–9, 37–8, 41, 43–4, and Ch. 6, n. 22.

[130] N 252. Rousseau, 'The Desert Fathers, Antony and Pachomius', 124, may be right to think that *λόγος* in this saying refers to 'teaching and reflection', not to speech alone. James 4 and Isidore of Pelusia 1 discuss the relation of word to action, as does Moses 17: *ἐὰν μὴ συμφωνήσῃ ἡ πρᾶξις μετὰ τῆς εὐχῆς, εἰς μάτην κοπιᾷ.*

[131] Syncletica 12 (following the variant reading given in PG).

[132] Or 7. Sisoes (45) apparently passed on the teaching.

[133] Poemen 174.

assuming that his question betrayed a culpable desire to impose his own will on his companions: 'They themselves wish that I should tell them what to do, Father.' But Poemen was insistent: 'No. Rather be an example to them, not a legislator.' 'Work' in this saying seems to have a very general meaning, referring to both the practices and virtues of the monastic life, while it is the teaching of a particular virtue which Or's saying illustrates. But the principle taught by both Poemen and Or, that even where someone is willing to accept orders, teaching by example should prevail, is further illustrated by a story which emphasizes that it is to thoroughly down-to-earth and practical activities, not just to spiritual qualities and virtues, that the Desert Fathers thought the principle of teaching by example should be applied:

Abba Isaac said, 'When I was young, I lived with Abba Cronius, and he never told me to do any work, even though he was old and frail. He himself did the work, and offered the water-jug to me and to all alike. Then I lived with Abba Theodore of Pherme, and he never told me to do anything, but even used to lay the table himself, and say, "Brother, if you wish, come and eat". I used to say to him, "Abba, I came here in order to profit; why do you never tell me what to do?" But the old man was always silent. So I went and told the old men, and they came to him and said, "Abba, the brother came to your holiness in order to profit, so why don't you tell him to do anything?" The old man said to them, "Am I the ruler of a cenobium, that I should give him orders? I will not tell him anything, but if he wants to, he too will do what he sees me doing." So from then on if the old man was about to do anything, I used to anticipate him and do it. If he did anything, he did it silently, and this taught me too to act silently.'[134]

Of interest in this saying is the self-conscious contrast drawn between the methods of instruction practised by the Desert Fathers and the more formal and hierarchical methods of a cenobium.[135] But this is not the only point of interest in the story, which is one of the most valuable of all for our understanding of the Desert Fathers' views on the ideals of the teaching relationship. As in the sayings of Poemen and Or, example is believed to possess a power of its own for the teaching of a disciple who really wants to learn. The last sentence however adds a further point of significance. It is not only what Theodore does that

[134] Isaac of Kellia 2.

[135] The only saying explicitly describing contacts between the Scetiote community and the cenobitic Pachomian monastic system (Macarius the Citizen 2) deals with precisely the problem of the permissibility of instructing those who live in the cenobitic community. Cf. above, n. 101, and Ch. 1, n.56.

constitutes the example, but his manner of doing it—the silent actions which express his reluctance to impose his own will on someone else. From this Isaac learns to behave in the same self-submitting way. The abba's renunciation of his own will both balances, on his side of the relationship, and encourages the submission which is expected of his disciple. It may be a difficult idea for the disciple to get used to, but a teaching relationship conducted on this principle both allows the abba to maintain his personal integrity—his own possession of the virtues he is trying to teach—and operates more efficiently in bringing home to the disciple the nature and importance of what he is trying to learn.

Other sayings emphasize or explain the importance of an abba behaving in such a way as not to impose his will on a disciple. 'When you have someone to take care of you', Sisoes said, 'you must not give him orders.'[136] Even where an attitude as strict as this, or as Theodore's refusal to speak to Isaac, was not always recommended, the importance of acting without anger towards a disciple could be recognized. 'How ought we to live,' Abba Romanus was asked by his disciples as he was dying. 'I do not think I have ever told any of you to do anything', he replied, 'without first deciding not to be angry if you did not do what I said. And thus we have dwelt together in peace for the whole time.'[137] Hyperechius similarly stressed that a monk's behaviour should be characterized by meekness rather than highhandedness in words (*καμπολογία*).[138] In general an abba should not think slightingly about (*καταφρονεῖν*) his disciple or servant, 'for you do not know whether the Spirit of God is on you or on him'[139]—a statement of humility about his own achievements which would remind an abba of the desirability of not imposing his own will on someone else. The proper spirit in which commands should be given is 'with fear of God and humility'.[140] If, this saying continues, someone who gives an order to a brother does so not with the fear of God but out of a desire to exercise power, then

[136] Sisoes 29. For this teaching put into practice, see Ammoes 3. This attitude is probably also the key to Joseph of Panepho 9, in which one old man discovers that another does not know his own disciple's name.

[137] Romanus. Cf. N 128: 'They used to say of an old man that he lived with some brothers; he used to tell them to do something once, and if they did not do it, the old man used to get up and do it without anger.' Also Cassian 5 (from *Institutions*, 5.28): 'I have never done my own will, nor taught anything which I had not done first.'

[138] Hyperechius, *Sentences* 122 (1485A). The text continues: 'Such a man is wise, and a steward of many brothers, for he is truly wise who does not teach by his word, but educates by his work.' The last third of this text alone is found in PJ 10.75.

[139] N 317.

[140] N 315.

'God who sees the hidden things of the heart will not make him hear or do it.' The different kinds of 'work' (that is, in this saying, the different ways in which an abba may behave) are clearly distinguishable, 'for that of God is done humbly and with exhortation, but that which is done in an authoritarian way is full of anger and disturbance, for it is a result of evil'. In such terms it is made clear that the teaching of an abba who is subjected to the passion of self-will is of no positive value in the sight of God.

Several of the examples which have been cited to illustrate the Desert Fathers' awareness of the dangers of teaching without proper experience, without offering a personal example, and with self-will rather than humility, have been in the form of warnings rather than encouragements. But the story of Theodore and Isaac is a positive statement of the practice of effective teaching; it shows that it was believed to be both possible and necessary for an abba to avoid anger and the exercise of his own will, and to respond to his disciple's needs by teaching through experience and example. Words alone (certainly not words accompanied by manifestations of anger and self-will) were not enough; the abba's teaching should be offered in the form of a united witness of word and life. This is a widely acknowledged point,[141] but it does deserve close examination. Not only the examples given here, but also such fundamental sayings on the importance of teaching as Poemen 65 and 73, quoted in the first section of this chapter, all imply that humility, fear of God, and indeed progress in the monastic life in general are most effectively taught by someone who possesses and displays these qualities in his own person—perhaps an obvious fact, but one which the Desert Fathers were concerned to stress.

6. The Response of the Abba: Openness and Involvement

Teaching by example is one way in which the integrity and efficiency

[141] Guy, 'Educational Innovation in the Desert Fathers', 46–7; Louf, 'Spiritual Fatherhood in the Literature of the Desert', 51; Regnault, 'Qui sont les Pères du désert?' 29, 32; von Lilienfeld, 'Die Christliche Unterweisung der *Apophthegmata Patrum*', 89–90, and 'Jesus-Logion und Vaterspruch', in J. Irmscher (ed.), *Studia Byzantina* (Halle-Wittenberg, 1966), reprinted in *Spiritualität des frühen Wüstenmönchtums*, 17 (where she speaks of the 'aus verwirklichtem Leben ablesbare Ordnung' which the example of an abba constitutes for his disciple).

of an abba's teaching is maintained and enhanced, but not the only way. In earlier sections of this chapter we have already discussed stories in which the process of responding to a disciple's needs involves an element of personal self-disclosure and openness on the part of the abba.[142] In Macarius 3, he persuades the brother to admit that his thoughts trouble him by confessing that he too is attacked by them: 'Behold, how many years I have laboured, and am honoured by all, yet the spirit of fornication troubles me, an old man.'[143] Similarly, in N 509 Zeno elicits the brother's disclosure of thoughts by the twice-made comment, 'I too am a man', meaning that as a human being, subject to temptation just like the brother, he is unlikely to be shocked by what he has to say, but on the contrary will be able to help him more easily. In Poemen 62, he gains the brother's trust by establishing a bond of common experience: 'you and I are subject to fornication.'

These sayings prompt reflection on the importance of self-disclosure of this kind as a component of the practice of teaching, and we will find several examples in which confession either of a sin or of some general weakness by an abba is reported. Sisoes was visited by three old men who wanted to question him about the fears of hell and punishment to which they were subject.[144] Sisoes' initial reply is rather curt ('I remember none of these things, for God is merciful, and I hope that he will have mercy on me'), and the old men are offended. So he changes his tack and explains to them that because they are continually aware of punishment, 'it is impossible for you to sin. But what shall I do, because I am hard-hearted, and it has not been granted to me even to know if there is a punishment for men, because of which I sin all the time?' The visitors then depart, assuring him that they now know the truth of what they have heard about him. Sisoes' response is marked by the exercise of discernment and flexibility as a teacher: his first response reminds the old men that the fear of punishment should not be a central element of faith in God; his second enables them to see their fears in a different, more positive light, perhaps even as a source of faith and hope, and thus probably helps to ease their distress to some extent. The important point to note however is that Sisoes exercises

[142] N 509, Macarius 3, Poemen 62 (above, pp. 32, 42–3, 45).

[143] Macarius 31 makes the general point about his behaviour that he preferred to speak to someone who treated him as a sinner than to someone who approached him 'with fear, as a great and holy old man'. He preferred, that is, to stress his solidarity with others rather than his achievements.

[144] Sisoes 19.

his discernment by exposing his own inner life to criticism and reassures his questioners by putting himself in a position inferior to theirs. Stark awareness of sin is a feature of Sisoes' attitude to himself which is not only found in this saying.[145] It is his humility and self-exposure, as much as his discernment, to which the visitors respond with thanks.

Other abbas respond to questioners with similar discernment and humility. Matoes answered a question about love of enemies by saying that he himself did not know how to love even those who loved him, while Ammoes, questioned by a brother, was silent for seven days before sending for him and saying simply, 'Pay heed to yourself; as for me, my sins have become a wall of darkness between me and God.'[146] A story about Agathon concerns some brothers who deliberately tested him, having heard about his discernment.[147] In response to their questions he admits (in humility rather than in truth) that he is a fornicator, proud, a blatherer, and a slanderer, but denies their final accusation that he is a heretic: 'The first things I ascribe to myself, for it is good for my soul, but heresy is separation from God, and I do not wish to be separated from God.' The questioners leave, duly astonished at his discernment, but again it is important to note that in order to teach this lesson, both about humility and about the overriding importance of his relationship with God, Agathon has taken a risk with his own reputation. What would have happened if the brothers had left without asking their final question?

A different kind of self-exposure is illustrated by Silvanus. His disciple Zacharias went out with some brothers and moved the fence of the garden to make it bigger:

When the old man found out, he took his sheepskin, and said to the brothers, 'Pray for me'. When they saw him, they fell at his feet saying, 'Tell us what is the matter, father.' He said to them, 'I will not go in, nor take off my sheepskin, until you put the fence back in its original place.' Then they moved the fence again, and made it as it was. So the old man returned to his cell.[148]

[145] Cf. Sisoes 5; the accounts of his final illness and death in 14, 49; and 35–6 (where the text acknowledges the existence of two Sisoes).

[146] Matoes 5; Ammoes 4 (Eth. Coll. 13.83 is a more circumstantial version). Achillas 4 also illustrates an abba's willingness to admit his sin in order to teach an important lesson; Theodore 22 demonstrates the abba's self-exposure in two ways: his willingness to accept the blame for his disciple's error, and the disciple's willingness to admit his own sin by using the story in subsequent teaching. See also the strategy employed by the abba in N 66.

[147] Agathon 5.

[148] Silvanus 8.

Silvanus' behaviour here is a response to a thoughtless and worldly act on the part of his disciple. But he reacts not simply by criticizing or rebuking him, but by threatening to leave his disciples, to put an end to the relationship between them. Undoubtedly the threat is meant seriously, but it should also be seen as a deliberate strategy, designed to draw attention in the most graphic way to the fact that something is wrong, and providing in itself a demonstration of the sort of detachment from possessions which a monk ought to attain.[149] Silvanus' conduct is self-exposing in so far as by threatening the relationship, he exposes himself to the possible charge of overreacting to the problem; even to the situation of having his bluff called by a disciple who might refuse to accept his fault. In fact the brothers immediately recognize their error, perhaps more readily than would have been the case had the old man simply told them off.

The method of teaching practised by Macarius, Poemen, Sisoes, and others involves the expression of common experience or solidarity with the disciple in his temptation.[150] In these cases the solidarity is generalized; the abba claims that he is subject to the same sort of temptations, or (in Sisoes' case) to a different spiritual problem which sheds light on his questioners' experience. In some cases however, the abba's personal involvement with his disciple is taken further, and he expresses solidarity with his disciple in the latter's actual, current sin or temptation and shares in his burden of penance or in combat against it. A brother came to Abba Lot and, after some hesitation ('he was agitated, coming in and going out, unable to sit down') told him that he had committed a great sin.[151] 'Confess it to me', Lot said, 'and I will carry [*βαστάζω*] it.' After the brother had confessed, Lot told him to 'Be confident that repentance is possible', and to go and fast, 'and I will carry half of the sin with you.' Here Lot apparently intends to undertake the same penitential discipline as the brother, and the result is that 'after three

[149] For willingness to leave one's cell as a mark of detachment from material things, see Agathon 6 (and, implicitly, 7), Ammoes 5, Megethius 1; on detachment also Silvanus 4 (cf. the last sentence of 2) and John Kolobos 10 (an instance of an abba being tested by his disciples). Or 1 (like Agathon 6) concerns the building of a new cell (cf. N 361) and shows that even this necessary task could be seen as a diversion from dependence on God to attachment to possessions: 'They said to one another, "What would we do if God visited us now?" And they left the clay, weeping, and each withdrew to his own cell.'

[150] 'Solidarity in experience' is noted by Stewart, 'Radical Honesty about the Self', 33, though his stress on it leads him to an exaggerated emphasis on the view that the abba was essentially a *witness* of his disciple's struggles rather than a teacher or counsellor.

[151] Lot 2.

weeks, the old man was convinced that God had accepted the brother's repentance'.

Another account of an abba's reaction to his disciple's temptations illustrates his willingness to expose himself to possible temptation or criticism. An old man encouraged his disciple to resist the temptation of fornication, but when the disciple replies that 'I will not be able to endure, Abba, unless I commit the act', the abba changes his tack from encouragement to involvement: 'I too am beset, child, so let us go together and commit the act, then return to our cell.'[152] When they arrive at a prostitute's dwelling the old man goes in, on the pretext that he will see her first, but when inside he makes her give him her word not to defile the brother. When the brother (presumably believing, for the moment, that the old man has already sinned) goes in in turn she persuades him to pray before they commit the act, and after 'twenty or thirty prostrations' the brother is seized by compunction, and goes out undefiled.

Thus far it seems as if this abba's intervention on behalf of his disciple is simply a clever trick by which he procures his escape. But this is not how the Desert Fathers saw it. It is the conclusion of the saying which illustrates the real significance of the abba's behaviour in this story: 'God, seeing the labour of the old man, relieved the brother of his warfare, and they returned to their cell glorifying God.' Far from simply indulging in a ruse, the abba has embarked on a dangerous course of personal involvement, and God responds directly to his action. This pattern of labour or involvement followed by God's response is repeated elsewhere. A brother proved himself willing to confess to a sin he had not committed, in order to persuade his companion (who had sinned) not to give up the monastic life but to accept a penance from the old men and perform it. The two start to do penance together and, 'God, seeing the labour of his love, within a few days revealed to one of the old men that, "Because of the great love of him who did not sin, I have forgiven the sinner" '.[153] It is presumably not until this moment

[152] N 44.

[153] N 179. Cf. N 180 where an old man encourages a brother to 'carry' his companion, because kindness rather than harshness is necessary and 'God, seeing your work of endurance, will support him.' To illustrate his teaching the old man tells another story about a brother who accompanied his companion to a village when the latter was determined to commit fornication, having been told by an abba that 'because of your labour, God will not let him fall'. In N 255 a brother who has sinned asks another to 'labour with me for two weeks', with the result that he is forgiven. In N 190 an abba labours in prayer on behalf of a brother who has sinned, and over the course of several

that the old men who have imposed the penance realize that the brother has acted out of solidarity with his companion rather than because of his own sin. In fact, there is cumulative evidence to suggest that the Desert Fathers saw this form of self-committing solidarity and laborious sharing in another's temptation or penitence as a vital element not only of the relationship of abba and disciple, but also, in general, of the relationship of one brother to another, and as part of the duty of the community as a whole towards its members.[154]

In evaluating the importance of this aspect of the Desert Fathers' practice as an element in the relationship of abba and disciple it is interesting to note that a brother could regard an abba's willingness to share in penitence as proof that in him he had found a good master. We are told that an old man, who wanted a particular brother to come and live with him, 'was pure, and never wished to hear that a monk had thoughts of fornication'.[155] The brother is reluctant to go to live with him. Perhaps he fears that, like Ibistion in Poemen 62, the abba will be unable to understand his problems; or, perhaps more likely, he does not wish to force the abba to listen to problems the knowledge of which might threaten his own purity of thought. At any rate, he replies that 'I am a sinner and cannot stay with you, Abba'. But the old man persists, and so the brother asks him to wait a week for a reply. At the end of the week the brother tests (*δοκιμάσαι*) the old man by telling him that during the week he has committed fornication in the village. 'Do you repent?' asks the old man, and when the brother tells him that he does, the old man makes what, as we can see from the story of Abba Lot, the Desert Fathers regarded as a proper response to this sort of confession: 'I will carry half the sin with you.' The old man's response (unexpected perhaps in the light of the previous comment about his

weeks the brother is assured of God's forgiveness by a series of visions. (Rousseau, *Ascetics, Authority, and the Church*, 28 n. 45, comments misleadingly on this saying as if the brother's visions were an end sought in themselves.)

[154] See N 389, which encourages suffering and weeping along with those who are troubled, and N 335: 'Go and carry the living.' Both of these could apply to the practice of sharing in penitence or helping someone who is tempted. For a story about the whole community, see N 165, where a brother confesses his temptation to the whole assembly, 'And they all laboured for him for a week, praying to God, and the warfare ceased.' In N 187 an old man asks the assembly to 'pray for me', when he returns to Scetis to resume his former way of life, having previously left the desert and committed fornication with a virgin who served him while he was ill. In N 64 a brother reveals his temptation to all and asks them to pray for him, though here his humility rather than the others' solidarity is the stated cause of the relief he gains from warfare.

[155] N 346.

unwillingness to listen to others' problems) overcomes the brother's doubts, and he decides that he will be able to live with him.

7. Bad Relationships

The teaching relationship can be seen to involve a complex pattern of attitudes of self-disclosure, endurance, and obedience, required, as the last two sections have shown, of both parties if the abba was to teach with integrity and efficiency. The teaching relationship is not of course always conducted in these ideal circumstances, and it remains in this chapter to consider some examples, apparent or real, of breakdown or failure in the teaching relationship. In a number of stories the question is considered of how an abba ought to respond to his disciple in circumstances where the relationship is under strain. We have already seen that an abba cannot force his disciple to be good or to obey him; the disciple must choose to co-operate in the educational process.[156] One important consequence of this is that the abba himself is potentially vulnerable to his disciple's misbehaviour, non-co-operation or simple carelessness; he cannot, the Desert Fathers believed, simply opt out of a bad relationship or shield himself from its dangers.

The old men said about another old man that he had a disciple living with him, and saw him doing something which was not good for him. So he said to him once, 'Do not do this thing', but he did not listen to him. As he had disobeyed, the old man left him to his own judgement. The young one closed the door of the cell where the provisions were, and left the old man to fast for thirteen days; but the old man did not say to him, 'Where are you?' or 'Where are you going?' The old man had a neighbour, who when he realised that the young one was [leaving the old man for] a long time, made some food and gave it to him through the window, and implored him to eat. But if he said to him, 'Why is the brother late?' the old man said, 'He will come when he has time.'[157]

The old man's stance towards the brother here conforms to the requirement not to impose his will on someone else, and is generally consonant with the practice of instructing a disciple to do something only once, as reported in N 128. It is the abba's refusal to speak critically to someone else about his disciple, or to take action against him or on his

[156] Isaac of Kellia 2, Sisoes 28, N 128. In N 281 an old man makes no move to rebuke his disciple, simply letting him have his way until he realizes his error.

[157] N 341.

own behalf, which is most obviously commended by the saying. The same applies in the two different stories in the anonymous series (originally combined as one, on the evidence of the Ethiopic collection) which discuss the reaction of an abba to a brother who steals from him. In one of these the old man concerned contents himself with the observation that 'No doubt the brother needs it', and takes no action, even though the theft (which is repeated) causes him hardship and means he has to work harder.[158] In the other case the old man resorts to leaving a note for the thief (who is stealing from him while he is out) asking him at least to leave half of the money.[159]

It is possible to see these three stories, like many *Apophthegmata*, as serving a purpose closely allied to the customary illustrative cases of traditional moral theology—simple examples designed to make clear the sort of material factors and motives which ought to affect behaviour in particular situations. The Desert Fathers clearly believed that a disciple ought to be given the benefit of the doubt, and that it was praiseworthy to endure hardship rather than criticize or denounce someone else. But the stories show that it was possible to compromise—to accept food from someone else or to try to strike a bargain in order to secure a minimum for yourself—provided that the principle of avoiding criticism was not breached.[160]

The two stories about theft both end in death. In the first, the old man is surrounded by the brothers at the time of his death, and seeing the thief calls him to his side and kisses his hands: 'I give thanks for these hands, because through them I am going to the kingdom of heaven.' As a result of this, the brother repents and becomes 'a tried [*δόκιμος*] monk as a result of the old man's actions which he saw'. The old man's endurance, and the fact that he continues to express himself right to the end in love rather than recrimination, work, in other words, to the ultimate benefit both of himself and the brother. In the other saying the brother is the one who is dying. He calls the old man and confesses his sin and asks him to pray for him. The old man does so,

[158] N 339.

[159] N 7.

[160] Contrast Euprepius 2 and Theodore of Pherme 29, two more stories about robbers taking a monk's possessions. Euprepius tries to make them take everything he has, whereas Theodore fights back and then bargains with the thieves to make them leave him the habit which he wears in church. In Eth. Coll. 13.79 an abba tells his disciple, who has been robbed by another brother, that rather than concealing himself from the robber he should actually have instructed him to take what he was stealing, in order to ease the brother's conscience later. See also Macarius 18, 40.

contenting himself with the mildest of rebukes: 'Why did you not speak sooner?' We are probably intended to believe that the brother dies in peace and is saved.[161]

Some more trivial stories (in the sense that they are not the result of a disciple's deliberate wrongdoing) may be noted to illustrate the endurance of various abbas. One insisted that when a disciple was away on an errand it was wrong to worry about when he might return—it is proper to imagine that death may come before the brother.[162] Another made no move to complain when his disciple accidentally gave him food made with lamp-oil rather than honey.[163] Here the disciple is worried by his abba's failure to tell him of the mistake immediately: 'Woe is me, Abba, because I have killed you, and you have laid the sin on me by not speaking.' But the old man regards the mistake as a sign of God's action: 'Do not worry, child, if God had wanted me to eat honey, you would have put honey in it.' A story recounted to Abba Isaiah by 'a faithful brother' who had heard it from Abba Sisoes reveals another facet of an abba's endurance of a certain form of mistreatment by his disciple.[164] Here Abba Athre tells Sisoes that his obedience to Abba Or (which Sisoes, who is visiting them, has just seen demonstrated) 'is not mine, it is the old man's'. This is an acknowledgement of the value of teaching by example, and Athre follows it up by a strategy to show Sisoes how obedient Or really is:

> He cooked the little fish, and spoiled it deliberately, and set it before the old man, and he ate it without saying anything. So he said to him, 'Is it good, Abba?' And he answered, 'It is very good.' Then he took him a bit which was very good, and said to him, 'I have spoiled it, old man.' And he said to him, 'Yes, you have spoiled it a bit.'

The story is similar to the story of Silvanus' testing of the obedience of his disciple Mark[165] and illustrates that an abba too might be faced with such a test of his behaviour, in however trivial an incident.

Finally, we should note two sayings in which a particular abba's ability to endure a bad relationship is seen as a special practice which

[161] In the (more reliable) parallel in Eth. Coll. 13.80 it is the thieving brother who dies, but the reconciling motif of the abba's words of blessing is present.

[162] N 522 (Evergetinos, 1.5.6.6).

[163] N 151. Stories like this also of course convey the message that the endurance of hardship is a good thing whatever its source; cf. Arsenius 18, Macarius 30, N 158.

[164] Isaiah, *Logos* 6, 6A (the quotation which follows is from paragraph d); transmitted under the name Pistus in the alphabetical collection.

[165] Mark 2.

is of advantage to the community as a whole as well as to the brothers concerned. If anyone had a disciple who was 'weak, or negligent, or proud', Abba Isidore would take on the brother himself and 'heal him through his long-suffering'.[166] A saying about Arsenius is less idealistic, but clearer about the motives involved. He took a monk who was stealing from the old men into his own cell, 'Wishing to gain him, and to give relief to the old men, and said to him, "If you want anything, I will provide it, only do not steal."'[167] However the brother starts stealing again, and the old men drive him away. If a brother is weak, the conclusion is, he must be carried, but a thief 'both harms his own soul and causes trouble to everyone in a place'. There are limits to endurance, at least when the whole community is being harmed, rather than just one old man who can take a personal decision to put up with a difficult relationship.[168]

'I heard from some of the saints', an old man once said, 'that there are young ones who lead old men to life.'[169] There follows a story about a brother who came to live with an old man who was a drunkard and stayed with him for three years despite the hardship which the old man's behaviour caused him. After the three years the brother is tempted to leave the old man, but overcomes the temptation. Immediately an angel appears before him and tells him that he is to die the following day. He repeats this to the abba, who tries to reassure him, but when the brother does indeed die, the abba realizes that the brother has been saved through his endurance, while he has been living carelessly. In several respects the story is parallel to the immediately preceding story in the anonymous series, about the death of the old man whom a brother had robbed, particularly of course in the part played by the death of the suffering monk, but also in the motif with which each story concludes, that the experience led to the survivor becoming *δόκιμος*. The difference of course is that in the second case it is the disciple, not the old man, who suffers as a result of a bad relationship. The proximity and similarity of the two stories illustrates that in the matter of enduring a bad relationship the Desert Fathers regarded the abba and disciple as

[166] Isidore 1.
[167] Daniel 6. For the meaning of 'gain', see Ch. 3, Sect. 2.
[168] In Poemen 131 some old men ask him how Abba Nisteros could bear with (*ἀνέχειν*) his disciple. His reply, though difficult, suggests that he recognizes Nisteros' own choice of this way, and perhaps, his own unwillingness or inability to follow it.
[169] N 340.

having similar roles and were well aware that strains and tensions do not arise from only one side of the relationship.[170]

It is of course difficult to tell from these examples how common such strained relationships were—only how the Desert Fathers thought it was right to respond and that they thought that even in these strained circumstances the relationship could bear spiritual fruit, for one party and sometimes for both. Similarly, it is difficult to tell how often the problem was expected to arise of an abba being unable to respond to a disciple's particular problems or temptations, exemplified by Poemen 62. There are several other examples of this problem. Zacharias found that his abba was unable to respond satisfactorily to a visionary experience which he had, only beating him and accusing him of being a victim of the demons; so he told Poemen, and then another old man, both of whom were convinced that the vision was from God.[171] The last speaker does not however regard the problem as a reason for breaking the relationship, but tells Zacharias to 'Go and submit to your father'. That a disciple can get access to another old man can in fact help to alleviate any strain in his relationship with his abba and allow it to continue even where, as in this case, the abba appears to lack the discernment or experience needed to be an effective guide.[172] On the other hand at least one saying, also involving Poemen, acknowledges that a breakdown in the relationship could be permanent and final:

A brother asked Abba Poemen, 'I am harming my soul through staying near

[170] N 551 (Evergetinos, 1.37.3.1), another account of a disciple's endurance of his abba's bad behaviour, also involves recognition by God of the value of what the brother is doing, and ends, again, with his death and (successful) intercession on behalf of his abba's salvation also. Other texts illustrate the theme of a disciple's endurance. N 451 (the Greek text is unpublished—see *Les Sentences ... série des anonymes*, 151–2; a Latin version is found in PL, lxxiii. 754–5) is a remarkable example in which a disciple mediates between his abba and a stranger of whom the abba is jealous. The abba eventually recognizes that his disciple is the real abba, and he the disciple. The same conclusion occurs in An Abba of Rome 2, where a difficult abba repents in the face of his disciple's humble endurance. In John of Thebes he serves an ungrateful abba for twelve years, until the abba, on the point of death, finally recognizes his virtue: 'He is an angel, not a man.' N 53 may be an example of endurance of a bad abba, as he is said to want to control his disciple; but it may be meant as a deliberate test. In Ammoes 2, if it is meant to suggest difficulties in the relationship, it is impossible to tell who is at fault. N 451 is discussed by H. Brünner, 'Ptahotep bei den koptischen Mönchen', *Zeitschrift für Ägyptische Sprache*, 86 (1961), 145–7, who claims that it echos a traditional virtue of ancient Egyptian ethical literature.

[171] Zacharias 4.

[172] This is the case in N 551, where another old man realizes what is going on and encourages the brother to bear his abba's behaviour; cf. Phocas 2 and Isaac of Kellia 2 (where, of course, the abba is not in error). On the consultation of more than one abba, see above, n. 39.

my Abba. Should I still stay near him?' The old man knew that he was being injured, and was astonished that he should ask him whether he should stay. And the old man said, 'Stay, if you want.' So he went away and stayed there. He came again and said, 'I am losing my soul.' But the old man did not say, 'Leave'. He came for a third time and said, 'I really cannot stay any longer.' Abba Poemen said to him, 'See, now you have been healed. Go, and stay no longer.'[173]

The disciple's reluctance to leave his abba, even when he realizes that something is seriously wrong with their relationship (we are not told what), is understandable in view of the Desert Fathers' teaching on obedience and submission. To leave might be seen as an assertion of improper self-will. Poemen's attitude is more complex. Outwardly he remains neutral, but in fact realizes that ultimately the brother will have to leave. Only when the brother had come to the end of his endurance does Poemen affirm his decision and assure him that he has acted for the best. In some ways this saying is an exception to almost all the rules which the Desert Fathers made for the behaviour of a disciple, valuing as it does the disciple's own judgement of his need and showing how an abba could allow him to make his mind up for himself.[174] The case is clearly a special one, but like the story about Arsenius and the thief, it acknowledges that there will be times when it is impossible (despite the rewards which endurance brings) to endure a bad relationship.

8. Teaching and Reluctance to Teach

The fact that relationships between an abba and his disciple might sometimes suffer serious strain and even a permanent breakdown leads naturally to a consideration of some of the many instances in the *Apophthegmata Patrum* in which teaching is silenced or offered only with reluctance. An abba's silence would, we might naturally expect, usually be a precaution against the dangers of harming himself or his disciple if he failed to teach in the recommended way; but it is perhaps possible that silence, or teaching offered with hesitation, may also sometimes have a positive function, a value in itself as a means of teaching important lessons of the monastic life. It is, at any rate, worth

[173] Poemen S 2 (Guy, *Recherches*, 29–30). The story continues with a comment about when it is right to question an old man about 'hidden thoughts' or 'open sin'.

[174] In Mark 3–4 he is portrayed as reluctant to obey his abba. Here too some strain in the relationship may be implied, and his action seems to be commended.

examining cases where silence or reluctance to teach is referred to explicitly.

'If, when you rebuke someone, you are moved to anger, you are satisfying your own passion. So do not destroy yourself in order to save others.'[175] This saying of Macarius clearly warns that an abba who cannot teach without passion cannot teach with integrity, and that his subjection to anger endangers his own soul, regardless of the good he may be doing to others.[176] It was probably in order to guard against dangers of this kind that another saying advocated a manner of teaching designed to avoid the appearance of any desire to control or to assert the superiority of the teacher to the disciple: 'If you say a word of life to someone, say it with compunction and tears to him who hears; and if not, do not say it, lest you die without profit through using alien words in wishing to save others.'[177] Here the 'alien [*ἀλλότριοι*] words' are perhaps the words of anger or of self-will which are foreign to the proper spirit of teaching, or to an abba who possesses the integrity of a good teacher. Both of these sayings warn any teacher or would-be teacher that, for fear of self-destructive behaviour, for fear of the temptation to be other than a humble exemplar of the monastic life, it may sometimes be necessary to be silent.

As a particular example of an abba deciding he is unable to teach, a story of Theodore of Pherme is particularly illuminating:

A brother came to Abba Theodore to be taught to weave, bringing some cord with him. The old man said to him, 'Go, and come back tomorrow.' Getting

[175] Macarius 17. For avoiding anger in teaching, see above, pp. 62–3. That a teacher should avoid harming himself, see Eth. Coll. 13.2 and Evagrius, *On Prayer*, 25. This may be a point for which Evagrius was dependent on his teacher Macarius: on their relationship, see G. Bunge, 'Evagre le Pontique et les deux Macaire', *Irénikon*, 56 (1983), 215–27, 323–60.

[176] Cf. Poemen 127 for another comment on the necessity of a teacher being 'whole and without passions [*ἀπαθής*]'. It may have been pessimism about the possibility of achieving this which led Poemen (157) to compare teaching with rebuke: *τὸ διδάξαι τὸν πλησίον ὅμοιόν ἐστι τοῦ ἐλέγξαι.* Terms related to *ἀπάθεια* are rare in the Sayings (cf. Longinus 5 for *ἀπαθής*), compared with the central role which passionlessness plays in Evagrius' writing. See *Praktikos*, 2, 33, 53, 56, 58, 59, 60, 64, 67, 83, 91 (= Evagrius 6 in the Sayings). The Sayings emphasize endurance and combat against temptation, rather than victory over it (cf. *Praktikos*, 68), although of course Evagrius too was profoundly concerned with the process of resistance to temptation and did not think that possession of *ἀπάθεια* necessarily implied freedom from all 'memories' or sinful impulses, only from being distracted by them (*Praktikos*, 67).

[177] N 433 (Evergetinos, 4.38.7.6; also found at the end of Nau's text as no. 396, second half). For 'alien word', see also Or 3 and Eth. Coll. 13.6, and Amoun of Nitria 2 and Ammoes 1, referred to below.

up the old man soaked the cord and prepared the first row for him, saying, 'Do this, and this.' Then he left him, and the old man went into his cell and sat down. At the correct time he made him eat, and sent him away. But he came back the next day, and the old man said to him, 'Take your cord and go away, for you have come to cast me into temptation and care.' And he did not let him come inside again.[178]

At first sight, this text suggests a somewhat uncaring example of an abba being unwilling to make the effort to teach the sometimes very mundane things of which the monastic life consists. But as the story in Isaac of Kellia 2 shows, Theodore was very conscious of the need to establish an effective teaching relationship with a committed disciple. In the story quoted here, too, Theodore does not reject his role as a teacher; he makes an effort to do what is required but, in the end, seems to find himself unable to deal with a brother who needs more precise supervision and instruction than Theodore is willing to give. His reason may be (this cannot be proved, though his reference to 'temptation' may imply it) connected with the problem of anger referred to by Macarius, or it may be that he is doing no more than sticking to the principle stated in the Isaac story, of not instructing his disciple like the ruler of a cenobium. Both of these would be adequate reasons for refusing to take on a brother who needed a lot of ordering around. But it is not illegitimate to see Theodore's attitude as informed by a more general pessimism about his own capabilities as a monk, and indeed about the potential of others. On another occasion a brother said to him, 'Speak a word to me, because I am lost,' and Theodore replied, 'I am myself in danger, so what can I say to you?'[179]

Similar considerations should probably govern our interpretation of a saying of Sisoes, who did not allow anyone else to serve him while his disciple Abraham was away: 'Am I to let anyone else become familiar with me, except my brother?'[180] Sisoes shared the belief that it was wrong for an abba to impose his will on his disciple, and clearly enjoyed a close relationship with his disciple Abraham, who is mentioned in a number of sayings.[181] These two facts together suggest that his reluctance

[178] Theodore of Pherme 21.

[179] Theodore of Pherme 20. His pessimism about his contemporaries' capacity for the monastic life is illustrated by 8, 16 ('Many take their rest [ἀνάπαυσις] before God grants it to them'—cf. 2 in which he denies having ever found rest himself), and even by the apparently trivial comment on manners in 6: 'The monks have lost their good breeding and do not say "forgive me."'

[180] Sisoes 46; cf. 7 for his spending a long period alone.

[181] Sisoes 29. For the depth of his relationship with Abraham, see esp. 51.

to allow anyone else to serve him derives from a fear of initiating a relationship less thoroughly tested for its conformity to the principles of effective teaching than that with Abraham (or Theodore's with Isaac, after Isaac had discovered the purpose of Theodore's behaviour), and therefore more likely to be based merely on Sisoes' imposition of his own will on the disciple. Sisoes also showed some reluctance, perhaps for similar reasons, to speak to visitors, an attitude which is sometimes shared by Arsenius;[182] but there was no absolute rule about this, and both did allow visitors to consult them on other occasions, as did Theodore.[183] In two of the cases where Sisoes refused to speak to visitors, his reason for eventually breaking his silence is interesting. In Sisoes 16 his visitors notice some baskets and ask Abraham what they are for. 'We dispose of them here and there,' says Abraham, meaning that they are for sale. At this point Sisoes breaks in: 'Even Sisoes eats now and then.' In the other saying, Sisoes 21, a visitor exasperated by Sisoes' silence exclaims, 'Why trouble the old man? He does not eat, that is why he cannot speak.' Sisoes replies by saying that he eats when he has to. Neither of these incidents is particularly significant in itself, but both illustrate Sisoes' unwillingness to give visitors a false impression about his own merits as an ascetic. This is recognized by the brothers in the first saying, who 'went away with joy, edified by his humility'.[184]

The purpose of this discussion is to suggest that on occasions abbas had reasons for refusing to teach which are connected with their personal worries or feelings of inadequacy, and not with a dismissive attitude towards the value of teaching as such. It is probably a feeling of his own unworthiness to answer a question (from an older and more experienced monk) which leads Zacharias to teach only when his questioner persists in asking him.[185] In the case of Arsenius we are told that, 'He never wanted to talk about any problem in the Scriptures, even though he could talk about it, if he wanted to; and he did not

[182] Sisoes 16, 21; in 50 his refusal to see a visitor appears to be connected with his reluctance to receive special treatment because he is ill. In 27 he refuses to allow even Abraham to see him, because *οὐ σχολάζει τὰ ὧδε*—now is no time for relaxation or rest. Arsenius (37) opens the door to a caller, thinking it is his servant, but falls to the ground and refuses to speak when he discovers it is a stranger.

[183] Sisoes 28 in particular suggests that on occasions he could treat callers in a friendly way. Arsenius (34) apologized to a group of travellers for not having received them on a previous occasion (when he was ill) and indicated that he had imposed a penance on himself as a result. In 27 his attitude to a caller is noticably more friendly than in 37. Theodore accepts visitors in 2, 9, 20, but remains pessimistic.

[184] Cf. Theodore of Pherme 28.

[185] Zacharias 1, 3 (see above, n. 55).

readily write a letter.'[186] His reserve here should probably be seen as an example of authentic humility, coupled perhaps with an unwillingness to obtain any prestige or advantage from the fact that he had received a good secular education before becoming a monk.[187]

This comment on Arsenius raises the question of the Desert Fathers' attitude to Scripture and to its use in teaching, and how this was related in other instances not only to an abba's feelings about himself, but also to the attitudes which he wished his disciples to cultivate.[188] Three of the most revealing and interesting comments on this subject are found in sayings of Sisoes, Poemen, and, first, Zeno:

> Some brothers came to him and asked him, 'What does it mean that is written in Job, "Heaven is not pure before him?"' The old man answered them, 'The brothers have left their sins, and inquire about the heavens. This is the interpretation of the saying: since he alone is pure, he said, "Heaven is not pure."'[189]

Zeno does not refuse to comment on the text, but his answer begins what is presumably a warning rather than a compliment, a warning against forgetting about the important task of attention to yourself and your sins, and turning instead to speculation and talk of things for which your behaviour does not make you worthy. A long story about Poemen provides the second example. A great anchorite came to see him in Egypt, and after they had greeted one another and sat down the stranger began to speak to Poemen 'from the Scriptures, concerning spiritual and heavenly things'.[190] 'But Abba Poemen turned away his face, and did not give him an answer.' The visitor asked Poemen's disciple what was wrong, and he went in to ask the old man. 'He is of above', replied Poemen, 'and speaks heavenly things. I am of below, and speak earthly things. If he had spoken to me about the passions of

[186] Arsenius 42.

[187] On Arsenius' rejection of his education, see 5, 6. For a comment on these texts, see F. von Lilienfeld, 'Paulus-Zitate und paulinische Gedanken in den *Apophthegmata Patrum*', *Studia Evangelica*, 5 (TU 103; Berlin, 1968), 293, reprinted in *Spiritualität des frühen Wüstenmönchtums*, 55.

[188] On the Desert Fathers and the Bible, see D. Burton-Christie, '"Practice Makes Perfect": Interpretation of Scripture in the *Apophthegmata Patrum*', *SP* 20 (Leuven, 1989), 213–18; Dörries, 'Die Bibel in ältesten Mönchtum'; L. Leloir, 'La Bible et les Pères du Désert', in *La Bible et les Pères, Colloque de Strasbourg (1er–3 Octobre 1969)* (Paris, 1971), 113–34; von Lilienfeld, 'Jesus-Logion und Vaterspruch', 'Paulus-Zitate und paulinische Gedanken', and 'Die Christliche Unterweisung', 98–103.

[189] Zeno 4. Job 15: 15.

[190] Poemen 8; cf. again Eth. Coll. 13.2 (above, nn. 77, 175).

the soul, I would have answered him. But if he speaks of spiritual things, I do not know them.' So the brother told the visitor, 'The old man does not readily speak of the Scriptures, but if anyone asks him about the passions of the soul, he will answer.' After this exchange the old man goes back in to Poemen, penitent (*κατανυγείς*), and confesses to him that the passions control him. Poemen now gladly speaks to him, and the old man leaves convinced that 'this is the true way', and thanking God that he was worthy to meet such a great saint.

In the third saying, someone tells Sisoes that when he reads Scripture he is tempted to formulate a question, in order to have something to ask.[191] The brother seems to realize that there is something wrong with this—perhaps that it is a mere quest for information, or nothing more than a wish to have something difficult to ask the old men in order to impress them with his perceptiveness. Sisoes denies the need for this: 'Rather, you ought to get to be free from cares, and to speak as a result of your purity of mind.'[192] Dörries comments that the Desert Fathers did not inherit Origen's interest in the speculative interpretation of Scripture.[193] In a sense this is obviously true. What these sayings do suggest is that for the Desert Fathers the interpretation of Scripture was not something to be lightly entered upon, not something to be regarded as an automatic subject of discussion. An easy approach to Scripture may hide your own real needs and your own real state of mind. Where the proper attitude is not present, it is implied, silence, the absence of teaching or of dialogue between abba and disciple, may be the best course of action.

It is in this general context that we should see some other stories which refer to the interpretation of Scripture, where silence is clearly advocated, though in each case the precise point made may differ. Some of these sayings may appear to cast doubt on the propriety of the use or interpretation of Scripture at all; but in the same way as sayings which have been examined earlier in this section convey not a general reluctance to teach but a reluctance based on perception of particular problems, so the reasons for silence about Scripture are realistic rather than negative, implicitly based, like those of Zeno and Sisoes, on awareness of sin and recognition that your own approach to Scripture

[191] Sisoes 17: *θέλει ὁ λογισμός μου φιλοκαλῆσαι λόγον, ἵνα ἔχω εἰς ἐπερώτημα.*

[192] On freedom from care or worry, cf. again Sisoes 43 (above, n. 32).

[193] Dörries, 'Die Bibel in ältesten Mönchtum', 254: 'Es ist nicht der Geist des Origenes der hier fortlebt', referring to Zeno 4 and Copres 3 (in which he refuses to discuss the significance of Melchisedek). Cf. Guy, 'Les *Apophthegmata Patrum*', 79–81.

may be wrongly motivated. This is true of a story about Antony. He once wished to test (*δοκιμάσαι*) some brothers, so he asked them what they thought of a particular passage of Scripture.[194] After each one had answered as best he could, only to be told by Antony that 'You have not found it', Antony asked Abba Joseph, 'What do you say this passage means?' Joseph answered that he did not know. 'Abba Joseph has really found the way', said Antony, 'because he has said, "I do not know."' It was the duty of an abba to test his disciple's development of the virtues of humility and recognition of his own failings; discussion of a passage of Scripture would be a particularly effective way of doing this, the differences of opinion clearly showing that the correct attitude is that of the experienced abba who is aware of his own limitations and humbly refuses to claim to speculate about what he does not know.

In a saying which stresses the different needs of the young who need to guard themselves (*ἡ νεότης γὰρ χρείαν ἔχει φυλακῆς*) and the old men who are already able to do so and 'do not have anything foreign in them which they could find to say', Poemen warns Amoun against the dangers of speaking 'alien words' to one's neighbour.[195] The designation is quite general, covering anything which is inappropriate to the monastic life. Amoun then asks what he should do: 'If I must speak with my brother; am I to speak of Scripture, or of the words of the old men?' Poemen replies that 'If you cannot leave in silence, it is better to speak about the words of the old men rather than Scripture. For to speak of Scripture is dangerous.' To understand this saying, it is necessary to take seriously its warning against improper subjects of conversation and unnecessary talking.[196] A similar point is made in a story about some brothers who visited Antony, spending the journey talking about the words of the Fathers, the Scriptures, and about their manual work, while an old man who was travelling with them remained silent.[197] When they met Antony he greeted them and the old man in turn, commenting, 'You have brought some good brothers with you, Abba.'

[194] Antony 17.

[195] Amoun of Nitria 2 (Isaiah, *Logos* 6, 4A). The quotations are from Isaiah's text, though there are no significant differences. As Chitty, *The Desert a City*, 79 n. 83, points out, this saying certainly does not concern the founder of Nitria of *HL*, 8, but a disciple or friend of Poemen, possibly the same Amoun (or Ammon) who is mentioned in Sisoes 17 and 26.

[196] Cf. Ammoes 1, where he takes steps to prevent *ξένη ὁμιλία* from slipping into his conversation with his disciple.

[197] Antony 18. The same pairing of Scripture and words of the Fathers is found in Eth. Coll. 13.2 and 77.

'They are good', he said, 'but their courtyard has no door, and whoever wishes can come into the stable and steal the ass.' We hardly need the comment of the compiler or transmitter that 'He said this because they spoke whatever came into their mouths'. It is true that neither of these stories expresses clearly what the dangers of thoughtless talk are supposed to be; but at least Poemen, unlike the anonymous old man, differentiates between the dangers of different subjects: using Scripture as a subject of irrelevant conversation is dangerous, but less so than the other topics.[198]

The attitude expressed here is certainly cautious—opposed, like Zeno's, to speculation and discussion about Scripture, and deeply aware of the possibility of error in interpretation.[199] But it would be wrong to think that this caution implies that the Desert Fathers had little regard for Scripture or (conversely) that their attitude was so reverential that Scripture was treated as a book too holy to be used.[200] The sayings concerned are merely warnings which serve to remind a disciple or an abba that silence is occasionally necessary; they should not be regarded as evidence of a general avoidance of the use and interpretation of Scripture. There are many sayings in which Scripture is used confidently in the practice of teaching.[201]

At the beginning of this section it was suggested that silence may sometimes have had a positive function in teaching. Some of the sayings which have been considered in this section and earlier in this chapter

[198] N 646 (labelled J 677 in the French translation. Evergetinos, 4.17.1.9; also, unusually for a piece in the later part of N, found in PJ 10.104) warns that when a brother is considering the meaning of a word (presumably of Scripture), the demons may intervene to suggest whatever meaning suits them, if God does not reveal it to him. It is not difficult to believe that all the sayings discussed see speculation and irrelevant conversation as a tool in the hands of the demons.

[199] As well as the sayings discussed in the text, see Pambo 9: 'In this he was superior to many, that if he was asked a question from the Scriptures, or a spiritual question, he did not reply immediately, but said he did not know the answer. If he was asked again, he gave no answer.' The version in *HL*, 10.7, speaks of him spending long periods considering the answers to questions, and of his words therefore being received 'as from God'.

[200] Cf. H. Lietzmann, *The Era of the Church Fathers* (London, 1951), 153–4, for this view on the basis of Amoun of Nitria 2. But Lietzmann is wrong to deny that the Desert Fathers made significant use of Scripture. Among older works a more balanced attitude is taken by Bousset, *Apophthegmata*, 82–3; and K. Heussi, *Der Ursprung des Mönchtums* (Tübingen, 1936), 276–80.

[201] See e.g. Antony 9, 32, Agathon 14, Ammonas 11, John Kolobos 38, John of the Cells 2, Moses 18, Matoes 2, Poemen 30, 34, 54, 60, 74, 86, 112, 115, 116, 117, 126, 131, 136, 153, Sisoes 44, N 225, 301. The value of Scripture is affirmed in general terms in Eth. Coll. 13.1, 13.

do seem to allow this. Here we should distinguish between silence, a simple refusal to speak or to answer a question, and something more specific and more discerning, a refusal to speak about the particular question a disciple wishes to raise, or to answer in the way he expects. Zeno 4 and Poemen 8 are good examples of the latter practice: Zeno refuses to embark on an interesting discussion; Poemen refuses to fall in with his visitor's assumptions about what is the right sort of thing for respected old men to talk about; both forcefully draw the attention of their questioners to what they should really be concerned with. Sayings of Matoes, referred to already in the discussion of an abba's exposure of his own inner life, and Pambo, one of those which manifests belief in the inspiration of an abba's words, are other revealing instances of this.[202] In his case, Pambo hesitates for a long time before answering a question, and when he does so, his answer effectively rejects the terms in which the question was posed and supplies a more considered, more significant, and more personal answer than the questioners originally desired (the same points are present in the Ethiopic version). Other abbas too refused to respond as their disciples expected, showing them that what they think they ought to do when they question an old man is not in fact how a monk should behave.[203]

In all these cases of 'unexpected response' the aim of the abba concerned was to express his own feelings of unworthiness and to teach his disciple something about himself and his needs. But perhaps the most straightforward explanation for an abba's *outright* refusal to teach would be not these complex ideas but a belief that his disciples or questioners were simply not listening. In section two of this chapter we saw that another of the sayings which clearly express a belief in the inspiration of the words of an abba portrays an abba as refusing to speak, and indeed claiming that God had taken away the gift of teaching because of the unresponsiveness of the brothers.[204] Isaac of Kellia expressed a similar pessimistic view: 'I will no longer offer you commands, for you do not keep them.'[205]

Rousseau has raised the question of whether there was a decline in the charismatic authority of the abba during the fourth century,

[202] Matoes 5, Pambo 2 (Eth. Coll. 14.21).

[203] Euprepius 7, N 482. Another possible example of unexpected response is Eth. Coll. 14.7.

[204] Felix.

[205] Isaac of Kellia 7. This pessimism about the dedication of his contemporaries to the monastic life is reflected also in 5 and 8.

accompanied by a growing stress on example as the principal means of teaching.[206] The sayings of Felix and Isaac do suggest that there were limits to the authority of the abba's words, and perhaps that these became more acute when standards declined. But it is doubtful whether this phenomenon betrays a change *over time* in the role of the abba or in the importance of charismata, rather than a recognition that the success of teaching was inherently dependent on the responsiveness of the disciple as well as the abilities or inspiration of the abba, combined with a general pessimism about the standards of the present generation in the monastic life.[207] Clearly the unresponsiveness of disciples would impede teaching by example as much as teaching by word. But in any case, the evidence which has been discussed in section five of this chapter suggests that example and word were generally seen as closely and necessarily combined, even if some, like Theodore, preferred to teach close disciples by example because of the problem of self-will.

Rousseau's attempt to separate the two forms of teaching chronologically is therefore unconvincing,[208] and sometimes involves a rather strained use of evidence.[209] He makes other related suggestions about the evolution of the monastic community over time. He suggests that the decline of charismatic authority was accompanied by an evolution in the pattern of the teaching relationship from one of encounters between abbas and disciples on 'isolated occasions' (requiring no special

[206] Rousseau, *Ascetics, Authority, and the Church*, 37: 'There are signs that the "charism of the word", which played so prominent a part in more primitive encounters, suffered a decline as the century proceeded; and that the example of the elders acquired increasing importance in the later stages of the ascetic movement'; cf. 29, 39, 69.

[207] When Poemen asked Macarius for a word, Macarius (25) said, 'The thing that you are seeking has gone now from the monks.' But Macarius is probably referring to the dedication to the monastic life which Poemen seeks. He does not mean that the gift of inspired speech is no longer present.

[208] Thus he acknowledges that 'change, when it came, did not entirely override former attitudes and customs' (p. 37); and that charismata persisted (pp. 42–3); on p. 38 he claims that teaching by example is present even in the 'earliest ascetic literature', in which case it is not easy to maintain that it was ever absent. Important here is the fact that Poemen 108, about an abba who lived well into the fifth century, refers explicitly to the charism of the word. As in Felix, the charism is not exercised, but this is because of Poemen's humility before his elder brother, not because the charism is absent or has been superseded by teaching by example.

[209] See his use of Macarius 31 (p. 37 n. 17 has '33', but this seems to be a misprint for 31) who allegedly represents the older, charismatic rather than exemplary form of teaching: 'Macarius the Egyptian, for instance, was seriously perturbed, when visitors showed more interest in his pattern of life than in revealing to him their problems and temptations.' In fact Macarius does want people to consider his way of life—as a sinner rather than as a 'great and holy old man'.

knowledge of the disciple by the abba, but giving him an opportunity to exercise his general spiritual wisdom) to one of 'more permanent relationships' in the context of which the abba addressed his disciples' individual needs. But this argument is imprecise and unconvincing.[210] Similarly he sees the presence of clergy in the monastic communities as a sign of the progressive institutionalization of teaching in the later fourth century: 'it was clerics, now, who gave spiritual assistance, when famous holy men were no longer able to "speak the word".'[211] But there is no evidence at all that the ordained monks to whose sayings he refers were able to exercise authority only *because* they were priests.[212] Finally, he suggests that the authority of tradition and the written word (rather than charismata) came to prevail in the later community; but this point too may be subjected to criticism.[213]

[210] Ibid. 36, esp. n. 14, where Joseph of Panepho 3, Joseph of Thebes, Cyrus, Macarius 3, and Poemen 62 are held to show that abbas continued an older practice of first outlining 'general principles' before going on to apply them to a particular disciple. But in Joseph 3 and Poemen 62 the emphasis is on the needs of different individuals, not on general teaching at all, while in Cyrus and Macarius 3 the dialogue is a way of approaching the needs of an individual and seems quite natural. Anyway, no evidence is cited to prove that the 'general' way of teaching was an older form. John Kolobos 8 does not, as claimed (n. 14), necessarily suggest that John had personal knowledge of all the individuals concerned. Ares and Ammoes 1, also seen by Rousseau as illustrating later forms, are virtually undatable (as in fact is Cyrus)—we know from Ammoes 4 that there was an Ammoes who may have been a contemporary of Poemen, though he may equally have been an old man when Poemen was young. As shown above, n. 39, patterns of teaching may have been generally much more flexible than fixed one-to-one relationships, and some of the evidence for this (e.g. Poemen 88–9, Sisoes 35–6) is quite late in date.

[211] Ibid. 63.

[212] See Isidore 1, Poemen 44, Isaac of Kellia 7, Pambo 2, and Esaias 4 (cited in Rousseau, *Ascetics, Authority, and the Church*, 63 nn. 40–1). It is surely more likely that ordination marked a *recognition* of a monk's qualities than that the presence of priests in the community competed with and was essentially unrelated to 'personal sanctity, or capacity for leadership' (p. 62—the one saying cited as evidence for this, N 254, is of questionable significance). In fact the evidence supplies no support for the claim that the 'proliferation of presbyters' (p. 62) was a late phenomenon marking a change from earlier charismatic forms of leadership. To use N 165 (p. 63 n. 41) as evidence that 'formal penance' replaced 'hearing the words of the fathers' is also mistaken. Bessarion 5 (ibid.) is seen as an instance of an 'old-style ascetic' being 'called in to rescue clerics from their own incompetence', but neither the chronological judgement nor the implication of a tension between lay and ordained monks is present in this text, nor in Bessarion 7 nor Moses 5 (ibid.) where, *contra* Rousseau, Moses is not 'publicly rebuked by the local clergy'. Similarly, priests are not even mentioned in Agathon 14 (p. 64 n. 47).

[213] Ibid. 68–76, with reference to a generation who 'always thought of themselves as disciples, dependent for their teaching on the insights of the past' (p. 71). The problem here is the false assumption that tradition, oral or written, and charismata are mutually exclusive sources of authority. Once it is recognized that the reuse of past teachings (p. 71 n. 15) is a normal element in the practice of the Desert Fathers, it can be seen that the growth of tradition carries no implication of a decline in the 'word' over time. Cf.

In other words, reluctance to teach or to speak of Scripture should be seen not, as Rousseau argues, as a stage of development in monastic life, but, as has been emphasized throughout this section, as a response to particular factors. It stems from an abba's fear of being found guilty of imposing his will on others; from his own feelings of unworthiness, humility, or inability to speak of spiritual or scriptural matters; from his desire for his disciples to recognize their own limitations; or from his recognition that they were unreceptive to teaching.[214] It should not be generalized, as if 'on the whole, the Egyptian tradition disapproves of monks taking it upon themselves to teach one another'.[215]

In certain circumstances not only the phenomenon of 'unexpected response' but even outright refusal to teach might perhaps serve to teach a disciple something positive. Naturally in sayings like Isaac of Kellia 7 no benefit is obtained by the brothers as a result of Isaac's rejection of teaching,[216] but in the case of Felix his pessimism at least serves to draw his questioners' attention to their own failures, and they express grief as a result. One story seems to embrace the view that silence itself may teach something positive about the detachment and virtue of the monastic life (compared, in this particular case, with that of an archbishop deeply involved in affairs of the world) which the exchange of any number of polite, interesting, or spiritual words will not communicate effectively to someone who is not willing to learn. It concerns Archbishop Theophilus, who came one day to visit Pambo in Scetis. 'Say a word to the Pope', the brothers said to Pambo, 'that he may benefit.' But he refused to speak to the visitor and told the brothers

Gould, 'A Note on the *Apophthegmata Patrum*', 134–5. On p. 191 Rousseau speaks of attitudes to Scripture 'tinged with misgiving', and notes Amoun of Nitria 2. But Antony 17, 18 show that this was not a later development connected with the decline of charismatic teaching; it would be quite arbitrary to discount this evidence by denying that the stories go back to Antony. Rousseau describes the interpretation of Scripture as a 'third and quite separable element' (that is, presumably, different from both the charism of the word and the use of tradition or example) in the practice of teaching; the view that interpretation of Scripture was not a part of the Abba's charismatic teaching is also criticized in 'A Note on the *Apophthegmata Patrum*', 135.

[214] Cf. Theodore of Pherme 3, where he refuses to teach someone who 'wishes to be glorified by [repeating] the words of others', and Arsenius 26 for a refusal to see visitors whom he regards (perhaps rather self-centredly) as badly motivated.

[215] Tugwell, *Ways of Imperfection*, 18, referring to Antony 17. He fails to distinguish between general attitudes to teaching and occasional warnings of its dangers, and also suggests wrongly that the 'habit of passing the buck', that is of reusing stories or sayings of other monks in teaching, is prompted by reluctance to teach.

[216] Nor in Isidore the Priest 7: 'When a brother came to him, he used to flee inside his cell.' But his refusal to teach is not total, as he is willing to explain his actions: 'Even the beasts are saved when they flee to their lairs.'

that 'If he does not benefit through my silence, he will not benefit through my speech'.[217]

9. Conclusion

It has been the purpose of this chapter to show that the Desert Fathers saw the teaching relationship as essentially two-sided. It certainly places great demands on the disciple, whose duty is to submit himself to his abba and to learn the virtues of endurance and renunciation of his own will which are considered essential to the monastic life. But as we have seen, especially in sections five to seven of the chapter, the relationship was important for the abba too, testing his own endurance, submission, and integrity in teaching by example and by personal involvement with his disciple's problems and temptations. On occasions he knew that he could not teach as his disciple wished. But even here, in what have been called circumstances of 'unexpected response', or of outright refusal to teach, he might still succeed, by drawing attention to his disciple's erroneous assumptions, in conveying an important lesson. But it was not just his disciple's limitations that he recognized, for he must also be aware of his own: here too the relationship is two-sided, and both parties learn through it about themselves and about how to live the monastic life.

In that its aim was to teach the disciple how to live (in a practical as well as spiritual sense), and in that, as many sayings illustrate, the disciple acted as a cook, servant, and nurse to an abba who might often be old and weak,[218] the teaching relationship was essentially functional.

[217] Theophilus the Archbishop 2. As it stands this is an anachronism, for Pambo died *c.*374 (Chitty, *The Desert a City*, 46–7, 56). If the name Pambo is correct, the archbishop was probably Athanasius; if Theophilus is the right name, the monk cannot be identified. Rousseau, *Ascetics, Authority, and the Church*, 60, comments, 'Theophilus had not come with the attitudes and aims of a disciple.' This is probably true, although it is not made explicit in the same way as in the texts cited in n. 214 above. Rousseau treats this saying too as marking an earlier phase when the identity of the monastic 'group' was jealously guarded against outside pressures (cf. 'The Desert Fathers, Antony, and Pachomius', 124). But he does not note that discrimination between visitors was not solely on the basis of whether they were members of the 'group'—monks could be rejected too. Nor does the rejection of Theophilus, a secular cleric, imply any tension between monks and clergy *within* the monastic communities, for which there is no evidence (cf. above, n. 212). On the rejection of lay visitors, cf. Ch. 4, n. 120.

[218] Among sayings quoted in this chapter, see e.g. Arsenius 37, Isaac of Kellia 2, John of Thebes, Sisoes 29, 46, N 151, 317, 341.

The Desert Fathers based their view of it on their understanding of the needs of a beginner and on their ideas as to how those needs were best met, rather than on the belief that such a relationship should be grounded in affection or love. But because the relationship *was* a personal one, rather than one based on the impersonal exercise of authority, it would be surprising if it had not produced many examples of tenderness and devotion,[219] and if such feelings were not occasionally articulated more clearly. Abba Isidore tried to describe the attitude of a disciple to his teacher, taking account of the fact that the disciple is both an obedient learner and a partner in a personal relationship: 'Those who learn must both love as fathers those who are truly teachers, and fear them as rulers; and neither lose fear through love, nor weaken love through fear'.[220] But even here, a stress on reciprocality remains: it is the abba who is a good teacher—a teacher, we may think, who teaches by example and involves himself personally with the well-being of his disciple—who deserves this respect and love.

The existence and strength of the bond of affection or love which may exist between a disciple and his abba is, finally, illustrated by another story about an Isaac, which clearly belongs to a period of *diaspora* and decline in the monastic community, and well expresses the sense of loss which a brother could feel at being separated, by death or by geographical distance, from his teachers in the monastic life:

> Abba Isaac and Abba Abraham were living together. Abba Abraham came in and found Abba Isaac weeping. And he said to him, 'Why are you weeping?' And the old man said, 'Why should we not weep? For where have we to go? Our fathers have died; manual work is not enough to pay the fare which we need to go and visit the old men, and so we are orphans. That is why I weep.'[221]

[219] See e.g. Arsenius 35, John of the Thebaid, Poemen 144, N 351. On friendship and love in the relationship, see Louf, 'Spiritual Fatherhood in the Literature of the Desert', 55–7.

[220] Isidore the Priest 5; cf. Evagrius, *Praktikos*, 100.

[221] Isaac of Kellia 3. It is unlikely that this is the same Isaac as the pessimist of 5, 7, 8; perhaps he is the disciple of Poemen of Poemen 107, 144, 184. The Abraham may be the 'Abraham of Abba Agathon' of Poemen 67. The story must be of mid or late fifth-century date. Another story about visiting the old men which may stem from this time is Eth. Coll. 13.6.

3

The Monk and his Neighbour

At the end of Chapter 1 it was claimed that not only the teaching relationship, but personal relationships in general feature prominently in the teaching of the *Apophthegmata Patrum*. The purpose of this chapter is to examine the evidence for this claim. It will concentrate on the more clear-cut statements of the Desert Fathers on the importance of relationships within the monastic community. It will be left until Chapter 4 to show in more detail exactly what kind of relationships the Desert Fathers thought it was right to pursue, and to outline their reactions to the particular problems posed by personal relationships as they saw them. The relationship between a teacher and his disciple was controlled by a complex pattern of accepted rules which governed both the conduct of the abba and the behaviour of the disciple; these prescribed self-abnegation and openness to others in the interests of the effective teaching of the virtues of the monastic life. A system of accepted custom and precedent also guided both parties in the matter of responding properly to situations of strain and breakdown in the teaching relationship. In what follows, an equally complex pattern of attitudes and rules for behaviour will be found to apply in the case of the Desert Fathers' teaching on relationships in general.

1. Recognizing the Importance of your Neighbour

How then did the Desert Fathers recognize and assess the importance of their relationships with their neighbours in the monastic life? To answer this question it will be necessary to examine both sayings and stories which deal explicitly with relationships, and sayings of a more general kind which illustrate the basic principles of the monastic life as particular speakers understood them. There are many sayings of this type, characterized by von Lilienfeld as 'mnemotechnische Hilfen', offering a two, three, or fourfold summary of what constitutes the life of a monk.[1] The first chapter of the systematic collection, 'On the progress of the fathers',[2] is a collection of sayings of this type.

Abba Sisoes said, 'Be despised, cast your will behind you, and do not worry, and you will have rest.'[3]

A brother asked Abba Poemen, 'How ought a man to live?' The old man said to him, 'We see Daniel, against whom no charge was laid, except in the matter of his service of the Lord his God.'[4]

Poverty, tribulation, austerity, fasting, these are the tools of the monastic life. For it is written, 'If there were these three men, Noah, Job and Daniel, as I live, says the Lord.' Noah is the personification of poverty, Job of labour, Daniel of discernment. If then these three practices are in a man, the Lord dwells in him.[5]

If a monk overcomes two things, he can be free of this world. . . . bodily rest and vainglory.[6]

God demands these three things of everyone who is baptized: right faith from the soul, truth from the tongue, restraint from the body.[7]

The questions answered here are the fundamental ones of the monastic life: how to live, how to attain peace, what is the work (ἔργον) of a monk, how can I please God,[8] and the answers given prescribe the basic practices of fasting, poverty, detachment from the world, right faith, humility, discernment, labour. One saying goes beyond the simple enumeration of three or four basic principles, and prescribes a long list of ascetic practices and virtues: 'I want a man to share a little of all the virtues. So rise early every day, and get started on every virtue and commandment of God, with great endurance, with fear and patience, in the love of God' and so on.[9] Other sayings describe alternative, equally valid practices or ways of life and leave the questioner to choose for himself which way he will follow:

Abba Joseph the Theban said, 'Three things are honourable before the Lord:

[1] von Lilienfeld, 'Die Christliche Unterweisung der *Apophthegmata Patrum*', in *Spiritualität der frühen Wüstenmönchtums*, 94–5.

[2] Latin (PJ) *De Profectu Patrum*; for the longer Greek title, see Guy, *Recherches*, 119.

[3] Sosoes 43 (PJ 1.17). See Ch. 2, p. 34.

[4] Poemen 53 (PJ 1.13).

[5] Poemen 60 (PJ 1.14). Quite possibly two sayings combined. The biblical citation from Ezek. 14: 14, 20 is left unfinished. The Latin version is slightly abbreviated.

[6] Poemen 66 (PJ 1.15).

[7] Gregory the Theologian 1 (PJ 1.3). Other 'mnemonic' sayings are found in Eth. Coll. 13.59, 66, 75, 76, 14.19, 30, 31.

[8] Zacharias 1 (PJ 1.6), Antony 3 (PJ 1.1).

[9] John Kolobos 34 (PJ 1.8); cf. Poemen 46.

when someone is ill, and temptations come upon him, and he bears them with thanksgiving; the second is, when someone makes all his deeds pure before God, and retains nothing human; the third is, when someone remains in submission to a spiritual father, and renounces his own will in all things. This one will obtain a great crown. But I have chosen illness."[10]

Among these sayings on virtues and ascetic practices of different kinds are several texts which explicitly recognize the place of a monk's attitude to his neighbour as one of the most important principles on which his life is based.[11] 'Abba Poemen said, "These three principles are valuable: to fear God, to pray, and to do good to your neighbour." '[12] This is not the only saying in which fear of God is associated with a particular attitude towards others: 'A brother asked an old man, "How does the fear of God come into the soul?" The old man said, "If a man has humility, poverty, and does not judge, the fear of God comes to him." '[13]

Similarly, Ammonas 8 is a saying which associates, though not as directly as does the saying just quoted, the fear of God with an attitude which avoids judging others. Antony told him that 'You will progress in the fear of God', and that he would become as impassive as a stone in the face of evil:

And it happened thus. For Abba Ammonas made such progress that because of his great goodness he saw no evil in anyone. When he had become a bishop, they brought him a young woman who was pregnant, and said to him, 'So-and-so has done this. Give them a penance.' But he sealed her [with the sign of the cross] on her stomach and ordered six pairs of sheets to be given to her, saying, 'It is in case when she comes to give birth, either she or the child dies, and nothing is available for the burial.' Her accusers said to him, 'Why have you done this? Give them a penance.' But he said to them, 'See, brothers, she is near to death, so what can I do?' And he sent her away, for the old man did not dare to judge anyone.

[10] Joseph the Theban (PJ 1.9). The last two sentences are absent in the Latin version. On giving thanks in illness, see Copres 1, 2, and N 209. Different ways of life are presented as of *equal* value in Poemen 29 and Nisteros 2 (PJ 1.11), a response to the question, 'What is good, that I may do it and live in it?' Pambo 2 (Eth. Coll. 14.21) regards different outward ways of life as irrelevant if the conscience (Pambo) or heart (Eth. Coll.) is not right. Eth. Coll. 13.37 sees renouncing all and working for a living as a greater way of life than keeping back some money in order to be able to offer charity to others.

[11] Cf. L. Leloir, 'Solitude et sollicitude: Le Moine loin et près du monde d'après les "Patérica" arméniens', *Irénikon*, 47 (1974), 312. Most of the sayings in the Armenian *Apophthegmata* have parallels in the Greek and Latin collections.

[12] Poemen 160 (no parallel in PJ).

[13] N 137 (PJ 1.19: also parallel to Euprepius 5).

The fear of God, for the Desert Fathers, was generally a positive quality, a means to the attainment of virtue.[14] In the sayings which have been referred to, the fear of God is closely associated with virtues which pertain to the relationship of a monk to his neighbour: charity, or doing good to your neighbour, humility, and not judging or condemning someone else even, as in the case of Ammonas 8, when the person is, in conventional terms, obviously guilty. For Poemen 160 the orientation of a monk's life towards God in fear of God and prayer is balanced by his orientation towards his neighbour in charity, while in N 137 the ascetic virtue of poverty produces the fear of God in combination with virtues which are mainly concerned with shaping a monk's attitudes to others—humility and an unwillingness to judge anyone else. Ammonas, we are told, *dared not* judge anyone. Clearly here the importance of a monk's relationship with his neighbour in his pursuit of a total life of virtue is recognized.

This is also the case in another, longer list of virtuous practices from the first chapter of the systematic collection:

> An old man said, 'The life of a monk is obedience, meditation, not to judge, not to slander, not to murmur, for it is written, "You who love the Lord, hate evil." For the life of a monk is not to fall in with the unjust, not to look at evil things, not to interfere, not to listen to irrelevant words, not to steal with your hands, but rather to give, not to be proud in your heart, nor evil in your thoughts, not to fill your stomach, but to do everything with discernment. A monk is these things.'[15]

The necessity of not condemning is here amplified to include all forms of slander and adverse comment, and despite the predominantly negative, proscriptive character of what is taught, the positive role of charity and doing good is emphasized. The same positive attitude to charity is present in another saying whose other prescriptions are negative: 'Do not live with heretics, nor have anything to do with those in authority,

[14] The fear of God is a lamp which illuminates the heart and teaches the virtues and commandments of God (James 3); fear of God and humility are as necessary as breathing (Poemen 49), or superior to all other virtues (John Kolobos 22), and lead to disregard of self (Eth. Coll. 13.64); fearing God causes the Spirit of God to dwell in you (Poemen 75); fear of God and discernment are brothers (Eth. Coll. 13.18). The fear of God is lost through relaxation of ascetic practices (Poemen 57, 181). Only Antony 32 seems to cast doubt on the generally high regard in which the attainment and practice of the fear of God was held: 'I no longer fear God, but I love him.'

[15] N 225 (PJ 1.22); Ps. 97: 10; referred to by Leloir, 'Solitude et sollicitude', 312.

and do not stretch out your hands to gather, but rather to give."[16]

From these sayings it is no great step to an exclusive concentration on a monk's relationship with his neighbours as the most important aspect of his monastic life:

Abba Paphnutius, the disciple of Abba Macarius, used to say, 'I besought my father saying, "Speak a word to me," and he said, "Do not do evil to anyone, and do not condemn anyone. Guard these things, and you will be saved." '[17]

For Poemen, with similar emphasis on his relations with his neighbour, a monk could be defined not only by uncomplaining acceptance of the conditions of his life (*οὐκ ἔστι μοναχὸς μεμψίμοιρος*), but also by restraint of the impulses of retribution and of anger towards others (*οὐκ ἔστι μοναχὸς ποιῶν ἀνταπόδομα, οὐκ ἔστι μοναχὸς ὀργίλος*).[18] Not to complain is admittedly an ascetic virtue, readily understandable in the context of the harsh conditions of a life of physical austerity, and yet it too has relevance to one's attitude towards others, as can be seen if the saying just quoted is compared with a saying of Abba Or: 'In every temptation do not blame anyone else [*μέμφου ἄνθρωπον*] but only yourself, saying, "This has happened to me because of my sins." '[19]

2. To Gain your Brother

The purpose of the previous section was to show that the Desert Fathers recognized certain attitudes towards others as basic to the monastic life along with practices such as asceticism and prayer. In the rest of this chapter, the significance of this recognition of the importance of relationships will be elaborated.

Abba John the Short said, 'It is impossible to build the house from above downwards, but only from the foundation upwards.' They said to him, 'What

[16] Chomai (PJ 1.18); for giving rather than receiving, see Matoes 10 (a threefold 'mnemonic' saying). See Matoes 11 (= N 330, PJ 1.23) for another text referring to humility and not judging (but rather considering your own sins), and also to not associating with heretics.

[17] Macarius 28; cf. Theodore of Pherme 13: 'There is no other virtue than not to despise.'

[18] Poemen 91, also referred to by Leloir, 'Solitude et sollicitude', 312. On *ἀνταπόδομα*, see *PGL*, 150b, which refers to this passage.

[19] Or 12 (= N 305). The various comments made in the last few paragraphs on the relationship between anger, humility, judgement, and blaming others anticipate some of the themes of Ch. 4.

does this saying mean?' He said to them, 'The foundation is your neighbour, whom you must gain [κερδάνῃς]. That is the first requirement. For on him depend all the commandments of Christ.'[20]

This saying explicitly teaches that any progress in the monastic life is completely dependent on a monk's attitude to his neighbour. It is however entirely general in tone, and it is difficult to be precise about what is meant by 'to gain your neighbour'. Does it mean simply to gain his friendship or to establish a good relationship with him, a relationship of love rather than one of judgement, bitterness, and blame of the kind censured in sayings which have already been quoted? Or is there perhaps a more precise meaning, deriving from the biblical use of the idea of gaining your neighbour? 'If your brother sins against you, go and rebuke him between you and him alone; if he listens to you, you have gained [ἐκέρδησας] your brother.'[21] To what extent did the Desert Fathers see forwarding the 'moral and spiritual benefit'[22] of their neighbours as an important goal of relationships? To some extent certainly: 'Rescue your neighbour from sin without reproach as far as you are able', said Hyperechius, 'For God does not send away those who repent.'[23] Theodore of Pherme also spoke of the duty of offering help to a sinner, although with a notable caveat:

> If you are friendly with someone, and it comes about that he falls into the temptation of fornication, give him your hand, and draw him out. But if he falls into heresy, and you cannot persuade him to return, then quickly cut yourself off from him, lest by delaying you are dragged down with him into the pit.[24]

In more general respects the Desert Fathers do seem to have been concerned that their actions towards their neighbours should be to their spiritual benefit. John Kolobos' concern to 'gain his neighbour' is illustrated by an anecdote about him: at a meal in Scetis a priest got

[20] John Kolobos 39. Matt. 22: 40. The only sayings to allude directly to Matt. 22: 39 are Eth. Coll. 13.85 (love of neighbour suffices for salvation), 86, and 14.64 (a threefold saying).

[21] Matt. 18: 15.

[22] *PGL*. s.v. κέρδος, 748a. John Kolobos 18 concludes with the comment that it was the work of the Scetiotes to 'do violence to themselves in order to gain one another for good'.

[23] PJ 17.13a (not preserved in the present alphabetical collection, but quoted from Hyperechius, *Sentences* 117, 1484D).

[24] Theodore of Pherme 4. Cf. the discussion in Ch. 2, pp. 67–8, of sayings like N 44 and N 179 (which describes the brother as wishing to 'gain' his companion when the latter has sinned).

up to offer a drink to all present, but only John accepted anything from him; the others present were shocked that he should dare to allow the priest to serve him, but he replied with a comment illustrating his understanding of the value of acts of service like this in the context of the monastic community: 'When I get up to offer the cup, I am glad if everyone receives it, because I have my reward. So I too received it, in order to give a reward to him.'[25] The reward here must surely be thought of as a spiritual one, a reward from God for the acts of kindness and concern which should characterize incidents of everyday life in the monastic community. Agathon, in fact, generalizes John's attitude into a description of the principle by which he has lived his life: 'I have never offered an *agape*; rather, to give and to receive has been an *agape* for me, reckoning that my brother's gain is a work which bears fruit.'[26] 'To give and to receive' could characterize John's attitude towards the shared cup. Agathon is certainly concerned with the well-being of his neighbour, but is also confident that his actions constitute an 'offering'[27] on his own behalf directed, presumably, towards attaining an eternal reward from God. In the parallel in N 353, 'a work which bears fruit *for me*' is made explicit.

The terminology of 'to gain your neighbour' or 'my brother's gain' which these sayings of John and Agathon employ also occurs in Antony 9: 'Life and death are from our neighbour; for if we gain our brother we gain God, if we offend our brother we sin against Christ.' A parallel to this saying occurs in one of the letters attributed to Antony, which both gives an interesting context to the thought and yet shows up some verbal differences.[28] The author of the letters writes that demons do

[25] John Kolobos 7.

[26] Agathon 17. A close parallel is found in N 353: 'I have never desired a work which benefits me and harms my brother, having this hope, that my brother's gain is a work which bears fruit for me.' Agathon's reference to the *agape* is to the monastic community's communal meal, on which see Ch. 5, Sect. 2.

[27] *PGL*, s.v. καρποφορία, 704a. Arsenius 39 belongs to the same world of ideas: when he was dying Arsenius told his disciples, 'Do not think to offer *agapes* for me. For if I have offered an *agape* for myself, I will find it.' Here *agape* probably refers to a memorial feast for a dead monk, though I know of no other relevant evidence in the Sayings to illuminate this practice.

[28] The *Letters of Antony* exist in Georgian, in Arabic, in a Latin version of doubtful reliability (PG xl. 977–1000), and fragmentarily in Coptic and Syriac. The Georgian is in *Lettres de S. Antoine: Version géorgienne et fragments coptes*, ed. G. Garitte (CSCO 148–9; Scriptores Iberici, 5 (text) and 6 (modern Latin translation); Louvain, 1955). For an English translation, see *The Letters of Saint Antony the Great*, trans. D. J. Chitty (Oxford, 1975). The letter discussed here is letter 4 in Georgian (text 17–31, trans. 11–20), letter 2 in Latin (981–8) and letter 6 in Chitty's translation (17–23), which follows the Arabic order (see the table on p. viii of Garitte's edition).

not act against humans by means of visible bodies of their own (they have none), but by means of the human soul which accepts their wickedness and manifests it bodily as evil acts.[29] To allow them to act thus is to stir up God's wrath against us, 'For they know that our perdition is from our neighbour, and equally our life is from our neighbour.'[30] 'Therefore he who sins against his neighbour sins against himself, and he who does evil to his neighbour does evil to himself; similarly he who does good to his neighbour does good to himself.'[31] God can only be sinned against by means of sin against other people, and therefore we should 'give ourselves over to death for our souls and for one another', not loving ourselves and therefore not being subject to the power of the demons.[32]

In the letter therefore the monk's contest against demonic temptation is directly linked to his attitudes towards his neighbour. The sin against our neighbours and against God to which the demons tempt us is to be resisted by a self-sacrificial attitude towards our neighbours; the avoidance of self-love is in the ultimate interests of all. The saying in the *Apophthegmata* lacks this demonological context, and instead directly links a monk's attitude to his neighbour with his attitude to Christ, bringing in the terminology of 'gaining' which, as we have seen, occurs in other texts. 'To gain your neighbour' is again left imprecise, but probably covers attitudes of concern, of giving and receiving, like those of John and Agathon. The text of the letter may well be the ultimate origin of this particular unit of the *Apophthegmata* (although the possibility that the saying and the letter originated separately from Antony cannot be ruled out, if the possibility of the authenticity of the letters can be entertained); but if this is the case, then the text has been modified (either in the process of oral transmission or in being extracted from the letter for inclusion in the written *Apophthegmata*) and brought into accord with the terminology and the teaching of the other sayings which have been quoted. In the context of the Sayings, this text reinforces the message of the essentially corporate, neighbour-oriented attitude to the monastic life which the Desert Fathers could clearly espouse.

[29] From Garitte's Latin translation, p. 15, v. 51; cf. PG, xl. 984B.
[30] Latin, p. 15, v. 53; cf. PG, xl. 984B.
[31] Latin, p. 16, v. 63; cf. PG, xl. 985A.
[32] Latin, p. 16, vv. 64–8; cf. PG, xl. 985A-B.

3. Charity and Work for your Neighbour

'Abba John said that our father Abba Antony said, "I have never put my own convenience before the benefit of my brother." '[33] At the most basic level, a monk's recognition of the importance of his relationship with his neighbour expresses itself in active charity towards others. Some of the examples of the practice of charity which are contained in the *Apophthegmata* are certainly very mundane, for example Agathon's insistence that a visitor should accept a small knife as a gift, or Theodore's sale of three books, despite their usefulness, in order to give the money to the poor[34]—a saying which reflects a high estimate of poverty rather than a positive evaluation of charity as such, and is accordingly translated in section six of PJ, on possessing nothing, rather than in section seventeen on charity. But, despite these commonplace examples, charity towards others was recognized and highly valued as a demanding discipline carried out in obedience to the commandments of Christ. To a brother who expressed a desire to fulfil all the commandments, it was proper to point out that Abba Theonas, when he had made bread to give to the poor, then given away his baskets and finally his cloak, still returned to his cell reproaching himself for not having fulfilled the commandment of God.[35]

In most sayings about charity the emphasis lies on the quality referred to by John the Eunuch in his saying about Antony—a desire to put his brother's benefit or well-being before consideration of his own convenience; or to push oneself to the limit of self-sacrifice and endurance in the service of someone else. Again a relatively mundane example may be cited: a brother gave the handles of the baskets he was making to someone who had none, leaving his own baskets unfinished.[36] Particular actions were recognized as heroic feats of charity towards others: a brother who was *τις τῶν ἀγωνιστῶν*—a real fighter, a champion—travelled from Scetis to Egypt to fetch some fresh bread

[33] John the Eunuch 2.

[34] Agathon 25, Theodore of Pherme 1 (PJ 6.6).

[35] Theodore of Pherme 18. On obedience to 'the commandment', see Regnault, 'Obéissance et liberté', 89–91. A saying which clearly relates fulfilling the commandment to a monk's love for his neighbour is Agathon 29: 'He was zealous to fulfil every commandment. If he embarked in a boat, he was first to take the oars, and when brothers came to him, he used to set the table immediately after the prayer, for he was full of the love of God.' Like N 451 (Ch. 2, n. 170), this saying has been interpreted as a reflection of a tradition of ancient Egyptian ethical thought: see M. Kaiser, 'Agathon und Amenemope', *Zeitschrift für Ägyptische Sprache*, 92 (1966), 102–5.

[36] N 347 (PJ 17.16).

for an old man who was ill. The old man refused to eat it: 'It is my brother's blood', but the old men persuaded him, 'Eat, for the Lord's sake, lest the brother's sacrifice be in vain.'[37] Service of the sick is, in various ways, highly valued and commended: Agathon is portrayed finding a sick man and staying with him for three months, working to obtain money and healing him, before returning to his own cell.[38] A brother who serves a sick abba fights against the temptation to give up and leave, and eventually God sees his endurance and heals the old man.[39]

These examples illustrate the value of self-sacrifice, or doing something which seems actively harmful to your own interests, on behalf of others. It is true that a distinction may be necessary here, in that openness to the needs of others is not held to extend to the endangering of your own *spiritual* well-being: Theodore of Pherme, quoted above, does not hesitate to commend offering assistance to a brother who has fallen into fornication, but a heretic must be shunned if he cannot be converted; and even Agathon is aware of the spiritual dangers of friendship.[40] But the general principle holds good for acts of charity, of self-sacrifice, of physical labour, or of 'gaining' your neighbour through endurance and love. A few more general sayings about charity and about the stance which a monk ought to take towards working or doing something for someone else may now be considered as illustrations of it.

> An old man said, 'If anyone asks you for something, then even if it is a struggle for you to grant it to him [*καὶ βίᾳ παράσχῃς αὐτῷ*], your thought too must be pleased with the gift, as it is written, "If anyone forces you to go one mile, go with him two." That is, if anyone asks you for something, give it to him with your soul and spirit.'[41]

Both the teaching itself and the biblical interpretation which is used to justify it are worthy of note: 'to go two miles' means struggling with yourself not only to give the assistance or object demanded, but to

[37] N 348 (PJ 17.17). Macarius 8 relates a similar incident. For other uses of *ἀγωνιστής*, see Arsenius 15 and N 172.

[38] Agathon 27. See N 355 (Eth. Coll. 13.12; PJ 17.18) for a general evaluation of ministry to the sick in relation to other ways of life. Agathon's self-sacrificing love is also recorded in the story of Agathon 30, and in general in his desire, if it were possible, to exchange his body for that of a leper (Agathon 26).

[39] N 356 (PJ 17.25).

[40] Theodore of Pherme 4; Agathon 23: 'If someone were especially dear to me, and I knew that he was leading me into sin, I would cut him off from me.' Cf. Ch. 2, n. 175.

[41] N 345 (PJ 17.15). Matt. 5: 41.

overcome your own resentment and offer it not grudgingly but with a willing thought. Giving charity with a wrong motive would fall under the censure implicit in this saying of those who give without bringing their own feelings into line with the act. Poemen 51 concerns a brother who is aware that when 'I give a little bread, or something else, to my brother' (clearly the description is meant to cover acts of charity or friendship in general), then 'the demons defile it, as if it is done with the aim of pleasing men'. Does the brother mean that he finds himself hoping for public commendation for his charity, or is he speaking purely of his motives towards the individual brother concerned, knowing that he is subject to a desire to win the brother's admiration or put him in his debt? Whichever of these is the case, the brother is aware that his motives are suspect. But Poemen tells him to carry on giving, reciting a parable about two farmers, and concluding, 'If we sow a few seed, even impure ones, then we shall not die in the famine.' Any act of charity, however soured by bad motives, gains some reward; but the tone of this saying, which hardly suggests that the brother's feelings are ideal, is such that it reinforces, rather than contradicts, the message of N 345 on the necessity of a correct attitude.

These explanations of the necessity of struggle and effort on someone else's behalf are supported by general teaching about the nature of the monastic life. The monastic life is not meant to be easy; whether the struggle is for someone else or for the achievement of the more personal goals of asceticism and virtue, it involves hard labour. 'What is a monk?' someone asked John Kolobos. 'Labour; because a monk labours at every work.'[42] Similarly, a monk 'does violence to himself [*ἑαυτον βιάζεσθαι*] in everything';[43] progress cannot be made or virtue acquired without labour and endurance in the work which has been undertaken.[44] Sayings

[42] John Kolobos 37.

[43] Zacharias 1 (cf. 3 and Eth. Coll. 14.34). For 'doing violence' to oneself in order to achieve a particular spiritual goal, cf. John Kolobos 18 (above, n. 22); N 211 (Ch. 2, n. 117), Ammonas 11, Theodora 3, Pistus (Isaiah, *Logos* 6, 6Ab), N 249 and 514 (Evergetinos, 1.15.4.5), and Eth. Coll. 13.22, 63, 67, 71 ('force your heart to go with the Lord'), 14.3, 17, 23 (constrain yourself to ignore your own will).

[44] N 297. See N 193 and 197 for the necessity of labour (*κόπος, πόνος*) in response to the threat of eternal punishment or the promise of reward; N 166 for labour as a response to temptation (cf. Olympius 2). Antony 35 asserts the need to direct labour towards the attainment of a particular virtue (cf. Alonius 2, 3 for related points). Esaias 5 teaches the need for labour by an acted parable. See also Isidore 5 and 9. Poemen 44 sees labour as both necessary and as bringing rest (*ἀνάπαυσις*). But on the other hand, see Poemen 141: 'Let go a part of your righteousness, and you will have rest in a few days.' Matoes 10 sees enduring tribulation as preferable to having rest. N 235 takes a somewhat different view again: though they labour, the saints receive some rest already because they are free

like those quoted above, which indicate an awareness that charity may involve a struggle against yourself and against the thoughts which make you shy away from the proper service of others, are a particular application of this view of life.

In many sayings 'work' (*ἔργον*) means simply manual labour, and this is viewed as an essential component of the monastic life and of ascetic discipline.[45] But two of the sayings referred to in the last paragraph seem to treat 'work' more generally as a term for the activities, the progress-making or virtue-seeking practices, of the monastic life as a whole. The importance of work in this wider sense is also emphasized by three related sayings which, taken together, directly link the concept of 'work' to a monk's duty towards God and his attitude towards his neighbour. 'When we were in Scetis', said Theodore of Pherme to John the Eunuch, 'the works of the soul [*ἔργα τῆς ψυχῆς*] were our work and we held manual work to be secondary [*πάρεργον*]. But now the work of the soul has become secondary, and what was secondary has become our work.'[46] This laconic, almost elliptical example of a 'pessimistic' *diaspora* saying is elaborated or explained in the other two texts. An alternative version of Theodore's saying is preserved under the name of his interlocutor, John the Eunuch.[47] In this the contrast between works of the soul and manual labour is replaced, or made more explicit, by a contrast between the work of God and the needs of the body: 'How were you [plural, meaning monks of the generation represented by Theodore] able to do the work of God in peace [*ἀνάπαυσις*]', John asks, 'whereas we are not able to do it even with labour?' The old man replies that 'we could do it, because we held the work of God to be more important and bodily needs least', and he goes on to offer the same criticism of the present generation's reversal of priorities as does the shorter version of the saying.

What are we to understand by the work of God, or the work of the

of worldly thoughts. So does Eth. Coll. 13.87: it was not God who gave sin and labour to man, but humanity which took them for itself. Eth. Coll. has several texts on the need for labour: 13.76, 94 (if a monk's work was easy 'Agathon would have entered directly into the kingdom'), 14.7. For another application of teaching on labour, see again the sayings noted above, n. 24, and Ch. 2, nn. 153–4.

[45] See e.g. Antony 1, Agathon 10, Achillas 5, John Kolobos 2, Lucius 1, Poemen 69, 103, 150, 168, Pistamon, Silvanus 5, N 86, N 168.

[46] Theodore of Pherme 10. On his pessimism, see Ch. 2, n. 179.

[47] John the Eunuch 1. Is this saying an elaboration of the other version, or do they stem from independent oral traditions? It is impossible to tell for certain, but the longer version is not found in PJ or the Greek systematic collection, or in the early Syriac version (*Les Sentences ... troisième recueil*, 218–19) and may be a late text.

soul, here? A brother asks Theodore this question in the third of the texts, and it is this saying which is the most revealing for its description of what constitutes true work and for the attitude which it expresses to the relationship between a monk and his neighbour.[48] 'Everything which happens because of the commandment of God is a work of the soul,' says Theodore, 'But to work and obtain things for our own reasons, this we ought to hold as a secondary work.' Examples follow:

Suppose you hear that I am ill, and you ought to visit me. You say to yourself, 'Am I to leave my work and go now? I will finish it first and then go.' Then some other pretext comes along, and you never go. Or again a brother says to you, 'Give me a hand, brother', and you say, 'Am I to leave my work and go and work with him?' If you do not go, you are breaking the commandment of God, which is the work of the soul, and doing what is secondary, which is your manual work.

'The work of the soul' in this account is defined in contrast to the practical aspects of the monastic life such as working for a living; but it is not defined, for example, as prayer or asceticism but as obedience to the commandments of God among which helping someone who needs it, and visiting the sick, are implicitly given priority.[49] The examples given, drawn from the daily life of a monk in contact with his neighbours, illustrate the importance of these ordinary incidents and contacts with others as occasions for the exercise of the proper practices and virtues of the monastic life.

But what happens if you cannot help when you are asked to do so? A brother who was too weak and ill to work asked John what he should do 'because of the commandment'.[50] If he cannot work, John replies, he should sit in his cell and weep because of his sins. Another brother told Joseph that he was unable either to suffer evil or to work to give charity. What should he do? 'Guard your conscience from your neighbour, from every evil, and you will be saved.'[51] Even, that is, when you cannot show your concern for your neighbour actively, perhaps even when you are confined to your cell through illness, or deeply affected

[48] Theodore of Pherme 11. This may have originated in the oral or written tradition of the Sayings as an explanation of Theodore 10, if it does not stem from Theodore himself.

[49] But see Theodore 19, in which he declines to visit a sick abba.

[50] John Kolobos 19.

[51] Joseph of Panepho 4. On the problem of not being able to bear evil, see Antony 19. For other references to guarding your conscience towards your neighbour, see Pambo 2, 11, where it is an essential feature of the monastic life, and (using 'heart' instead of conscience) Eth. Coll. 13.40.

by some sense of personal inadequacy, like this brother, your attitude towards your neighbour is important; harmful thoughts of any kind must be avoided.

The Desert Fathers' attitudes to charity and work on behalf of others should not be over-simplified. The self-sacrificial attitudes of the giver were valued, but in some sayings the possibility of charity having a harmful effect on the recipient is canvassed. Poemen was unhappy that a merchant who did not need them should have bought the lamp-wicks which the brothers had to sell: 'I will not harm someone who does not need them, lest he suffers loss as a result, and takes away what I have gained.'[52] In a simpler story, a brother complains to another who has been secretly placing his own possessions among the speaker's property: 'Because of your fleshly things you have mocked my spiritual things.'[53] This brother clearly believes that he has suffered a spiritual loss because of the augmentation of his possessions, but prior to being told this the other was no doubt convinced that he was simply doing what was right in giving away, secretly and without making a show of it, what he did not need. In Poemen's case unnecessary dependence upon someone else is to be avoided as detrimental to the (spiritual) value for a monk of working for his own living. This is the case for Poemen however, not just because work is good in itself or because charity is harmful, but because the merchant has suffered unnecessary injury. Though apparently reserved about charity therefore, Poemen is not reserved about relationships. There is a close link between his attitude to his own 'gain' and his desire for the good of others.

In another story, a brother inconveniences himself and his abba in order to help another old man to sell his manual work. 'Forgive me', says the other when he finds out, 'because your great charity has taken away my reward.'[54] The old man here has failed to realize that the brother was putting himself out and has therefore unwittingly been

[52] Poemen 10. The merchant's charitable act is twice described as a 'work' on behalf of the brothers. In N 259 the brothers do not need the money which a layman offers (cf. *HL*, 10.2–4). This text distinguishes between the motives and reward of the giver ('God has received your charity') and the belief that charity is not always necessary, or good for, the recipient. On charity given by monks *to* poor lay people, see N 281, 282, 287, 358, Ch 257. Except for N 287 these all warn in one way or another against meanness on behalf of the giver, but John Kolobos S 7 (Guy, *Recherches*, 24) puts the care of the monastic community before charity to lay people, and N 286 warns that a monk who supports his poor lay brother may be harming him: it is better for him to work for himself.

[53] N 6.

[54] N 344.

responsible for causing inconvenience. Unlike Poemen however, he cannot give back what he has received and has to be content with an expression of sorrow. There are therefore two sides to a charitable act: the attitude of the giver who must give with a willing heart and work without hesitation for others when he is required to do so, and the effect on the recipient, for whom unwanted material things are harmful, and who must avoid presuming upon the actions of the giver and therefore injuring him unnecessarily. The problem of how a monk ought to react to the dependence on others which results from being ill and unable to work is one which introduces further complications discussed in a number of texts;[55] views differed, but despite the variety of their opinions, sayings on charity all manifest the concern of the Desert Fathers to keep their relationships with others in good repair.

4. The Monk, his Neighbour, and God

Some of the most general and most profound sayings about the importance of the relationship between a monk and his neighbour, such as Antony 9 and Agathon 17, maintain that a monk's relationship with his neighbour and his relationship with God or Christ parallel one

[55] N 213 assumes that a sick monk should accept affliction as from God and depend on others, but in N 260 an old man will not accept charity when he is ill because God has always provided for him; Arsenius (20), *per contra*, gives thanks that God has made him worthy to receive charity. In N 350 a brother who has been too ill to help with the harvest refuses to take his share of the wages and is grieved when an old man decides that he must accept it. N 592/41 (Evergetinos, 1.43.1.1 plus 3.49.1.3) is a theoretical discussion: if you ask for what you need when you are ill and are not given it, you should not be grieved, for 'if I was worthy, God would have compelled the brother to give.' Then a distinction is drawn between three classes of ascetic, the 'perfect' who do not readily receive anything from anyone else, the 'intermediate' who do not ask for anything but receive as if from God when someone gives to them, and the 'very weak' who is unable to work, and has to ask for what he needs with humility, blaming himself in everything. None of these attitudes can be regarded as wrong in itself: each monk has different spiritual and material needs and different understandings of his relationship with his neighbour. The brother in N 350 is no doubt concerned both to maintain his material dependence on God and not to harm his companions in the harvest by taking from them what in his view belongs to them alone; cf. N 258 and 263 (though the latter does not concern monks). Two other sayings on the Desert Fathers' attitudes to charity may be noted: John of Persia 2 praises his freedom in giving away his own possessions and lack of concern for getting back what he is owed or has lent; Poemen 33 is by contrast a rather cynical saying about the misuse of charity and about its outcome for a brother who has some money to give away, but who is likely to gain no reward, or to become negligent, as a result.

another closely—that a monk reaps a spiritual harvest (even if the seeds he sowed were few and impure, as in Poemen 51) from his attitudes and actions towards others. Just as some sayings about charity are comparatively mundane, so the most frequent use of the parallelism between the two relationships in the *Apophthegmata* is a simple and obvious one, based on the biblical command to forgive others their sins, in order to obtain forgiveness oneself.[56] A monk's attitude towards his neighbour is seen as directly determining his acceptability to God. 'Have mercy on all,' said Pambo, 'for mercy leads to freedom of speech [*εὗρεν παρρησίαν*] before God.'[57]

It is worth drawing attention to another text which explicitly teaches that acceptability with God depends on your attitude to your neighbour. 'How can a man obtain the gift [*χάρισμα*] of loving God?' asks the questioner in the dialogue *On Thoughts*.[58] The reply directs the attention firmly towards a monk's prayers on behalf of his neighbour, as the means by which he himself deepens his relationship with God: 'When someone sees his brother in sin, and cries to God concerning him, to come to his help, then he receives knowledge of how it is necessary to love God.' The dialogue also teaches that prayers are not acceptable from anyone unless he has not committed an offence against his neighbour, or at least has taken steps to be reconciled with him, 'For it is written that whatever you bind on earth will be bound in the heavens.'[59] The biblical quotation here is used to refer not to the apostolic or priestly ministry of absolution, but to the responsibility of everyone to see that he is reconciled with those against whom he has sinned, if his own sins are to be unbound in heaven.[60]

[56] Matt. 6: 14–15; Mark 11: 25. See Isidore S 1 (Guy, *Recherches*, 24–5): 'When he spoke to the brothers in the church, he said only this, "Brothers, it is written, *Forgive your neighbour, that you too may receive forgiveness*"'; also Eth. Coll. 13.60, N 226 (an old man teaches the necessity of mercy and forgiveness), Evagrius, *On Prayer*, 104, and PJ 17.13b (Hyperechius, *Sentences* 118; PG, lxxix. 1485A): 'Do not nurse a word of evil or wickedness in your heart against your brother, that you may be able to say, "Forgive us our trespasses", and what follows.' In Poemen 86 he teaches that God always forgives, for he would not do less than he commanded men to do, which was to forgive 'seventy times seven' (Matt. 18: 22).

[57] Pambo 14.

[58] *On Thoughts*, 28, ed. J.-C. Guy, 'Un Dialogue monastique inédit: ΠΕΡΙ ΛΟΓΙΣΜΩΝ', *RAM* 33 (1957), 171–88. Passages from the dialogue are quoted in N 506–8 and N 623–4.

[59] *On Thoughts*, 31. Matt. 18: 18.

[60] Cf. Pseudo-Macarius, *Homily*, 53.3, in *Macarii Anecdota: Seven Unpublished Homilies of Macarius*, ed. G. L. Marriott (Harvard Theological Studies, 5; Cambridge, Mass., 1918), 30: 'Prayers become acceptable by means of good deeds, that no-one should hate his neighbour, or speak against anyone.'

Other sayings co-ordinate a monk's relationships with his neighbour and with God in various different ways. Isidore of Pelusium 4 teaches simply that evil both separates people from God and divides them from one another. Other sayings describe acquiring the grace of God in quite explicitly social and co-operative terms:

A brother asked an old man, 'How is it that now some labour at their ways of life [πολιτείαις], but do not receive grace like the ancients?' The old man said to him, 'Then there was love, and each drew his neighbour up, but now love has cooled, each drags his neighbour down, and because of this we do not receive grace.'[61]

Abba Theonas said, 'When someone gains a virtue, God does not give the grace to him alone, for he knows that he did not become faithful as a result of his own labour. But if he turns to his companion, then it remains with him.[62]

'It remains' here may refer to the virtue (a virtue can only be gained and kept when monks co-operate and encourage one another) or perhaps to God himself: 'he remains' with a monk whose attitude to others is positive and open.

Abba Apollo used to participate joyfully in any work to which the brothers called him, saying, 'Today I am working with Christ for my soul, for this is its reward.'[63] The precise significance of this saying is not perhaps entirely clear; if it is to be taken at face value, the reward of the soul is not something additional to its participation in the work of Christ for its own salvation; it *is* the privilege of sharing in this work. But nothing is said which would indicate that Apollo's joyful co-operation with the brothers is only an *opportunity*, one among many, for 'working with Christ'; rather, his love for others is the primary means of his encouraging and forwarding of the work of his own soul for its salvation.[64]

A story from the anonymous series, whose unusual conclusion sheds

[61] N 349. For πολιτεία as a way of life or an ascetic activity, cf. Aio, in which an old man is constrained to eat the food offered to him when he is ill; this is a 'labour', which God guards (i.e. rewards) for him because he does not eat willingly. But the brothers who look after him also have a 'reward'. On πολιτεία, see Ch. 6, pp. 173–4 and n. 33.

[62] Poemen 151.

[63] Apollo 1. Apollo (3, a quotation from *HM*, 8.55–6) also believes that in your brother you encounter God. Cf. *HL*, 19.8, for working for your neighbour as an ascetic discipline contributing to your own fight against temptation.

[64] Cf. Evagrius, *On Evil Thoughts*, 11 (PG, lxxix. 1213B): a little compunction and compassion for others when they are suffering makes the soul less careless about itself too.

light on the relationship between a monk, his neighbour, and God, also deserves attention here.[65] Like other sayings it describes the acceptability to God of a monk's labour on behalf of someone else—in this case his willing endurance of the hardship of a long journey to visit a disciple, rather than summoning the disciple to visit him. The twist in the story comes when, undertaking another journey the following day, presumably with the intention of obtaining a further reward from God, the old man meets the other monk whom he intends to visit, coming in the opposite direction. The first says, 'I possessed a treasure, and you have tried to steal it.' The implication is that by himself undertaking the journey the second has robbed the first of the reward which God gives for his charity and labour.[66] The second however rebukes this presumption and self-centredness, commenting, 'Does the narrow gate have room for you alone? Let me enter with you.' An argument seems imminent, but an angel is on hand to intervene and say to the two monks, 'Your rivalry has gone up to God like a fragrant perfume.' The implication seems to be that both are acceptable to God for their zeal in doing good to one another. There is no question that one will benefit at the expense of the other.

In sayings like this one, as well as Antony 9, Agathon 17, and John 7, the reward which is hoped for or promised is implicitly an eternal, heavenly one, a divine response to the way in which Agathon or John have chosen to live the monastic life as a life of concern for their neighbours—a concern which extends, in the case of John 7, to the hope that his neighbour too will receive his heavenly reward as a result of his actions. To end this chapter, two other sayings may be noted which reflect, in different ways, on the eternal significance of personal relationships. One text refers to the role of the abba as an intercessor on behalf of his disciples when he is in heaven. Abba Daniel recalled that one day Arsenius summoned him and said, 'Give comfort to your father, that when he goes to the Lord, he may beseech him on your behalf, and it may be well with you.'[67]

Finally, a curious and moving story about Macarius. He finds the skull of a pagan priest in the desert, and speaks to it about the condition of those undergoing eternal punishment: 'You are Macarius, the Spirit-bearer [*πνευματοφόρος*]', it says to him, 'and when you have mercy on those suffering this punishment, and pray for them, they receive a little

[65] N 441 (Evergetinos, 3.36.4.33–5).
[66] Cf. N 344 discussed above.
[67] Arsenius 35.

relief.'[68] Macarius asks what the nature of the punishment and relief is. 'We stand immersed in fire from head to foot', the skull replies, 'and not face to face, so that we can see anyone, but with each person facing his neighbour's back. But when you pray for us, each can see the face of his neighbour a little.' The story requires no comment, other than to point out explicitly that it recognizes the gift which an inspired old man receives of intercession on behalf of those who are undergoing punishment, and that it teaches, in some sense, the importance of relationships, even in hell.

In the light of the evidence of this chapter, it can be accepted that, as Rousseau comments, the Desert Fathers were, 'intent upon creating a new society. Their spirituality reflected that aim, catering for relationships as well as personal goals.'[69] In addition to this basic affirmation of the importance of the communal as well as individual aspects of the monastic life, some indications have been given of the kind of relationships which the Desert Fathers wished to cultivate: relationships in which judgement and criticism were avoided, and mutual service and encouragement valued. The next chapter will concentrate on the obstacles to the proper conduct of relationships which the problems of anger and judgement create.

[68] Macarius 38. For *πνευματοφόρος*, cf. Antony 30: 'He became a Spirit-bearer, but because of men did not wish to speak of it, for he declared both what was happening in the world and what was going to happen.' For an example of his awareness of distant events, see Antony 14. In *VA*, 34, he is portrayed as commenting on the ability of the human soul to know the future when it is pure, and in 59–60 distant events are revealed to him in prayer. In *HL*, 11.5, Evagrius is described as *διακριτικὸς καὶ πνευματοφόρος*. On the development of the idea of being a Spirit-bearer, see P. Nagel, *Die Motivierung der Askese in der alten Kirche und der Ursprung des Mönchtums* (TU 95; Berlin, 1966), 69–75.

[69] Rousseau, 'The Desert Fathers, Antony and Pachomius', 120.

4

The Problems of Anger and Judgement

1. Introduction: Rejection of Relationships

The previous chapter has shown that there is good evidence for the belief that the Desert Fathers saw relationships within the monastic community as an important feature of the monastic life. They sometimes suggested that good relationships contributed directly to their acceptability to God. But there is another aspect of the Desert Fathers' teaching to be considered. There are sayings in which relationships are, or appear to be, rejected, or in which pessimistic comments are made about the deleterious effects of relationships with others on a monk's relationship with God. These sayings exist alongside those we have already considered in which a positive view of relationships is put forward. It cannot be assumed that either of these classes of saying represents the 'true' viewpoint of the Desert Fathers and the other not. Their existence requires an explanation, in the form of a further exploration of different aspects of the Desert Fathers' teaching on relationships which will occupy the remaining chapters of this work.

Arsenius and Theodore of Pherme are two monks who feature in the *Apophthegmata* as the subjects of sayings which suggest isolationism, or an unwillingness to engage in relationships:

They used to say about Abba Arsenius and Abba Theodore of Pherme that, above all others, they hated the praise of men. Abba Arsenius did not readily meet anyone, and Abba Theodore, though he would meet people, was like a sword.[1]

They used to say about Abba Theodore of Pherme that, above many, he held these three things to be fundamental: poverty, asceticism, and flight from men.[2]

Again he [Theodore] said, 'Unless I cut myself off from these feelings of compassion they will not let me be a monk.'[3]

[1] Arsenius 31.
[2] Theodore of Pherme 5; cf. Eth. Coll. 13.75.
[3] Theodore of Pherme 15.

Similarly reserved attitudes to relationships are not difficult to discover, sometimes with, sometimes without any indication of the reasons why avoidance of others is advocated:

Abba Alonius said, 'Unless someone says in his heart, "I and God are alone in the world", he will not have rest.'[4]

Abba Moses said, 'Someone who flees is like a ripe bunch of grapes, but someone who remains among men is like an unripe fruit.'[5]

Sever your relationships [*σχέσεις*] with the many, in case your mind is distracted, and you disturb the habit of stillness [*τὸν τῆς ἡσυχίας ταράξῃ τρόπον*].[6]

A monk who loves stillness remains unwounded by the enemy's arrows, but he who mixes with the multitude continually receives wounds.[7]

Alonius' saying introduces the view that 'rest', an important goal of the monastic life,[8] can be achieved only by a concentration on your own relationship with God which appears to exclude any consideration of your neighbour. Moses in turn suggests that progress to perfection in the monastic life can be achieved only by someone who chooses solitude rather than a life of community. These are general remarks, but some rather more personal stories and exchanges offer an illuminating insight into the attitudes of doubt or pessimism about relationships which appear in these sayings. 'Why do you flee from us?' Arsenius was asked by his disciple Mark; he replied: 'God knows that I love you, but I cannot be with God and with men. The thousands and myriads above have only one will, but men have many wills. So I cannot leave God and be with men.'[9] 'Flight from men', which Theodore considers to be 'fundamental' and Arsenius to be necessary in order to enable him to 'be with God', is also the subject of two sayings of Macarius, which make slightly different points from these:

Abba Macarius the Great said to the brothers in Scetis, as he was dismissing the congregation, 'Flee, brothers.' One of the old men said to him, 'Where can we flee that is further than this desert?' He put his finger to his lips, saying,

[4] Alonius 1; cf. N 267.

[5] Moses 7.

[6] Evagrius 2 (parallel to Doulas 2), a quotation from Evagrius, *Outline of the Monastic Life*, 8; PG, xl. 1260C. For *σχέσις* as 'relationship, attachment, ... especially of soul to earthly or heavenly things', see *PGL*, 1358a (definition 8).

[7] Nilus 9.

[8] On rest, cf. Ch. 2, nn. 9, 179; Ch. 3, nn. 44; also Ch. 6, nn. 15–16 and other sayings to be referred to in Chs. 4 and 5: Joseph of Panepho 2, Poemen 159, S 4 (Guy, *Recherches*, 30), N 318.

[9] Arsenius 13.

'Flee this.' And he went into his cell, shut the door, and sat down.[10]

Abba Aio said to Abba Macarius, 'Speak a word to me.' Abba Macarius said to him, 'Flee from men, sit in your cell, and weep for your sins; and do not love the conversation of men, and you will be saved.'[11]

In what follows we will meet other sayings which, like these, put forward what seems to be a negative view of personal relationships. Several of these texts, maintain what may be called the 'hesychastic' motive for flight—the view that a monk cannot achieve stillness (*ἡσυχία*) or rest when he is in the company of others.[12] How are we to understand these comments, which as they stand appear to conflict with the Desert Fathers' otherwise manifest concern for the proper conduct of relationships within the monastic community?

One approach, of course, would be simply to accept that there was a contradiction in the Desert Fathers' understanding of the monastic life between the community-oriented views which have been examined in Chapter 3, and the goals of solitude, *hesychia*, and a relationship with God which these sayings express. Or we could suggest that the different views expressed in the *Apophthegmata* represent the variety of opinion which was inevitably current in a loosely organized community without central direction or control. Both of these views may be accepted in part. It would always be wrong to deny that different attitudes existed, or to claim that a view expressed in one saying must be consistent with the views of others. Similarly, no attempt will be made in the following chapters to argue that there is no tension between the different views which are expressed, or to minimize the Desert Fathers' own emphases, where they existed, on solitude and on the problems which relationships can cause. There *is* an irreducible element of conflict between the different aims of a solitary life and of a life of interaction with others. But not all of the sayings which have been cited above in fact need to

[10] Macarius 16; cf. Sisoes 37: 'When the congregation was dismissed, he used to flee to his cell. They used to say that he had a demon, but he was doing the work of God.'

[11] Macarius 41; cf. 27. For the command 'Flee from men, and you will be saved', see Arsenius 1.

[12] On *ἡσυχία*, cf. Arsenius 2, where God tells him to 'Flee, be silent, be still [*ἡσύχαζε*], for these are the roots of sinlessness.' The term *ἡσυχία*, which has so far been translated 'stillness', certainly has a range of meanings. In Nilus 9 it refers to the fact of physical separation from others; but in Evagrius 2 it denotes an inward disposition of freedom from distraction, perhaps equivalent to the 'rest' of Alonius 1. For other comments, see Ch. 6, pp. 171–3 and n. 27. For a discussion, see K. Ware, 'Silence in Prayer: The Meaning of *Hesychia*', in M. B. Pennington (ed.), *One Yet Two: Monastic Tradition East and West* (CSS 29; Kalamazoo, Mich., 1976), 22–47.

be, or ought to be, explained in this way. It has been shown above[13] that sayings about refusal to teach do not cast doubt on the general acceptance of the importance of teaching; in the context of the Desert Fathers' views in their entirety, they can be seen as a response to particular problems in the conduct of the teaching relationship. In the same way, if we wish to understand why the Desert Fathers sometimes rejected relationships in general, we must not read sayings in which they do so as isolated units. They have a context—the entire corpus of sayings which explain what sort of relationships the Desert Fathers did recognize as good, and what problems they wished to avoid.

Theodore's worries about the conduct of relationships, illustrated above, may for instance be viewed in the same way as examples of his refusal to teach in certain circumstances—that is, as an illustration of his general pessimism about his own and other people's ability to live the monastic life properly,[14] rather than as a denial in principle of the value of relationships. His saying on the dangers of 'compassion' may be just a much more forceful expression of his conviction that a monk's relationships with others, however constructive he might wish these, in general, to be, should not be allowed to endanger his own spiritual well-being.[15] Perhaps this calculating approach does not quite equal the self-sacrificial approach espoused by the Apostle Paul,[16] but at least it is far from thoroughly dismissive of all relationships.

More generally, we need to ask whether reservations may not be expressed about particular situations rather than about relationships in general. Arsenius 31, for example, refers to Arsenius' and Theodore's dislike of receiving *δόζα*, praise or glorification, from others. Another story which refers to what may perhaps be called the 'problem of praise' concerns John Kolobos:

> He was very fervent in spirit. Someone came to him once and began to praise his work (he was working at a rope). But he was silent. Again he spoke to him, and he was silent. The third time he said to the one who had come, 'Since you came here, you have taken God from me.'[17]

[13] Ch. 2, Sect. 8.

[14] See Ch. 2, n. 179.

[15] Theodore of Pherme 4 (Ch. 3, n. 40).

[16] Rom. 9: 3.

[17] John Kolobos 32. This is the text as it stands in the *Apophthegmata*, but it appears to be a quotation (with some adjustments) from a longer story about John, making a slightly different point: for the text, see R. Draguet, 'À la source de deux apophtegmes grecs (*PG* 65, Jean Colobos 24 et 32)', *Byzantion*, 32 (1962), 53–61; cf. L. Regnault, 'Le Vrai Visage d'un Père du désert: Abba Jean Colobos', in E. Lucchesi and H. D.

The text states clearly that contacts with others may cause distraction from attention to God.[18] But it is only a specific kind of relationship—a bad, and avoidably bad, one—which is censured.

Arsenius 13 also leaves open the possibility that it is only bad relationships which Arsenius rejects, relationships involving strife or disagreement, the product of the 'many wills' of men.[19] Another story about John Kolobos illustrates what may have been Arsenius' attitude to bad relationships too:

> They used to say about Abba John, that he came to the church in Scetis, and heard some brothers arguing. He returned to his cell, and walked round it three times, and then went in. Some brothers who saw him wondered why he had done this, and went to ask him. He said to them, 'My ears were full of the argument, and so I walked round in order to clear them, and thus to go into my cell in peace [ἡσυχία] of mind[20]

Other stories imply that relationships are rejected for different personal, but not *necessarily* isolationist or anti-social reasons. Even the sayings of Macarius recommending flight do not imply a sheer rejection of the values of community. One emphasizes that flight is a response to awareness of sin and solitude a form of compunction; the other refers by implication to the sins of the tongue which will figure later in this chapter. Neither actually precludes a positive conception of good relations with others. Some brothers visited another John, and found him working; he greeted them, and then turned straight back to his work.[21] 'Who gave you the habit, who made you a monk?' they complained, 'Didn't he teach you to take the brothers' sheepskins, and tell them to pray, or to sit down?' But he replied that 'John the sinner has no time for these things'. The business of recognizing your own sin sometimes takes precedence over the rituals of greeting.

Apparently isolationist sayings like those of Macarius, Arsenius, and Theodore could be analysed further for evidence of such qualifications of their message as have been noted in the last few paragraphs. It may even be justifiable to interpret sayings such as Moses 7 and Alonius 1

Saffrey (eds.), *Antiquité Païenne et Chrétienne: Memorial André-Jean Festugière* (Cahiers d'Orientalisme, 10; Geneva, 1984), 225–34, reprinted in *Les Pères du désert à travers leurs Apophtegmes*, 37–53, esp. 43–5 of the reprint.

[18] Cf. John Kolobos 27, 30, 31.

[19] Arsenius, like Theodore, was in fact selective, rather than generally negative, about relationships (see Ch. 2, nn. 182–3). He could encourage good relationships with his disciples: Arsenius 24, 35.

[20] John Kolobos 25; cf. 35 (although here anger is not specifically mentioned).

[21] John of the Cenobium.

(where the threat posed by relationships is put in starker terms) in the light of these more qualified remarks, or at least to see them as representative of only one particular, rather than a universal view. But in any case, enough has been said already to show that if we do wish to understand why relationships could sometimes be rejected, then we must in the first instance at least look at those situations of anger, conflict, and praise which for the Desert Fathers constituted the worst examples of problems in the conduct of personal relationships.

2. Anger and Dispute

With the exception of the conduct of the teaching relationship, there is no area of personal relationships with which the Desert Fathers show themselves more concerned than the problems arising from anger, judgement, dispute, and slander. In Chapter 3, in reviewing the positive comments which the Sayings contain about the importance of relationships, we have already seen some indications of this. Not judging or despising others is emphasized,[22] and a general comment on what a monk's life should be like warns against judgement, slander, murmuring, interfering, and 'listening to irrelevant words'.[23] It is considered essential to be despised, or to humble yourself, before others,[24] and not to be angry, retaliate, or blame others, whatever difficulties you may face.[25] Another comment of Poemen that 'In every labour which comes upon you, victory over it is to keep silence',[26] should probably be understood in the light of these views.

Several sayings illustrate the fact that control of the tongue, advocated by Poemen in times of trouble, was seen in general as a matter of primary importance, sometimes linked, in what seems to have been a traditional pairing, to control of the 'stomach', that is to the practice of fasting and asceticism.[27] 'How can I guard my heart?' a brother asked Tithoes (enquiring, probably, about the attainment of a proper inward

[22] Theodore of Pherme 13, Macarius 28, N 137 (Ch. 3, pp. 90–2).

[23] N 225. Cf. Nisteros 5 for a list of sins of speech: 'Judge no one. These things are foreign to a monk: swearing, perjury, lying, cursing, abusing, laughing.' Abba Or seems to have lived up to this: 'He neither lied, nor swore, nor cursed anyone, nor spoke without necessity' (Or 2, taken from *HL*, 9).

[24] Poemen 158, Sisoes 43 (Ch. 2, p. 34).

[25] Poemen 91, Or 12 (Ch. 3, p. 92).

[26] Poemen 37.

[27] Antony 26, Poemen 62, 178, Matoes 11 (= N 330).

condition of awareness of and resistance to temptation, complacency, and self-deception).[28] 'How can we guard our hearts', Tithoes replied, 'when our tongues and our stomachs are open?'[29] As in this saying, sins of the tongue could be seen as a door by which other passions entered, or as a symptom of a monk's subjection to temptation:

An old man said, 'Strife hands a man over to anger; anger hands him over to blindness; and blindness makes him a worker of every evil.'[30]

He who does not control his tongue in a time of anger will not control the passions either.[31]

That the Desert Fathers believed anger to be incompatible with the monastic life as they wished to lead it is obvious. 'Even if an angry man should raise the dead,' said Agathon, 'he is not acceptable to God.'[32] An inward struggle to restrain the expression of anger, and flight from situations in which the temptation to be angry is present, are often described in such a way as to suggest that the simple fact of being angry is something always to be avoided. 'I was once going up from Scetis with my rope', John Kolobos said, 'when I saw a camel-driver speaking, and he moved me to anger. So I left my things and fled.'[33] Ammonas spent fourteen years asking God to grant him victory over anger.[34] Isidore

[28] Tithoes 3; for guarding the heart, cf. Gerontius (many avoid bodily sin but fail to guard their hearts), and Eth. Coll. 13.38, 91, 14.12, 31, 54 (various analyses of the relation between interior and exterior virtue); see Ch. 2, nn. 125, 129; also N 592/24 (Evergetinos, 2.28.7.9).

[29] The Latin parallel in PJ 11.27 (attributed to Sisoes, of which Tithoes is probably a variant) refers only to control of the tongue, suggesting that, as it stands, Tithoes 3 has been assimilated to the texts referred to in n. 27. Cf. Eth. Coll. 13.73 (attributed to Sisoes) where guarding the tongue is 'that which is appropriate to a monk', and the longer version of Poemen 21 in Eth. Coll. 13.84: inner passions must not be allowed to express themselves through the tongue.

[30] N 634 (Evergetinos, 1.42.2.2).

[31] Hyperechius 3.

[32] Agathon 19.

[33] John Kolobos 5. John Kolobos 6 and Isidore 7 convey a similar message, and all three concern the involvement of the monk in economic activity—in selling his manual work or in helping with the harvest. It was possibly to avert anger and dispute in these circumstances that Agathon (16) and Pistamon advocated avoiding haggling over prices when selling goods. Cf. Evagrius, *Outline of the Monastic life*, 8, 1260D-61A. Brown, *The Making of Late Antiquity*, 83–8, has linked the Desert Fathers' teaching on anger with an established tradition of self-sufficiency and isolationism (ἀναχώρησις) among Egyptian peasant proprietors who wished to avoid the socio-economic and inter-personal frictions of fourth-century village society. This theory is not unattractive, but there is little to suggest that the practice of the monks and the attitudes of the farmers cited by Brown were directly linked by contemporaries. For criticism of Brown's view, see C. Lubhéid, 'Antony and the Renunciation of Society', *Irish Theological Quarterly*, 52 (1986), 304–14.

[34] Ammonas 3.

was asked why the demons feared him so much: 'Because ever since I became a monk, I have striven not to allow anger to rise in my throat.'[35] The struggle against anger cannot be expected always to be successful. Sisoes once expressed his failure freely (*μετὰ παρρησίας*), drawing his hearer's attention to the seriousness of sins of the tongue (in general, though anger would certainly be included), and yet also probably with the intention of counselling him against despair: 'Have courage. For thirty years I have never prayed to God about sin, but I pray like this, saying, "Lord Jesus, protect me from my tongue." Yet until now I fall daily and sin because of it.'[36]

John Kolobos 25, quoted above, expresses the view that argument disturbs a monk's inner stillness; but with exceptions like this, these sayings on anger or sins of the tongue in general, memorable as they are, do not in fact analyse in any detail the effects of anger and dispute either on the individual or on the quality of relationships within the community. We shall see that this is the general pattern of the Desert Fathers' teaching on the subject. They are much more concerned to recommend the avoidance of anger than to analyse its effects. Nevertheless, what they have to say does add up to a clear statement of how it is right to respond to situations in which anger arises—including situations of personal conflict, in which a monk is subjected to ill-treatment or criticism.

> He [Poemen] said, 'There is no greater love to be found than this, to lay down one's life for one's neighbour. For if someone hears an evil word, that is, one which causes him grief, and is in a position to say the same in return, and struggles not to say it; or if he is taken advantage of, and bears it, and does not retaliate—such a person lays down his life for his neighbour.'[37]

[35] Isidore 2 (the parallel in Eth. Coll. 14.38 attributes his ability to perform miracles to freedom from anger). See also Isidore 3, where he claims to have been tempted in thought for forty years, but never to have succumbed to ἐπιθυμία or θυμός. Poemen 115 advocates that θυμὸς should always be 'cut off'. See also Poemen 68: 'God has given this way of life [πολιτείαν] to Israel, to abstain from what is contrary to nature, that is anger, rage [θυμοῦ], hatred, and slander against the brothers, and everything else which belongs to the old way.' Evagrius, *Praktikos*, 24, makes θυμός a weapon to be used against the demons—who of course try to tempt us to use it against people; cf. *On Prayer*, 24. Other sayings referring to anger in general are Cassian 4 (*Institutions*, 5.27), Poemen S 16 (Guy, *Recherches*, 30), and Eth. Coll. 14.51 ('If you are angry, you are the devil').

[36] Sisoes 5. His willingness to speak freely about himself is of course an example of his acceptance of the necessary openness of a good teacher. Pambo (5, 8) and Anoub (2) were more optimistic about their success in avoiding sins of the tongue. Cf. Hierax 2.

[37] Poemen 116. John 15: 13 (also quoted in Eth. Coll. 13.40). Cf. Eth. Coll. 14.17 (do violence to yourself in order not to say anything unpleasant to someone else), and Evagrius, *On Prayer*, 12: in order to calm the urge to retaliation, think of prayer.

We may well think that the scriptural text used here has been stripped of much of its significance and power by being applied to the comparatively mundane problem of personal conflict, rather than to the practice of Christian self-sacrifice and martyrdom. But the fact that Poemen chose to apply the text to the monastic life in this way itself illustrates the importance which the Desert Fathers attached to the proper conduct of personal relationships. It also shows that in Poemen's view, it is the effect of his words on his neighbour, rather than on himself, which a monk must consider. It is for his neighbour that he struggles, not (although it is not of course explicitly excluded) because he fears that anger will damage his own inner life. This is illustrated, in a specific case, in another story about Poemen:

A brother asked Abba Poemen, 'If a brother has a small amount of money which is mine, do you want me to ask him for it?' The old man said to him, 'Ask him once.' The brother said to him, 'What shall I do, for I cannot control my thought?' The old man said to him, 'Never mind your thought—just do not trouble your brother.'[38]

The rules of behaviour laid down in these sayings—not to retaliate, not to injure others, even when you have a legitimate grievance against them—are illustrated in many other texts. Whether the harm you have suffered is the result of someone's oversight or simple error, or of deliberate action, malicious or not, you have a duty to do nothing to cause distress through anger or recrimination. John and his companions were once travelling from Scetis at night, when they realized that their guide had led them astray.[39] 'If we tell him,' the old man said, 'he will be grieved and ashamed.' So they pretended that the old man was ill and unable to continue, and thus managed to arrange to cease travelling until morning, when, presumably, the guide realized his error and was able to correct it without comment from the others. 'And they did not cause offence to [*οὐκ ἐσκανδάλισαν*] the brother.'[40] But most sayings on

[38] Poemen 169. 'Never mind your thought' represents *Ἄφες τὸν λογισμόν σου λακκâν*. *PGL* 790b, suggests 'stagnate'. The meaning is probably stronger: 'to hell with your thoughts'.

[39] John Kolobos 17. On the importance of not grieving others (in an entirely different situation), see N 68.

[40] In Sisoes 30 a brother asks him what should be done in similar circumstances: 'Are we to let him lead us astray?' 'What else,' replies Sisoes, 'could you take a stick and beat him?' He then tells a story similar to that involving John, but in which the brothers, knowing they are being led astray, battle (*ἀγωνίζειν*) all night not to speak; in the morning the guide discovers his error and is astonished to find that the brothers said nothing. The relative priority of this story and that involving John is impossible to determine.

the subject of retaliation probably envisage a deliberate act of harm.

The temptation to retaliate is discussed again in another saying off Poemen:

Another brother asked him, 'What does "Do not render evil in return for evil" mean?' The old man said to him, 'This passion has four ways of working. The first is of the heart, the second of the face, the third of the tongue, and the fourth is not to do evil in return for evil. If you can cleanse your heart, it does not come to your face. But if it comes to your face, be on guard so as not to speak. But if you speak, stop quickly in order not to do evil in return for evil.'[41]

The analysis is not quite verbally coherent, but the point is clear: the passion afflicts both inward feelings and outward behaviour, but even if the heart is tormented by it, the essential thing is to attempt not to speak, not to harm the other person, even though his words or actions are the cause of your suffering.[42] John Kolobos was once insulted by another old man and responded by embracing him and saying, 'You have spoken the truth, Abba.'[43] Later he was asked whether he had not been inwardly disturbed by the incident. 'No', he replied, 'What I am outwardly, I am inwardly too.' John had succeeded in cleansing his heart, as Poemen put it, of the temptation to retaliate, and there was no danger of his rendering evil for evil. Moses, on the other hand, illustrates the struggle not to speak: when questioned in similar terms after being insulted, he replied that 'I was disturbed, but I did not speak'.[44]

This struggle not to speak, assisted by prayer for deliverance from the passion of anger, is discussed in other texts:

One of the old men came to Abba Achillas and saw him spitting blood out of his mouth, so he asked him, 'What is this, Father?' The old man said, 'The

[41] Poemen 34. 1 Thess. 5: 15. Cf. N 360 for a similar analysis using a sequence which runs, thought—inner consent—speech—action; though this saying is not related specifically to problems of relationships.

[42] Poemen's reference to the 'face' indicates that it is not speech alone which is harmful. Cf. Esaias 8: 'If someone wishes to render evil in return for evil, he can injure the conscience of his brother even by a nod of his head.'

[43] John Kolobos S 6 (Guy, *Recherches*, 24). John Kolobos 8 also shows him being insulted, but the point here is his humility as well as his control over his thoughts: he claims that inwardly he is even more sinful than he appears outwardly. See Ch. 2, n. 129.

[44] Moses 3 (Ps. 76: 5, Septuagint); cf. 4. In both cases, the insult, a comment on Moses' race, is a deliberate test of his humility and ability to bear evil. Young, *From Nicaea to Chalcedon*, 49–50, comments that 'One suspects that such incidents of racial prejudice were not always mere pretence'. Cf. P. Frost, 'Attitudes towards Blacks in the Early Christian Era', *Second Century*, 8 (1991), 1–11, which includes evidence from the *Apophthegmata*.

word of a brother grieved me, and I struggled not to tell him, and asked God to take it from me. The word has become like blood in my mouth, and I have spat it out, and I am at rest and have forgotten the grief.'[45]

A brother was moved to anger against someone, and stood praying and asking for patience towards the brother, and for the temptation to pass harmlessly. And immediately he saw smoke coming out of his mouth.[46]

Situations of conflict can thus be defused either, as in these sayings, by the successful struggle not to retaliate, or by making attempts to avoid and resolve conflict when it occurs. Thus, 'I have never gone to sleep holding anything against anyone', said Agathon (speaking quite generally of the resolution of conflicts), 'nor, as far as I have been able, allowed anyone to go to sleep with anything against me'.[47] Other anecdotes illustrate the desire to resolve conflicts in action. In order to overcome the grudge which an old man bears against him, Poemen visits him and convinces him of his goodwill and humility by patiently waiting to be admitted, even after the old man has tried to send Poemen and his companions away.[48] Even heretics, according to two or three stories, should not be argued with (except to the extent of reading to them from an orthodox writing!) or driven away but persuaded to leave in peace, 'escorted by charity', if they will not renounce their views.[49]

[45] Achillas 4.

[46] N 372. A number of other stories which refer to not returning evil for evil may be noted. Poemen (177) again speaks of doing good as 'taking away' the effect of evil. Antony (19) told some brothers that if they could not turn the other cheek when struck, at least they should endure being struck on the one (presumably he means, 'endure in silence'); and if they could not do that, at the very least they should not retaliate. A story about a woman who visits an old man in order to expose him to the temptation of fornication ends when she dies during the night; but he prays for her, commenting, 'It is written, "Do not render evil in return for evil"', and she revives (N 189). The importance of being able to bear evil with humility is often noted: Antony 15, John Kolobos 41, John the Persian 3, Matoes 10, Phortas, N 71, 302. In N 352 two monks try to argue but cannot. In Serapion 4 (paralleled in Cassian *Conferences*, 18.11) an old man exposes a brother's false humility and teaches him that he must really learn to bear criticism without being grieved. Poemen 118 discusses the meaning of being angry without cause (Matt. 5: 22): however much someone takes advantage of you or harms you, you should not be angry, but, 'If he separates you from God, then be angry.' The same point of view is taught by Agathon 5 (Ch. 2, p. 65).

[47] Agathon 4 (cf. Epiphanius 4). The allusion to Eph. 4: 26 is clearer in Syncletica 13: 'It is good not to be angry, but if it does happen, he [the Apostle Paul] does not allow a full day for the passion, saying, "Let not the sun go down."' The saying continues with a recommendation for how to avoid thinking ill of someone who has harmed you: 'Why hate someone who has grieved you? It is not he who has done wrong, but the devil. Hate the disease, not the one who suffers from it.'

[48] Poemen 4.

[49] Lot 1; the reference to the orthodox book is in Sisoes 25; cf. Poemen 78.

This suggests that sayings which list the avoidance of heretics among the essentials of the monastic life may be seen as motivated not only by fear of the heresy itself, but by reluctance to become involved in the arguments accompanying doctrinal disagreement.[50] Matoes followed up this view to its logical extreme, and advised against getting involved in any arguments at all: 'If someone speaks to you about anything whatever, do not argue. If he has spoken well say "Yes". If he has spoken wrongly say "You know what you are saying". But do not diasagree with him about what he has said. This is humility.'[51]

'Humility', to which the Desert Fathers sometimes attributed prime status among the virtues,[52] is, in the saying just quoted, a convenient designation for the attitude of surrender to others which they advocated in contexts where avoidance of conflict and non-resistance to evil are required.[53] Humility can be seen, at its simplest, as the capacity to resolve situations of conflict by renouncing your own right to expect reparation or penitence when you have a grievance against someone. Humility, said an old man, 'Is when your brother sins against you and you forgive him before he repents'[54] In another saying about the resolution of conflicts the responsibility of the party who has caused the grievance to seek reconciliation is taken for granted, but the

[50] Matoes 11 (= N 330), Sisoes 48, Chomai. Cf. Sopatrus: doctrinal discussion involves both parties in *ἰδιωτεία καὶ φιλονεικία*.

[51] Matoes 11; cf. 12: 'Cut off from yourself controversy [*φιλονεικίαν*] about anything'. Cf. N 232 ('If a word which causes grief comes between you and another and he denies it saying, "I did not say the word," do not argue with him and say, "You did say it," or he will change his mind and say, "Yes I did say it, and so what?"') and Eth. Coll. 14.3 (on giving way to someone who contradicts you, even when he is wrong); but see N 234 for a different perspective. Cf. Nisteros the Cenobite 2 and N 29 for other comments on not intervening in discussions or disputes. Quarrels may be demonically inspired: Nicetas, N 397 (Evergetinos, 3.2.8.30 is a slightly shortened version of the text translated in *Les Sentences ... série des anonymes*, 132).

[52] Eth. Coll. 14.55. The anonymous series' chapter on humility covers N 298–334. But on the importance of humility in general, see also N 381: 'It is humility which enables a monk to progress'; N 552 (Evergetinos, 1.44.3.8): 'Humility has often saved many without labour. The tax collector and the prodigal son are witness to this'; N 558 (Evergetinos, 1.44.3.4): '[Humility] is able to draw a man out of the abyss itself, even if he is sinning like a demon. This is why the Lord blessed the poor in spirit first of all' (cf. John of Kellia 2); N 569 (Evergetinos, 1.45.1.78). Humility (sometimes in the context of human relationships, sometimes directed at the demons themselves) is often seen as a weapon against demonic temptations; Antony 7, Daniel 3, Theodora 6, Macarius 11, 35, N 77, 298, 310, 312, 313, 499 (Evergetinos, 1.45.1.56). John Kolobos 20 sees humility specifically as not speaking out against evil.

[53] Cf. Eth. Coll. 14.60: humility lies in abandoning your will with respect to your brother. See N 324, 325, 329, for further comments on bearing evil.

[54] N 304.

discussion ends by probing the motivation of the monk involved in such a way as to indicate that in the opinion of the abba concerned, the aggrieved party too ought to seek forgiveness:

A brother asked an old man, 'Why is it that even though I have made a prostration before someone who has something against me, I see that he has not been reconciled with me?' The old man said to him, 'Tell me the truth. When you make a prostration before him, aren't you justifying yourself in your heart, thinking that he has sinned against you, and that you are repenting before him because of the commandment?' The brother said, 'Yes, it is so.' So the old man said to him, 'This is why God has not convinced him to be reconciled with you—because you are not making a prostration before him with sincerity, as if you had sinned against him; rather you hold that he has sinned against you. Even if he has sinned against you, set it in your heart that it is you who has sinned against him, and justify your brother; then God will convince him to be reconciled with you.'[55]

Poemen's attitude to a similar situation also deserves quotation. If a brother whom you have harmed will not accept your repentance, he advises,

Take two other brothers and repent before him. And if he is not persuaded, take five. And if he is not persuaded by these, take a priest. And if he is not persuaded by this then pray to God without disturbance, that he may convince him, and you may be free of worry.[56]

Poemen's concern is that the unresolved dispute should not continue to disturb the brother who originally caused it; but by demanding that the brother's future prayer should be undisturbed (*ἀταράχως*), he may also be making the more specific point that the brother should not use prayer as a means of expressing his grievance (that his repentance has not been accepted) against the other. This would be consistent with the teaching of Poemen 116 and 169, that however troubling he found it to his inner life to do so, a monk's primary aim should be to avoid

[55] N 334 (the text continues with an illustration of the old man's teaching which is not entirely apposite and which may be an independent unit). 'The commandment' probably refers to Matt. 5: 23–5 on the settling of disputes. N 319 is a close parallel. Eth. Coll. 13.85 demands 'Go, love your neighbour as yourself, and all your enemies will fall at your feet.' Does this assume that only they are at fault, or does blame lie on both sides?

[56] Poemen 156. The procedure advocated bears some relation to that described in Matt. 18: 15–17, but with the difference, which is perhaps illustrative of the Desert Fathers' approach to situations of conflict, that in the Gospel the intention is to draw attention to the other person's sin, in the saying, to your own.

harming his antagonist by acts of retaliation which are likely (according to N 232) to do nothing other than intensify and perpetuate bad relationships.

The teaching on unwillingness to become involved in argument and dispute which has been examined in this section may sometimes suggest that the monks involved were pessimistic about the possibility of conducting good relationships and essentially concerned only to avoid what they perceived as bad. This may appear to be done even at the risk of seeming uncaring: Poemen refused to intervene in a fight between two of his younger brothers and told Anoub, who criticized him for allowing them to go on fighting, to 'Set it in your heart that inwardly I was not here.'[57] But a saying as negative as this is exceptional, and even this one may perhaps be interpreted in a somewhat more positive way, as a refusal to intervene in and possibly worsen a conflict which, after all, will eventually solve itself. 'They are brothers,' Poemen says, 'they will be at peace again.' In most cases which have been examined there is an implicit, if not explicit, awareness that non-resistance to evil and the avoidance and resolution of situations of conflict are practised not only in the interests of your own inner life, though this is certainly important,[58] but also for the sake of your neighbour, to avoid harming him or grieving him, so that 'both enjoyed great peace'.[59]

[57] Poemen 173. See also *On Thoughts*, 22: (Question) 'Is it good to intervene in an argument between brothers?' (Answer) 'Flee such things. For it is written, "He who stops his ears in order not to hear a judgement of blood, and shuts his eyes in order not to see unrighteousness"' (Isa. 33: 15). Both of these texts are in accord with John's behaviour in John Kolobos 25.

[58] See N 592/53 (Evergetinos, 4.14.2.3): 'If you hear that someone has insulted you and he comes to see you, do not show him that you know, but entertain him and smile at him, that you may have confidence [*παρρησίαν*] in your prayers'; also N 227, in which a single *λόγος οἰκτρὸς* which an old man hears completely distracts him from saying his office. Evagrius, *Praktikos*, 25, notes the danger of offending a brother so that he takes flight: 'you will never escape the demon of grief, which will be an obstacle to you at the time of prayer.'

[59] The conclusion of N 319. Poemen 175 also illustrates the primacy of the desire not to blame or harm *others*: if you find that you have not profited from a brother's visit, examine your own thoughts (i.e. not what *he* has done) to see why: then 'You will be blameless towards your neighbour, bearing your own sin'; cf. Eth. Coll. 13.53, and GSC 10.33 (unpublished; translated in *Les Sentences ... troisième recueil*, 82): salvation is to blame yourself and not harm your brother.

3. Slander

Anger and slander are closely related problems, but it is worth considering what the *Apophthegmata* have to say about the problem of slander in its own right:

It is better to eat meat and to drink wine, than to eat the flesh of the brothers in slander [καταλαλιαῖς].[60]

The serpent drove Eve out of paradise through whispering. He who slanders his neighbour is like the serpent, for he both loses the soul of the one who listens, and does not preserve his own.[61]

Slander is, in general, often warned against or compared with other sins;[62] but it is the fact that it involves a third party ('the one who listens' in the second saying quoted above) which makes it a particularly serious problem of relationships, analysed in somewhat different terms from anger, which tends to concern situations of confrontation between two individuals. If you hear a rumour about someone's ill behaviour, you should not trust the person who utters it, for if he was a faithful brother he would never have said it. Even if you are convinced that the rumour is true, you should not treat it as an excuse for leaving the place where you are—the proper course of action is to consider your own sins, and regard those of the other person as insignificant.[63] A monk, an old man said, 'Must be neither a hearer, nor a slanderer, nor easily offended [σκανδαλίζεσθαι]'.[64] He must, that is, neither listen to nor spread rumours, nor be easily discouraged or disturbed by what he hears, against others or against himself.

The sin of slander against your neighbour prevents you, according

[60] Hyperechius 4. N 225 (above, n. 23) is also important.

[61] Hyperechius 5.

[62] See Poemen 154 and Matoes 8 for comparison of slander and fornication. N 509 (Ch. 2, nn. 23, 25) includes the instruction not to slander anyone. Cf. Hierax 1 and Eth. Coll. 13.68, 69.

[63] N 391. It can in fact be considered necessary to behave better towards those who have a bad reputation than towards the good. Thus in Achillas 1 he agrees to make a fishing net for a brother because, 'If I do not make it for him he will say, "The old man does not wish to make it because he has heard about my sin." Then we will break the bond between us. So I raised up his soul, so that he would not suffer grief.' Cf. Poemen 70 (first half), and Eth. Coll. 13.41.

[64] N 386. For being scandalized by the temptations experienced by your neighbours, cf. N 177 and 200. In the latter case, the *tempted* party should not leave the area until the temptation has passed, in case his sudden departure troubles the others who live there.

to the dialogue *On Thoughts*, from entering the presence of God.[65] The same dialogue is pessimistic about the possibility of conducting relationships into which slander does not intrude: 'As he who takes fire into his bosom will be injured, so he who accepts the conversation of men will not be delivered from slander.'[66] But in the Sayings, procedures for avoiding slander or for alleviating its effects are sometimes suggested: 'If you have slandered your brother, and your conscience is troubling you, go and make a prostration before him, and say, "I have slandered you", and promise not to indulge in it again. For slander is death to the soul.'[67] It is possible, this means, to bring the matter out into the open with the victim, as an incentive for not repeating the sin in the future. An old man discusses how it is right to respond if someone slanders another in your presence. You must be careful not to fall in with the slander by agreeing with him. Either be quiet or say that, as a sinner, you are unable to judge him. 'Thus you will save both yourself and him'—that is the slanderer.[68]

But what constitutes slander? The expanded anonymous series contains two sayings, one of them unfortunately unpublished, which define slander clearly, and which differentiate between those circumstances in which saying something about someone is slanderous, and those in which it is not. 'Everything which someone could not say in front of his brother is slander. If for instance someone says that a particular brother is fine and good, but he is careless and lacks discernment—that is slander.'[69] On the other hand, to quote the second saying, if you see a brother doing something and you want to tell someone else, is that slander?[70] No, an old man comments, provided that what you say is

[65] *On Thoughts*, 12.

[66] Ibid. 25. For the text's pessimism about the possibility of conducting good relationships, see 9: 'Why am I not able to live with some brothers?' (Answer) 'Because you do not fear God. For if you remembered what is written, that Lot [alone] among those in Sodom was saved, because he judged no-one, you would cast yourself into the midst of the beasts and dwell with them.' Also 10: if a brother has offended you you should repent before him but then 'cut him off from you. For Abba Arsenius said, "Have love for all, but hold back from all."' This must refer to Arsenius 13 or a similar story.

[67] Or 15.

[68] N 592/40 (Evergetinos, 2.49.2.4). On not responding to words you hear, see N 303: here however the abba stresses the importance of not rebuking the one who says unwanted words to you; it would be hypocritical, since you too may be unable to avoid saying such things. 'If we want to be silent, this habit is enough for our neighbour.'

[69] N 417 (Evergetinos, 2.49.2.3); cf. the parallel (though with different examples of criticism and slander) in N 503.

[70] N 475. This summary is based on the translation in *Les Sentences ... série des anonymes*, 158–9.

free from passion and grievance against the brother of whom you speak. In this case, what you say is good. But, all these sayings imply, speaking about someone else is dangerous, and avoiding slander or repenting of having committed it play an essential role in the maintenance of good relationships within the community.

4. Judgement and Sin

The saying which defines slander in such stringent terms follows its definition with an explanation of what it is to judge or condemn someone else: 'If someone says that the brother is a trader and a money-lover, then that is to judge [κατακρίνειν], for he has condemned his actions and his whole life. This is worse than slander.'[71] The number of stories illustrating the necessity of not judging others, and the urgency with which abstaining from judgement was commended, confirms the importance of the problem of judgement in the Desert Fathers' understanding of relationships within the community. The problem of judgement, in fact, is the subject of what must rank, precisely because of its urgency and the memorable form in which the teaching is put, as one of the most remarkable of all sayings from the *Apophthegmata*:

> Abba Poemen said, 'It is written, "Bear witness to what your eyes have seen." But I say to you, even if you have touched with your hands, do not bear witness. A brother was once deceived in such a way as to see his brother sinning with a woman. Greatly troubled, he kicked them (he thought it was them) with his foot, and said, "Stop, how long will you go on?" But it turned out to be some sheaves of corn. That is why I told you not to rebuke, even if you have touched with your hands.'[72]

The point is not just that the brother's haste has led him to make a foolish mistake, or that his action would not have been wrong had the sin been real, but that he has been the victim of a demonic deceit which has led him to commit the sin of judgement. The term translated 'troubled' (πολεμηθείς), supports this: the brother has, literally, been 'warred against' by the demons. One other saying at least supports this interpretation, referring explicitly to deceit through demonic activity in a context which is somewhat similar to that described by Poemen:

[71] N 417. The saying also includes the definition, 'To slander is said to be concealed and secret, but to judge applies to open sins.'

[72] Poemen 114. Prov. 25: 7, Septuagint.

Abba Elias said, 'I saw someone carrying a flask of wine under his arm. And in order to shame the demons (for it was an illusion), I said to the brother, "Be charitable, and take this from me." He took off his cloak, and proved not to be holding anything. I say this so that even if you hear or see anything, you should not accept it. Even more, guard your reasonings, desires, and thoughts, because they [the demons] interfere with them, in order to pollute the soul and make it think about things which are unfitting, and to distract the mind from its sins, and from God.'[73]

Poemen himself more than once teaches that it is necessary to overlook the sins of another, even if they are real. Someone asked him whether it was right to 'cover' (that is, ignore or conceal from others) the sins of his brother if he saw them.[74] Poemen said to him: 'When we cover the sin of our brother, God covers ours. In the hour in which we reveal that of our brother, God reveals ours.' On another occasion he was asked whether a brother should be rebuked if he was seen sinning.[75] 'If ever I have to pass that way', he replied, 'and see him sinning, I pass by, and do not rebuke him.' Poemen's reaction to another quite trivial incident also illustrates his unwillingness to condemn others:

Some of the old men came to Abba Poemen and said to him, 'If we see the brothers sleeping at the *synaxis*, do you want us to wake them, so that they may keep watch in wakefulness?' He said to them, 'If ever I see a brother sleeping, I lay his head on my knees and give him rest.'[76]

Attitudes like this are not of course peculiar to Poemen. Another quite striking saying concerns Macarius who 'Became, as it is written, a God upon earth [θεὸς ἐπίγειος]'.[77] Whatever the origin of this designation, what it means in the context of the *Apophthegmata* is clear from what follows: 'As God covers the world, so Abba Macarius came to cover sins, treating what he saw as if he did not see and what he heard as if he did not hear.'[78] Another remarkable and related viewpoint

[73] Elias 4.

[74] Poemen 64.

[75] Poemen 113.

[76] Poemen 92.

[77] Macarius 32.

[78] R. D. Williams, *The Wound of Knowledge: Christian Spirituality from the New Testament to St John of the Cross* (London, 1979), 96, views Macarius' attitude in the context of an abba's exposure of his own weaknesses in teaching, and of the monks' sharing with one another in penitence for sin. For the meaning of θεὸς ἐπίγειος, see von Lilienfeld, 'Anthropos Pneumatikos—Pater Pneumatophoros', 389–90, who suggests (390 n. 1) that the text's 'as it is written' is to be seen not as an (unidentifiable) biblical allusion but as an indication that the compiler of the *Apophthegmata* was using a written source in which the phrase 'God upon earth' occurred, and that he felt uncomfortable about it.

is expressed by Alonius, when asked how someone can control his tongue in order never to lie:

If you do not lie, you are going to commit many sins ... Suppose that two men have committed murder before you, and one of them has fled to your cell. Then the magistrate comes to look for him, and asks you whether you have seen a murder. If you do not lie, you are handing the man over to death. You should leave him before God without censure, for God knows everything.[79]

One among the reasons which leads the Desert Fathers to renounce judgement is the belief (effectively expressed by Alonius) that God alone is the true judge. For a human being to judge is to appropriate a divine function, and this (notwithstanding the comment about Macarius) is always an act of presumption and pride. An anchorite accepted the truth of an evil rumour about a priest who used to bring him the eucharist and would not let him in the next time he came. When he had done so he heard a voice saying to him, 'Men have taken away my judgement.'[80] 'If God who made them does not burn them, who am I to rebuke them,' said an old man when he saw a brother committing a sexual sin with a child.[81] Another old man said merely that a brother who had fallen into fornication had 'done wrong'; but a few days later an angel appeared to him carrying the soul of the brother (who had died) and asked him to decide whether he should go to the Kingdom or to punishment.[82] The old man realized his error and spent the rest of his life in penitence for the sin. We are not told whether the brother was punished by God or not, but the essential message is that it is not for the old man, or any human being, to pronounce judgement on God's behalf.

[79] Alonius 4.

[80] N 254. The rest of the story justifies an *ex opere operato* doctrine of sacramental validity.

[81] John the Persian 1. On sexual temptations arising from relationships with children, or afflicting monks with respect to one another, see Achilles 6 (even an old man can admit to being tempted by another), Eudemon, John Kolobos 4, Isaac of Kellia 5, Poemen 176, N 181 (an old man shows that a brother's allegation that two others sleep together is false: 'Shut the brother in the cell alone, for he has the passion in himself'), N 456–8 (Evergetinos, 2.29.12.14–16), 545 (Evergetinos, 2.29.12.3). But not all sayings about children are about sexual temptation; some concern more simple forms of disturbance: Macarius 5, Poemen 155, and N 338.

[82] N 477 (Evergetinos, 3.2.8.33); cf. Isaac of Thebes 1. Sisoes 1 is another story about denying God the sole right of judgement and punishment: a brother expresses a wish to avenge himself on someone who has harmed him. The old man gets up to pray and says, 'God, we no longer need you to take care of us, for we will avenge ourselves.' The brother then realizes his error. Cf. Eth. Coll. 13.20.

Other reasons for not judging are of course given. 'Do not judge the fornicator if you are chaste yourself', said Theodotus simply, 'or you too transgress the law, for he who said, "Do not fornicate" also said, "Do not judge." '[83] In circumstances similar to those related in N 254, Mark the Egyptian refused to condemn a priest: 'It is written, "Do not judge, lest you be judged." Even if he is a sinner, the Lord will save him. For it is written, "Pray for one another, that you may be healed." '[84] Not only must the commandment be obeyed, but it is obviously more constructive to pray for others than to condemn them. This is vividly illustrated in an anonymous story. A monk and a virgin visited an old man, and during the night committed fornication together. In the morning they left, but wondering whether the old man knew what had happened, they returned to him to ask him and found out that he had been aware of it: 'They said to him, "What were you thinking at that time?" He said to them, "At that time my thoughts were standing where Christ was crucified, and weeping." '[85] Not surprisingly, the result of the old man's forbearance is that the sinners are converted and become 'vessels of election'.

Of the many sayings on judgement some of the most interesting show an abba teaching the more judgementally-minded the necessity of leniency. The fact that leniency rather than severity often has the desired effect of stirring someone to repentance is a perfectly valid practical reason for not rebuking a sinner, especially if he denies he is at fault.[86] But in addition, someone who holds authority will, ideally, maintain an awareness of his *own* sins which will lead him to be chary of exercising his authority to censure others in particular cases. 'Don't you too sometimes have something of the old man in you? Have you cast him off?' said Poemen to a priest who had taken their habits away from some negligent brothers.[87] 'So you are like the brothers; for if you share

[83] N 11.

[84] Mark the Egyptian. Matt. 7: 1; Jas. 5: 16. His refusal to judge is rewarded by a vision of the priest being glorified by God while celebrating the eucharist.

[85] N 13.

[86] Poemen 23. The Desert Fathers' attitude to the correction of others' sins does not fit easily with the 'rebuke' of Matt. 18: 15 (see above, n. 56 and Ch. 3, p. 93).

[87] Poemen 11. For the refusal of those in authority over others to judge, cf. Dörries, 'The Place of Confession in Ancient Monasticism', 294–8. For another example, see Ammonas 10: he adopts a ruse to conceal 'for the sake of God' the sin of a brother whom some others wish to expose and punish, and simply advises the brother to 'pay attention to yourself'. Mercy is, implicitly, more effective than punishment. Cf. the act of kindness towards a sinner which results in his repentance in GSC 9.20 (Evergetinos, 3.2.8.22; cf. PL, lxxiv. 378A-B). For a comment on Ammonas 10, see Tugwell, *Ways of Imperfection*, 15–16.

a little in the old way, you likewise rest in sin.' The priest's own doubts about the rightness of his actions were confirmed, and he repented before the brothers and reinstated them. Antony too is shown persuading the members of a cenobium to take back a brother whom they had driven away when he sinned,[88] and in another case (together with Paphnutius) convincing some brothers that they ought to receive back one of their number without rebuking him for a sin—which, as it happened, he denied having committed, though this is irrelevant to the basic principle of not judging.[89] In each of these cases leniency allows the sinner a chance to repent and resume his monastic life without enduring the shame of judgement; trying to prove he is guilty and correct him is a less constructive approach.

These stories are some of the most attractive in the entire corpus of the Sayings. In an example from the Ethiopic collection, an old man appeals to the fact of divine mercy as his reason for dissenting from the judgement of his colleagues and allowing a brother who had sinned to continue living in Scetis.[90] Another case concerns the two Macarii.[91] Macarius the Citizen excommunicated two brothers who had sinned; when Macarius the Egyptian heard about it, he responded by saying that it was not the brothers but Macarius who was excommunicated, 'for he loved him'. The Citizen fled to the swamp near the river, where the other found him:

> 'You have excommunicated the brothers, and see, they have withdrawn to the village. I have excommunicated you, and you have fled here like a beautiful girl to her inner chamber. I have summoned the brothers, listened to them, and told them that nothing has happened. See then, brother, whether you have been deceived by the demons—for you have not seen anything—and do penance for your sin.' He said, 'If you wish, give me a penance.' When the old man saw his humility he said, 'Go and fast for three weeks, eating once a week.' For to fast the whole week was his normal practice.

It is perhaps necessary to qualify the impression that the Desert

[88] Antony 21.

[89] Antony 29.

[90] With the old man in fact, with the result that the brother starts to care for his soul: Eth. Coll. 13.14. Cf. Poemen 6, where he convinces an anchorite of his error in advising the abba of a cenobium to drive away a sinful brother; also 90, a somewhat different incident, but one which displays the same principles.

[91] Macarius 21. On the two Macarii, see *HL*, 17–18 and *HM*, 21; 23 (esp. 23.2–4); for the problems surrounding the attribution of sayings to the two, see A. Guillaumont, 'Le Problème des deux Macaires dans les *Apophthegmata Patrum*', *Irénikon*, 48 (1975), 41–59.

Fathers invariably disapproved of judgement, or of revealing another person's sin, or that they always pointed to the possibility of demonic deceit when tempted to condemn others. To maintain life in the community it would sometimes be necessary to speak and act against sinners. But even sayings permitting such action suggest that the Desert Fathers worried about it. 'If I am living with some brothers, and see something unfitting', someone asked an old man, 'do you want me to speak?'[92] Sayings like Poemen 64 and 113 would certainly suggest the answer no, but the old man answers with careful discrimination, allowing that some criticism of others is necessary, but guarding himself against giving the brother licence to condemn:

> 'If they are older than you, or the same age, you will have more rest [ἀνάπαυσιν] by being silent, for in this way you make yourself less important, and free of worry.' The brother said to him, 'What am I to do, for the spirits [πνεύματα] trouble me?' The old man said to him, 'If you are struggling, speak once, humbly. If they do not listen, leave your labour before God, in order to renounce your own will, and attend to yourself; do not make yourself known, that your concern may be for God. As I see it, it is better to be silent, for that is humility.'

The old man's caution, and emphasis on silence, humility, renunciation of the will, and attention to yourself rather than to the sins of others, mean that this is only just, in fact, a qualification of Poemen's view.[93] More interesting perhaps is a discussion of a problem that must have been relatively common. If a brother asks an abba whether he ought to live with someone, and the old man says that it would not be good for him, is the old man judging the other brother in his thought?[94] The answer given is that if the old man answers with passion or hatred against the brother then, 'he harms himself, and his word has no value. It would be better for him to say, "I don't know", and clear himself.' To answer properly he 'will not condemn anyone, but accuse himself and say, "In truth, I am careless, but perhaps it is not good for you."'

[92] N 318.

[93] Poemen himself is asked a similar question in 45 (though it does not explicitly concern the actions of another person), and he answers that the brother should wait to be asked before speaking (Prov. 18: 13). N 478 (unpublished) much more explicitly instills the importance of correcting others—but with charity.

[94] N 476 (Evergetinos, 3.2.8.32). The printed text is slightly longer than that translated in *Les Sentences ... série des anonymes*, 159. My summary removes these additions (which appear to be for the purposes of clarification). The only real exception to the rule about not judging others, in the sense of a saying which justifies thinking adversely about someone, seems to be Or 5: 'If you see that I have a thought [λογισμόν] against someone, know that he has the same against me.'

If the questioner is sufficiently perceptive, he will realize he should not go to live with the other. The distinction made here parallels, in fact, the discussion of slander in the preceding saying; but the question here applies to a real problem of the monastic life which evidently requires some easing of the rules about not judging in order to answer it.

To the various reasons for not judging which have been illustrated in the last few pages—abuse of authority, usurpation of God's prerogative, the possibility of being subject to demonic deceit—must be added a further comment on a monk's awareness of his own sins. The continued, indeed ineradicable, presence of sin in a monk's life, however great his achievements in asceticism and combat against the demons, was a factor which the Desert Fathers were concerned to stress.[95] Despite his confidence that he had never, since he became a monk, eaten bread which he had not worked for, nor spoken a word which he had regretted, Pambo commented that 'I am going to God as one who has not even begun to serve him'.[96] A number of sayings reveal, or instil the necessity of maintaining, similar feelings, and often refer to compunction or weeping for sin as a monk's constant occupation.[97]

What is important in this context is the way in which these feelings of sin are explicitly related to a monk's attitude to others. Two stories concern abbas who were unwilling to join in an assembly convened for the purpose of judging a sinner, and who convinced the others present of the necessity of mercy by acted parables drawing attention to their own sinfulness.[98] One of the more general sayings on the monastic life includes the instruction to, 'Beseech God, that he may give your heart compunction and humility; attend to your own sins and do not judge

[95] Of the sayings cited already, see esp. Poemen 11. Cf. Regnault, 'The Beatitudes in the *Apophthegmata Patrum*', 25, 28–31.

[96] Pambo 8; cf. Sisoes 14.

[97] See Ch. 2, nn. 33, 146, and many other texts: Arsenius 3, Ammonas 1, Matoes 2, 3, Sarmatas 1, N 332, Eth. Coll 14.50 on awareness of sin; Arsenius 41, Dioscorus 2, Macarius 37, Poemen 39, 119, S 21, 22 (Guy, *Recherches*, 31), N 140, 141, 142 on weeping. Probably related to awareness of sin is the view that it is always possible to make a new 'beginning': Poemen 85, Silvanus 11; cf. N 10 and Antony 6 ('Do not worry about what is past'); also Ch. 2, pp. 45–6 and n. 70. N 5 illustrates how penitence could become perverted. A brother subjects himself to great hardship: 'I know that God has forgiven my sins, but I endure this hardship, so that in the day of judgement I may contemplate those who are being judged.' The major study of teaching on compunction is I. Hausherr, *Penthos: The Doctrine of Compunction in the Christian East* (CSS 53; Kalamazoo, Mich., 1982).

[98] Moses 2, Pior 3. Cf. Bessarion 7. Agathon 14 also shows him declaring the verdict of a council to be incorrect.

others, but be less than all.'[99] It was another old man's practice to say, when he saw someone sinning, 'If this has happened to-day, it will certainly be my turn tomorrow.' 'Even if someone sins before you,' the text continues, 'do not judge him, but hold yourself to be more sinful than he is.'[100] The way to avoid speaking evil of someone else, according to Poemen, is for a monk to blame himself: then his brother will appear to him to be good; but if he thinks himself good, he will start to think of his neighbour as evil.[101] A self-critical assessment of your own achievements thus leads to a less judgemental, a more understanding, attitude to others. It is a monk who considers himself to be a sinner, according to Moses, who is heard by God—that is, someone who bears his own sins and does not think about those of his neighbour.[102]

The attitude which a monk should take to the quality of his own life could easily be illustrated further. What emerges as the basis of non-judgemental attitudes to others is a consistent pattern of self-disregard and self-denigration[103]—but a thoroughly realistic one, without any trace of pathological self-hatred, false humility, or mere form. It would however be a fair point to remark that in the majority of these sayings the focus of attention is on the effect of judging on the one who judges, rather than on the victim. A relationship which involves judgement is in fact precisely one of those bad relationships which detracts from the

[99] Matoes 11 (= N 330).

[100] N 327. The parallel in Pa 16.3 (1039C) ends by making an exception if the sin you see is a blasphemy against God.

[101] Poemen 148. On blaming (*μέμφεσθαι*) yourself—the converse of not blaming or judging others (above, n. 25), cf. Theophilus the Archbishop 1, John Kolobos 21, Poemen 95, 134; also above, n. 59.

[102] Moses 16; cf. Paphnutius 1, where he prays for his own sins when tempted to judge others, and an angel tells him that for this humiliation of himself his name is written in the book of the living. Two other related comments are Eth. Coll. 13.40, which holds that 'there is no greater love' than to say 'I have sinned' rather than condemn a sinner, and 86: unless you say 'I have sinned' it is impossible to love your neighbour.

[103] See Tithoes 7, in which the way of humility is defined as 'Self-control, prayer, and holding oneself to be less than all creation'. The same attitude is described in a related text, Sisoes 13, as more important than having the thought of God continually in your mind. N 384 comments that 'It is written about idols, "They have mouths and do not speak, they have eyes and do not see, they have ears and do not hear." (Psalm 115: 5–6) This is what a monk should be like. And because idols are an abomination, he too should hold himself to be an abomination.' In Poemen 97 a brother asks him, 'But how can I regard myself as less than a murderer?' The answer is: 'If someone has attained this saying, and sees someone committing murder, he will say, "He has committed only this sin, but I commit murder every day."' Cf. Xanthias 3, Poemen 98, 142 ('To hate evil is when someone hates his sins and justifies his neighbour'), Or 7 and 11 (= N 299), N 323, Eth. Coll. 14.58, Ch 271, for related attitudes of blaming yourself, justifying others, and avoiding self-esteem.

inward stillness and peace which are the goals of the monastic life according to sayings quoted in the first section of this chapter. For example:

When he [Agathon] saw something, and his thought wished to judge it, he would say to himself, 'Agathon, do not do this.' And thus his thought was still [*ἡσύχαζε*].[104]

Abba Poemen said to Abba Joseph, 'Tell me how to become a monk.' He said, 'If you wish to find rest [*ἀνάπαυσιν*] both here and in the future, in every situation say, "Who am I?" and do not judge anyone.'[105]

If you see someone fall say immediately, 'Anathema to you, Satan, for he is not to blame.' Guard your heart so as not to judge your brother, in case the Holy Spirit leaves you.[106]

In the eyes of the Desert Fathers, judgement is an action which denies its perpetrator the favour of God, the indwelling presence of the Holy Spirit.[107] But this does not mean that judging was avoided for solely inward, individualistic reasons of personal spirituality. As we have seen, judgement is avoided for a number of different reasons: its offensiveness to Christ's explicit command; its openness to demonic exploitation (as in the story of the brother who kicked the sheaves of corn); its human arrogation of God's sole right to judge or have mercy; its absurdity as the act of one who is himself a sinner; its harmful effect on the sinner who would repent and return to full participation in the monastic life. Judgement would surely not have been seen as an action so disturbing to the peace of a monk's inner life unless, for these other reasons, it had been recognized as one of the worst of sins against other people. Prayer for the sinner; consideration of your own faults; kindness for the sake of repentance; leniency for the sake of allowing a sinner back into the community where (despite his sin) he really wants to be—these, not in judgement, are the ways to respond to sin. The Desert

[104] Agathon 18 (Eth. Coll. 14.45 is parallel but does not have the conclusion).

[105] Joseph of Panepho 2.

[106] N 592/39 (Evergetinos, 3.2.8.35, which continues with another comment on sympathizing with those who have sinned unwillingly). Withdrawal of divine favour from someone who judges is also portrayed in N 20 and 255.

[107] As in Moses 16; for the Holy Spirit, cf. N 575 (Evergetinos, 2.31.4.1), where holding others to be better than you is so that 'the Spirit of God dwells in you. But if you despise anyone, the grace of God withdraws from you, and hands you over to defilement of your flesh; your heart is hardened, and no compunction is found in you'. Or 13 is basically similar: it is wrong to 'Speak in your heart against your brother saying, "I am more sober and austere than he is." Submit yourself to the grace of Christ in the spirit of poverty and unfeigned love, that you may not fall into the spirit of boasting, and lose your reward.'

Fathers' treatment of the problem of judgement, like their treatment of anger, is a central element in the articulation of their concern for the smooth functioning and harmonious relationships of the monastic community.

5. Praise and the Metaphor of Death

The Desert Fathers believed that to be angry with, slander, or judge someone else was contrary to the essential values of the monastic community. In certain circumstances it was certainly good for a monk to bear others' insults or criticisms of himself with humility; but it would be absurd to suggest that for this reason, he should try to 'do good' to others by insulting or criticizing them.[108] This absolute prohibition on slandering or judging others, and strict insistence on non-resistance to evil, must have had the main purpose of avoiding the gradual establishment and creeping acceptance within the community of attitudes to others which were not guided by humility and the desire for peace; of avoiding the view, in other words, that bad relationships are somehow unavoidable and therefore acceptable even in the monastic life.

The Desert Fathers' strong aversion to attitudes and behaviour which seemed to involve harming anyone else (especially if such behaviour also involved a monk in failure to recognize his own sins) could be expressed in very strong terms—by what in the title of this section is called 'the metaphor of death'. This metaphor is especially prominent in some sayings attributed to Abba Moses, but it is found elsewhere:

> A brother said to Abba Moses, 'I see something before me, but I am not able to grasp it.' The old man said to him, 'If you do not become dead like those who are in the tomb, you cannot grasp it.'[109]

[108] For the two sides of the coin, cf. again Sisoes 43 (Ch. 2, p. 34) and Theodore of Pherme 13 (Ch. 3, n. 17). Tugwell, *Ways of Imperfection*, 19, comments, 'If it was considered improper to interfere with other people, it was considered eminently proper to allow other people to interfere with you.'

[109] Moses 11.

Abba Moses said, 'A man must die to his neighbour [*ἀποθανεῖν ἀπὸ τοῦ ἑταίρου αὐτοῦ*], so as not to judge him in anything.'[110]

He said again, 'A man must kill himself as regards every evil deed, before he leaves the body, so as not to harm anyone.'[111]

Abba Longinus said, 'As a dead person does not feel anything, so a humble person cannot judge anyone, even if he sees him worshipping idols.'[112]

The metaphor of death (especially 'death to your neighbour') sounds as if it might have essentially negative connotations, perhaps referring to the rejection of relationships or the belief that the attempt to achieve good relationships is futile; but this is far from the case. These sayings witness to a positive desire to attain the goals of the monastic life and to cultivate good relationships through self-restraint from harming and judging others.[113]

In the first section of this chapter the term 'problem of praise' was used as a label for one of the reasons for which relationships were sometimes avoided by the Desert Fathers.[114] Now in one sense a relationship involving praise is to be commended, for to praise someone excludes the vices of anger, slander, and judgement from your relationship with him. 'I am not worthy of the old man's words', said Matoes—he had been called 'A true Israelite in whom there is no guile' by Abba John of the Cells—'but know this: when you hear an old man glorifying his neighbour more than himself, he has achieved a great stature. For this is perfection, to glorify one's neighbour above oneself.'[115] In certain circumstances Poemen too was given to praise, in order to avoid allowing himself a chance to criticize or argue with someone else: 'They used to say about Abba Poemen that he never wished to state his opinion after

[110] Moses 14; cf. 12 for another comment on how to obtain death to one's neighbour. Another saying using the metaphor of death is Poemen 2: his brother has struck up a relationship with someone, and Poemen tells Ammonas that because of it 'I have no rest'. Ammonas tells him to 'Go and sit in your cell, and set it in your heart that you have already been a year in the tomb'. That is, a monk should not allow himself to be adversely affected by the behaviour of others, which is no business of his. In Arsenius 29 and Cassian 8 the metaphor of death serves only to emphasize the detachment of monks from the secular world, and especially from possessions.

[111] Moses 15.

[112] N 559 (Evergetinos, 1.45.1.24).

[113] Cf. Eth. Coll. 13.45, where 'death' is a concept with similarly positive implications for good relationships; 13.48, 49 also refer to death. All these are attributed to Poemen. The positive aspect of death to one's neighbour is recognized by Williams, *The Wound of Knowledge*, 97: '"Death" is withdrawal from the possibility of imposing the violence of selfishness on others.'

[114] Above, p. 110, referring to Arsenius 31 and John Kolobos 32.

[115] Matoes 7. John 1: 47. For similar compliments, see Hilarion.

another old man; instead he praised him in everything.'[116] Nevertheless praise has its dangers. In the same way as it is obviously wrong to insult someone, even though it can be good to receive insults, so, though it can be good to praise someone, it can be bad to receive praise:

He who is honoured or praised more than he is worth suffers great loss. He who is never honoured by men will be glorified above.[117]

He who praises a monk hands him over to Satan.[118]

When someone is praised, he should think of his sins, and believe that he is not worthy of what was said.[119]

Praise could be avoided by flight from a situation in which a monk was about to be praised or honoured by others,[120] or by silence in the face of compliments: 'If I answered them,' said Alonius, when praised by some old men whom he was serving at a meal, 'I would seem to accept their praise.'[121] Living an inconspicuous life, differing in no way from the others in the place where you live, and avoiding making a name for yourself, are other means of avoiding the attentions of those who seek out a highly-reputed figure, and thus help to maintain your own humility and freedom from disturbance.[122] The upshot of these reservations about the value of praise is that praise should probably be considered only as a second-best. It may be better to praise your neighbour than to insult

[116] Poemen 105.

[117] Or 10 (= N 300); cf. John Kolobos S 2 (Guy, *Recherches*, 23). According to Eth. Coll. 13.10, reputation among human beings is of no value compared with reputation before God.

[118] N 498 (Evergetinos, 2.2.6.2); cf. N 336: those who bless monks cause damage to the soul, and Eth. Coll. 13.34: 'to please men is to slay men' (cf. 13.36, 99). Evagrius, *On Prayer*, 41, also warns against seeking praise.

[119] James 2.

[120] Macarius 1, a remarkable story about accepting blame and avoiding praise. The evasion practised by Moses (8) and Simon (1, 2) in order to avoid meeting lay visitors also implies unwillingness to accept praise, as does the behaviour of an old man in N 61 when about to be greeted by some seculars (cf. Ammonas 9). Daniel 3, Longinus 3, and Sisoes 18 imply similar reasons for reluctance, though not complete refusal, to associate with laity. In Poemen 3 he refuses to speak to some visiting priests, perhaps for the same reason, although the reason given in the text is simply, 'I have nothing to do with it, for I have died, and a dead man does not speak.' Cf. Ch. 5, nn. 84–5.

[121] Poemen 55.

[122] Motius 1. Arsenius 16 probably implies a similar attitude: the brothers do not share with him some figs which they have been given, because they do not want to insult him. When he discovers that he has been missed out, he complains about their actions, and they are edified by his humility. Arsenius avoids appearing different from the rest on other occasions too: by pretending that a vision he has had was experienced by someone else (33—the vision concerns humility); and by making his disciples sit with him during a night of temptation, in order to humiliate himself (43).

or harm him, but in the view of Pambo, quoted by Poemen, 'It is better to be silent.'[123] A monk should realize that *anything* likely to harm his brother should be avoided.

One of the most interesting sayings dealing with praise goes beyond this fairly simple message, and by extending some consideration to the effects of a monk's actions on others, reaches a somewhat more balanced conclusion. It is therefore worth quoting in full:

Abba Abraham the Iberian asked Abba Theodore of Eleutheropolis, 'What is good, father, to obtain glory for myself or dishonour?' The old man said, 'I prefer to obtain glory than dishonour, for if I do a good work and am glorified, I can condemn my thoughts because I am not worthy of this glory. But dishonour is the result of foul deeds. How can I reassure my heart, if people are offended because of me?' Abba Abraham said, 'You have spoken well, father.'[124]

The way of seeking dishonour and avoiding praise may, by bringing with it allegations (true or false) of 'foul deeds' against the monk concerned, be a source of scandal or discouragement to others.[125] Resistance to the temptation of pride, Theodore concludes, should not be based on doing nothing to obtain glory, but on an inner struggle to 'condemn my thoughts'. This is a monk's own affair and does not rebound destructively on his relationships with others. What right has a monk to be at peace with himself through being humble, if others are shocked because of him or tempted to take up attitudes of criticism or rebuke?

The inner struggle is to render yourself entirely indifferent to praise and insult. With this achievement, Macarius comments, together with regarding poverty and riches as indifferent, 'You will not die.'[126] Another saying speaks of the inner struggle to treat equally well someone whom a monk knows to love him, and another whom he knows to hate him.[127]

[123] Poemen 47.

[124] Theodore of Eleutheropolis 1. The concluding comment suggests an awareness that the teaching was unusual, even controversial, but recognized in this case as the product of *διάκρισις*.

[125] N 316, 'I prefer a defeat with humility to a victory with pride,' possibly expresses the attitude which Theodore is criticizing as potentially bad for a monk's relationship with others; cf. N 328, where a brother in a cenobium accuses himself of many sins, and the others start murmuring against him (that is, his behaviour provokes them into behaving in a way they ought not to); here however his action is commended by his abba. Cf. above, n. 64.

[126] Macarius 20; cf. N 518 (Evergetinos, 3.29.3.4; Eth. Coll. 13.29) and Eth. Coll. 14.64.

[127] Abraham 1. On avoiding favouritism, see N 105: 'I warred for twenty years against one thought, in order to see all men as one,' and Poemen S 19 (Guy, *Recherches*, 31).

It is in describing the attainment of this degree of indifference that the 'metaphor of death' once again comes into its own. A brother asked Macarius to 'Speak a word to me; how may I be saved?'[128]

The old man said to him, 'Go to the cemetery, and abuse the dead.' So he went and abused them and threw stones at them. Then he came and told the old man, and he said to him, 'Did they say anything to you?' He said, 'No'. The old man said to him, 'Go tomorrow, and glorify them.' So the brother went and glorified them, calling them apostles, saints and righteous men ... The old man said to him, 'You see how much you dishonoured them, and they answered you nothing, and how much you glorified them, and they said nothing to you. You too, if you wish to be saved, must become dead. Consider neither the evils of men, nor their glory, like the dead. Then you can be saved.'

But it is in another story, concerning Poemen and his brothers, that the full significance of the cultivation of this indifference emerges for the proper conduct of relationships. The text concerns the flight of Poemen, Anoub, and their five brothers from Scetis after the first devastation by the Mazices and their temporary settlement in an abandoned pagan temple at Terenuthis.[129] 'Be charitable', Anoub said to Poemen, 'and let us each remain alone [ἡσυχάσει], and not meet with one another for a week.' They did this, and every day for the week Anoub went out and threw stones at a statue, and in the evening went out and apologized to it. At the end of the week Poemen asked him why he had acted in this way, and Anoub explained, like Macarius speaking of the dead, that the idol's failure to speak or be angry taught an important message:

We are seven brothers. If you want us to remain together, let us be like this idol, which is not disturbed, whether it is insulted or glorified. If you do not want to live in this way, see, there are four doors in this temple; each can go where he wants.

A time of disturbance such as that occasioned by the devastation might well be an appropriate time to think about the future, about whether it was possible for a group to remain together, and if so how its members should set about trying to live with one another in community. The story shows that, negative as it may seem in itself, teaching about being unresponsive to praise and insult alike did help to serve the vital purpose

[128] Macarius 23.

[129] Anoub 1 (Isaiah, *Logos* 6, 2). My discussion is based on the Isaiah text. The message of the story in summarized in Poemen S 11 (Guy, *Recherches*, 30). The first barbarian devastation is usually dated to AD 407—for references, see Ch. 1, n. 34.

of permitting and encouraging monks to live with one another in peace and love.[130]

6. Conclusion

The purpose of this chapter has been to show the extent of the Desert Fathers' concern with a group of related problems—anger, slander, judgement, and praise—which were dealt with with consistent and severe attitudes of rejection. The most detailed summary of the stance towards personal relationships advocated by the Desert Fathers is a saying of Moses which is certainly, as it stands, a composite of different sayings and fragments. After exhortations to seeking the help of God in time of temptation, to humility, weeping, and non-resistance to evil, and to concentration on your own sin rather than on the faults of others, it continues with the following observations:

> To die to your neighbour is to bear your own sins and not to worry about anyone, whether this one is good and that one is bad. Do not do evil to anyone, nor think evil against anyone in your heart. Do not despise anyone who does evil. Do not trust the one who does evil to his neighbour, nor rejoice with the one who does evil to his neighbour. Do not slander anyone, but say, 'God knows each one.' Do not agree with the slanderer, nor rejoice in his slander; do not hate someone who slanders his neighbour. This is not to judge. Do not be at enmity with anyone, or hold enmity in your heart. Do not hate someone who is at enmity with his neighbour. This is peace.[131]

Perhaps there still remains the problem of whether the attitude of the Desert Fathers was not fundamentally a negative one—a prescription (motivated by a desire to preserve a personal inner stillness) for avoiding problems, not an active quest for good relationships. There is no doubt that as a matter of fact relationships could be bad, and that many sayings

[130] The story concludes with some reflections of Poemen on the practice of living together and on the attainment of peace. D. Sutherland, 'Impassibility, Asceticism and the Vision of God', *Scottish Bulletin of Evangelical Theology*, 5 (1987), 203–4, comments on Anoub 1 that 'We may smile at this cultivation of the Stoic spirit'. But he considers the text exclusively as a witness to a defective understanding of the spiritual life as a quest for impassibility (encouraged by the doctrine of divine impassibility which he wishes to criticize) and fails to consider its importance as a pointer to the Desert Fathers' understanding of relationships. For being like a stone in the face of evil, see also Ammonas 8 (Ch. 3, pp. 90–1). This saying too is positive in outlook; being like a stone turns out to involve compassion and generosity in the face of sin.

[131] Moses 18.

do adopt a defensive posture advocating non-involvement in various ways.[132] But these do not imply that avoidance and defensiveness were the ideal. Similarly, sayings about the distracting effects of judgement on the quest for *hesychia* and rest clearly do not imply that all relationships should therefore be avoided, but presuppose that good relationships *are* possible.[133] Still more, stories such as that of Poemen, Anoub, and their brothers show that the Desert Fathers valued highly the relationships which make up community life.[134] These conclusions support those of the previous chapter on the importance of relationships; however serious the Desert Fathers thought the problems of anger and judgement were, they never, for the most part, lost sight of the fact that 'The foundation is your neighbour'.[135]

[132] See e.g. Arsenius 31, John Kolobos 25, Poemen 2, 173.

[133] See e.g., Agathon 18, Joseph of Panepho 2, Or 13, N 575 (above, p. 131 and n. 107); but the problem of *hesychia* as a motive for isolation, raised in Sect. 1 of this chapter, will need to be referred to again.

[134] Sayings such as Agathon 4, Poemen 4, and N 319 on the settlement of grievances should also be recalled here.

[135] John Kolobos 39.

5

Solitude and Interaction

1. Introduction: Solitary, Semi-Anchorite, and Cenobite

This chapter will examine the Desert Fathers' reactions to different situations in which they were, or felt themselves to be, forced to choose between the conduct of relationships and the practice of solitude. Their response to these situations may in some cases be seen as a further outcome of their views, already examined, on anger, judgement, and praise—in so far as anger and other problems of community life could not be avoided altogether, then community life has broken down, and solitude should be chosen. But other reasons for the choice of solitude will emerge in the course of discussion. There are three main questions to be considered: how the Desert Fathers viewed the formal opportunities for contacts with one another which were provided by the community's common meal or *agape* and by the practice of hospitality; what importance they attributed to the solitude of the monk's cell; and how they identified and reacted to those situations which seemed to require flight from others.

It should perhaps be noted that it is not the intention of this chapter to contrast a *strictly anchoritic* or solitary life with a *strictly cenobitic* or communal one. Comments have been made at various points on sayings which refer specifically to the behaviour appropriate to 'a cenobium', rather than to the anchoritic life familiar in Nitria and Scetis.[1] But in comparison with the total number of texts in the *Apophthegmata*, these sayings are rare, and sayings which explicitly contrast anchoritic and cenobitic ways of life are even rarer.[2] In my view this is no accident;

[1] Cf. Ch. 2, nn. 101, 135 (with reference to Isaac of Kellia 2), Ch. 4, nn. 90 (where some sayings were discussed which imply that an anchorite or recluse served as adviser to or critic of a cenobium and its head), 125, 127 (Poemen S 19). Cf. sayings to be referred to or discussed in this chapter: Joseph of Panepho 8, Poemen 152, Paphnutius 5, N 62, 201, 284.

[2] N 70, 461 (Evergetinos, 4.5.2.36–8) compare the lives of the head of a cenobium

the *Apophthegmata* are not intended to propagandize in favour of one particular form of monastic organization: they represent a pattern of life which was very varied, in which monks could live alone or in small groups, in permanent or in changing patterns of relationships; in which no doubt the options of complete solitude and permanent, ordered community, though they were known, were rarer than a wide range of intermediate possibilities.[3] To discuss 'solitude and interaction' is not therefore to discuss 'anchoritism and cenobitism', but to examine the varied practice of a semi-anchoritic community whose organization allowed monks the possibility of choosing between several different patterns of life, and therefore forced them to assess the relative value of different amounts of contact with and avoidance of their neighbours. In the light of this, we shall need to ask whether the choice between solitude and interaction is as real as it seems. Could the two lives, in fact, be combined?

Before proceeding with this discussion, a comment on John Cassian's understanding of the monastic life may help to illustrate and clarify the statements of the last paragraph. Cassian certainly believed in principle that the lives of the hermit and the cenobite were clearly distinct from one another.[4] The life of a hermit is superior to that of a cenobite, in that it allows him the possibility of contemplation and union with Christ, and it can be undertaken only after training in a cenobium.[5] The distinctive virtue of the cenobite, by contrast, is the freedom from care which dependence on the community for his food and work enables him to attain.[6] Yet despite this contrast, Cassian's attitude to the solitary life is not especially positive. He refers to the worries about work and food which it entails, to the problems of entertaining and speaking to visitors, to the danger of pride, and to the ascetic laxity of many current

and an anchorite—in the first case refusing to judge between the value of the two ways of life.

[3] *HL*, 7.2, refers to living singly or in pairs or small groups. For the flexibility of living patterns in the context of the teaching relationship, see Ch. 2, n. 39. The awareness that Pachomian monasticism was more strictly cenobitic than that of the *Apophthegmata* (cf. Ch. 1, nn. 55–7) does not mean that variety was not recognized *within* the Sayings. P. Rousseau, 'Christian Asceticism and the Early Monks', in I. Hazlett (ed.), *Early Christianity: Origins and Evolution to A.D. 600. In Honour of W. H. C. Frend* (London, 1991), 117, 119, 122, asserts the propagandist (and therefore unreliable) character of early sources when they claim to give accounts of different forms of monastic organization; but it would not be correct to apply this to the *Apophthegmata*.

[4] Cassian, *Conferences*, 14.4 (on the difference between a solitary and the ruler of a cenobium); 18.4–8 (on the different kinds of monks in general); 19.

[5] *Conferences*, 19.4, 8.

[6] Ibid. 8.

practitioners of the hermit life; and he portrays Abba John as returning to the cenobitic life after twenty years as a hermit, in the hope that if he loses something in purity of heart, he will at least gain in humility and freedom from care.[7]

More significantly, the distinction which Cassian draws between the hermit and the cenobite is not strictly maintained in his works. Each kind of life is only a partial perfection, Abba John tells Cassian, and a few have attained perfection in both ways. But perfection is not found in alternating between complete solitude and the life of a community (in the way that John had done) and attaining perfection in each successively, but in combining a search for austerity and loneliness in the desert with free, gracious, and uncomplaining acceptance of disturbance, and of the responsibilities of teaching and entertaining others.[8] In other words, when Cassian comes to describe perfection he drops his reference to the cenobitic life, in the strict sense, altogether, and concentrates on the ability of the good anchorite to live a life of openness to and freedom from irritation against visitors.[9] In doing so he conforms more closely to what has been asserted to be the generally accepted pattern of monastic organization in accord with which different ways of life are evaluated in the *Apophthegmata*—a semi-anchoritic pattern in which exactly how much and what kind of contact with others is desirable is a significant subject of discussion. But even this concession to the reality of life in the Egyptian desert fails to allow for the variety of attitudes which, we shall see, are characterisitic of the *Apophthegmata*—perhaps because Cassian's attitude is that of a systematizer and a legislator, rather than that of a faithful recorder of the desert tradition.

[7] Ibid. 5–6. Cassian's thought undoubtedly underwent some change, perhaps to a point where he ceased to see contemplation as the exclusive property of the hermit: see P. Rousseau, 'Cassian, Contemplation and the Cenobitic Life', *Journal of Ecclesiastical History*, 26 (1975), 113–26; and R. A. Markus, *The End of Ancient Christianity* (Cambridge, 1990), 181–93.

[8] *Conferences*, 19.9.

[9] It is the mark of a bad anchorite, by contrast, to dislike human contact and get angry with visitors (10); the rest of *Conferences*, 19, is about the means of overcoming these faults.

2. Interaction: Problem and Necessity. The *Agape* and Hospitality

The monastic life of the Desert Fathers offered a formal occasion for contact with others in the institution of the communal meal, the *agape*, of Scetis and other monastic communities, to which the Sayings contain many references.[10] Many of these texts address, implicitly or explicitly, the question of whether or not it is right to attend the *agape*, and so raise the problem of 'solitude and interaction', in the precise form of whether and how it is right to share in the communal meal.

A brother once asked Sisoes what he should do, for when he went to the church an *agape* often took place, 'and they detain me'.[11] Sisoes began to answer, saying, 'It is a difficult business', but his disciple Abraham distracted him from the question of principle, whether the brother should stay or not, by asking him whether three cups of wine is a lot to drink at a meeting on the Sabbath or the Lord's Day. 'If Satan did not exist,' Sisoes replied, 'it would not be a lot.'[12]

'It is a difficult business.' What Sisoes would have gone on to say in explanation of this answer is not clear, but his words show that in the eyes of some the *agape* could be a problem, an occasion of unwanted contact rather than a welcome opportunity for fellowship. Why might these contacts be rejected or be regarded as problematic? One important reservation, certainly, is not strictly connected with attitudes to other people at all, but arises from fear of breaking an ascetic regime. This is evidently the case in several instances in which a monk refuses to attend a meal or imposes conditions on himself and others before he will do so. It was the practice of a brother, we are told, to fast even during Easter week; so when a gathering for a feast took place in church he fled in order to avoid eating there and ate only a few beetroots in

[10] For evidence about the conduct of the *agape*—what was eaten, where, when, etc., see C. Donahue, 'The Ἀγάπη of the Hermits of Scete', *Studia Monastica*, 1 (1959), 97–114; also Regnault, *La Vie quotidienne*, 177–88.

[11] Sisoes 2.

[12] That the two questions were originally attached, though not certain, does not seem unlikely. For other references to the third cup as a limit, see Sisoes 8 and Xoius 1, the second half of which is closely parallel to the question about wine in Sisoes 2. It, rather than Sisoes 2, may of course retain the original context. The first half of Xoius 1 (on food) occurs separately in Abraham 2. Chitty, *The Desert a City*, 44 n. 129, suggests that Xoius and Sisoes are the same person and gives other instances of comments on wine. That monks who drank wine at all could sometimes be criticized is implied by Xanthias 1. For rejection of wine, see Poemen 19, Peter the Pionite 1, N 144, 157.

his cell.[13] Macarius' practice was to accept wine from the brothers when he was eating with them, but to deny himself water for a day for every cup of wine he drank.[14] This situation persisted until his disciple told the brothers to stop offering him wine: 'For the Lord's sake, do not give it to him, or he will kill himself in his cell.' Macarius' approach is certainly strictly ascetic, but it does not imply that he was at all reserved about the value of meeting with the brothers. On another occasion he was asked to explain why he conducted himself so freely with everyone, and replied that he had served the Lord for twelve years to receive this gift (*χάρισμα*).[15]

A particularly striking example of fear of breaking an ascetic regime concerns Isidore, who when invited to a meal replied that 'Adam was deceived by food, and forced to dwell outside paradise', and who was accustomed to warn against wine by reminding his hearers of the temptation into which Lot fell.[16] This is probably an unusually negative view; Macarius and Antony are more appreciative of the needs of others, and as we saw when discussing discernment in Chapter 2, value could be ascribed to adjusting one's own ascetic regime in order to fit in with the practices of others.[17]

Sisoes again—or perhaps, actually, a different Sisoes—exemplifies an approach of this kind to the problem, one which indicates that for him too the main problem about meals was not a problem of relationships but of personal asceticism. He was invited by the brothers to share in the Easter feast.[18] There is certainly no problem here with the attitude of the brothers concerned—they approach him with due deference

[13] N 160.

[14] Macarius 10.

[15] Macarius 9. His attitude should be compared with that of Antony. In *VA*, 45, he is portrayed as being ashamed to be seen eating, and as maintaining that the minimum possible time should be devoted to the needs of the body. Yet he is willing to eat with the brothers, because they benefit from his words. Cf. Antony 13, where he explains the necessity of relaxing strict asceticism in the interests of the brothers. In N 155 some old men are encouraged to relax their asceticism for a day and eat more 'for the Lord's sake'.

[16] Isidore the Priest 1. By contrast Poemen 17 shows him attending a meal even against his will in order to avoid grieving a brother who has invited him. Arsenius 19 illustrates a much more positive attitude to food in general.

[17] See above, p. 47. In N 148 a brother in Kellia is accused of vainglory when he makes a show of refusing to drink wine with others. Here however an abba tells his accusers to leave him alone and commends his action.

[18] Sisoes 52. Like 32, 35 (cf. Ch. 2, n. 145), and 37, this story concerns 'Sisoes the Theban', who is probably to be distinguished from the Sisoes of Petra (cf. Eth. Coll. 13.73) whose disciple was Abraham, the subject of the majority of the sayings, whose attitudes have been discussed at several points.

(*μετάνοια*) when asking him to come. But, it is stated, 'He used not to eat bread,' and this practice is the basis of his insistence that 'Either I will share in bread, or in all the dishes which you have prepared'. The brothers reply that he should eat only bread, and he agrees to this. His conundrum is presumably meant to illustrate that whatever he does, it will be a breach of his regime; but, perhaps because of the special importance of Easter, he is willing to consent to this.

A different kind of problem surfaces in a story of John:

> The fathers used to say that once when the brothers were eating at the *agape* a brother laughed at the table. When Abba John saw him he wept, saying, 'What has this brother got in his heart, that he should laugh, when he ought rather to weep, because he is eating the *agape*?'[19]

There could be more than one reason for this attitude. John evidently believes that the *agape* should be eaten in a mood of penitence, perhaps agreeing with other comments on the inappropriateness of laughter in the monastic life.[20] But in addition, his comment suggests a more specific doubt about the value of the *agape*; perhaps he disliked the dependence on others for food which participation in the meal suggested, or regarded the practice as a misuse of resources which ought to be used for other purposes, so that the end of the saying should be translated, 'because he is eating charity'. There is no direct, but some indirect, support for this view; others would no doubt reject it.[21]

Others, for various reasons, put forward different views of the meal. Agathon, as we saw in Chapter 3, never involved himself in the practice of the *agape*.[22] Bessarion, the priests at Scetis knew, would not come to the church if summoned to fulfil some special task or obligation, so they were forced to wait until he came at his normal time, and then to resort to a ruse to get him to exorcize a demon.[23] The desire to avoid

[19] John Kolobos 9.

[20] N 54, 139.

[21] Poemen 33 perhaps supports John's view. If a brother gives some money he has to the church, 'They will make feasts with it': This is clearly pejorative. But Arsenius 16 suggests (again indirectly) that he would take a different view, for he wishes to share in whatever is given to the monks as a group. For other sayings on money or other gifts being given 'to the church' for the use of the brothers, see Achillas 2, Benjamin 1, John Kolobos 1, N 259. The *agape* was eaten in the community church of each monastery (see Peter the Pionite 3 which also gives some details of seating arrangements); hence the assumption that Poemen 33 refers to a monastic church, not to an ordinary village. Cf. Donahue, 'The Ἀγάπη of the Hermits of Scete', 102–5, 109.

[22] Agathon 17 (Ch. 3, p. 94).

[23] Bessarion 5; cf. Sisoes 18.

praise probably explains his behaviour. Motius included the *agape* and the *synaxis* among the things in which a monk should normally participate with the others, if he was to maintain his humility and his anonymity.[24] An anonymous story, more positive and explicit about the importance of the common meal in the monastic life than any of the other sayings noted so far, comments that 'These three things are honourable among the monks, which we must approach with fear, trembling, and spiritual joy: communion in the holy mysteries, the table of the brothers, and the washing of feet'.[25] And the text goes on to comment on the different attitudes with which the brothers approach the meal, some praying continually with the fear and trembling which are recommended, others thanking God for his gifts, still others complaining about what they are given. The communal meal could be, on other occasions, the forum in which virtue was recognized and applauded.[26]

Of the sayings which have been discussed which are in some way negative about the *agape*, none rejects it for reasons which are clearly anti-social, rejecting in principle contact or fellowship with others. Agathon's attitude is, above all, highly positive in his approach to the value of relationships—even if in being positive in his own way, he rejects the formal occasion for contacts provided by the community. Is the *agape* ever rejected through fear of contacts with others? Three sayings need to be noted as possible instances: two of these have been quoted in Chapter 4 and though one of them suggests that the danger of sins of the tongue was responsible for Macarius' caution, neither is particularly revealing.[27] The third relevant story supplies a far more precise explanation of similar behaviour and sheds light not only on attitudes to the *agape*, but also on the interrelation between the conduct of relationships and a monk's attainment of *hesychia* and prayer. Discussion of this important text is therefore postponed to the final chapter, when the possibility that the pursuit of *hesychia* and rest is a force making for conflict with the acceptance of community-life will be reconsidered.[28]

John Cassian, as was noted above, regarded hospitality as a burden

[24] Motius 1.

[25] N 85. Sisoes 20 also implies a high regard for the *agape*, since it is implied that abstention from it was involved in doing penance for a sin. Eth. Coll. 13.7 however implies a penance which excludes all contacts with others *except* the communal meetings.

[26] John Kolobos 7, Poemen 55. In the latter case, however, the problem of praise is posed by open recognition of someone's virtue.

[27] Macarius 16, Sisoes 37 (Ch. 4, n. 10).

[28] Isaac the Theban 2 (Ch. 6, pp. 172–3, and Ch. 4, nn. 8, 12).

which the hermit may bear well or badly, depending on his success in adjusting to the contacts with others which even the hermit life involves. Yet in other passages he speaks positively of the duty of hospitality. A monk should always break his fast in order to entertain visitors.[29] Fasting is good, but it is a matter of free will, whereas 'the requirements of the commandment demand the fulfilment of a work of charity'. When a monk receives another he receives Christ in him, and 'the children of the bridegroom cannot fast while the bridegroom is with them'. If he wishes, he will make up his fast later on.[30]

These teachings of Cassian are quoted in the *Apophthegmata* and form a suitable prologue to a discussion of the Desert Fathers' approach to the problem of hospitality—of how and when a monk should break his own fast in order to entertain a visitor in his cell.[31] Their views on this question are related to those we have already discussed on the subject of the *agape*, in that the effect of fellowship with others on a monk's ascetic regime is considered an important issue. It hardly matters whether sayings such as Macarius 10 and Poemen 17 are referred to the communal meal or to private acts of hospitality. Some texts accordingly set out to show that it is possible for one monk to visit another without breaking his ascetic regime,[32] or that when two meet it is the spiritual fellowship which they enjoy, not eating together, which occupies their minds. Thus an old man visited another, who prepared some food for him. Before they ate it they decided to say a *synaxis*. 'And the one completed the whole Psalter, while the brother recited two major prophets by heart. And when it was early [the next day] the old man who had come withdrew, and the food was forgotten.'[33]

One of the most interesting and vivid stories about the problem of hospitality well illustrates the ascetic attitude typical, say, of Macarius, and the problems which a visitor might cause. It too concerns Sisoes.

[29] Cassian, *Institutions*, 5.23.

[30] Ibid. 24. Matt. 9: 15. Cassian suggests however that only private fasts are broken, not the public fasts of Wednesdays and Fridays, when presumably any visiting monk would be fasting himself.

[31] Cassian 1 (*Institutions*, 5.24), 3 (ibid. 26). For a discussion of the practical aspects of hospitality—the length of visits, prayer together, etc.—in the *Apophthegmata*, see Regnault, *La Vie quotidienne*, 153–63; and (including other monastic writings too) D. Gorce, 'Die Gastfreundlichkeit der altchristlichen Einsiedler und Mönche', *JAC* 15 (1972), 66–91.

[32] Sisoes 32, in which Sisoes the Theban decides to visit an old man who is ill but not to allow the brothers there to make him eat, since he is fasting that day.

[33] N 150; cf. 149.

Abba Adelphius, bishop of Nilopolis, came to visit Abba Sisoes on the mountain of Abba Antony. When they were about to leave, early in the morning, he made them eat something, though it was a fast-day. As they were setting the table, some brothers knocked at the door. He said to his disciple, 'Give them a little gruel, for they will be tired.' Abba Adelphius said to him, 'Don't, in case they say that Abba Sisoes eats early in the morning.' The old man looked at him and then said, 'Go on, give them something.' When they saw the gruel they said, 'Have you visitors; is the old man eating with you?' The brother said to them, 'Yes'. They were troubled and said, 'May God forgive you for letting the old man eat now. Don't you know that he will labour for many days?' When the bishop heard them he made a prostration before the old man and said, 'Forgive me, Abba, because I was thinking humanly. But what you have done is of God.' Abba Sisoes said to him, 'If God does not glorify a man, the glory of men is nothing.'[34]

Sisoes is aware of the practical value of hospitality—the brothers who arrive early in the morning have presumably been travelling all night—and he is unwilling to conceal from them the fact that he has already broken the fast because of the bishop's visit; but the new visitors (who seem to know Sisoes well enough to be able to criticize his disciple for thoughtlessness) are quick to see that beneath the surface he is worried, and that his breaking of his fast now will (like Macarius' use of wine with the brothers) be followed by a more stringent asceticism later. The bishop finally realizes both that he has afflicted Sisoes by allowing him to break the fast, and that his attempt to conceal this fact was mistaken. Sisoes' final comment deflects Adelphius' unwanted praise and reinforces the determination which he once again displays not to give a false impression about his own way of life.[35]

There are other sayings about hospitality whose concern is simply to answer questions about how and when a fast should be broken in order to entertain others.[36] But several texts offer a more thoughtful assessment of hospitality, treating it not as a distraction to asceticism but as an important duty whose practice bears on a monk's conduct of relationships and on the way in which the solitary life should be lived.

Joseph was once asked whether it is right to 'consort and be familiar'

[34] Sisoes 15.

[35] Sisoes 16 and 21, of course, illustrate the same unwillingness.

[36] Matoes 6: he is questioned by a brother who is worried about breaking his fast when he has visitors, and explains that 'If you eat with the brother, you do well'. But if you eat alone, 'it is your own will'; Silvanus 1: even if a monk has eaten 'through love' (that is during a visit) he should not treat it as an excuse to drink (or, presumably, eat) again that day, if it would normally be a fast.

with visiting brothers.[37] He pre-empted their question by acting out a curious charade, in which he disappeared into his cell and came out again first dressed in rags and then in his proper clothes. Questioning them about what he had done, he extracted the answer that he had not been changed or harmed by wearing either set of clothes:

> The same should apply as regards receiving visiting brothers, according to the Holy Gospel. For it says, 'Render to Caesar what is Caesar's, and to God what is God's'. So when brothers come, we should receive them with familiarity. When we are alone, we need compunction to stay with us.

The point is that, as what someone is really like is not affected by what clothes he is wearing, so the inner life of a monk is not affected by living cheerfully with the brothers on some occasions, and with due penitence before God on others. We should not underestimate the significance of this conclusion. We have seen that John the Cenobite and even Macarius (whose attitude towards relationships is otherwise open) could regard awareness of sin and the practice of compunction as a reason for an occasional shirking of the conventions of community-life.[38] Joseph's approach to the possibility of combining a life of compunction with a life of community is an answer to their greater pessimism. The biblical text is taken to show that the hermit does not only owe to God a direct duty whose performance visitors impede. Even someone who is normally alone has a responsibility to others which is an equally important part of his life.

This responsibility involves treating visiting brothers as if in greeting them you were entertaining God himself,[39] and obedience (as Joseph saw) to the explicit command of God. The fact that hospitality is a form of relationship which, like all relationships, can be misconducted is not of course overlooked. Not only the host, but the visitor too must recognize that he has a duty he must be willing to break his fast in order to receive hospitality from someone whose special work (*ἐργασία*) is to give rest to others.[40] A hospitable monk's kindness can act as the agent of the conversion of a Manichee to orthodoxy,[41] but someone who practises hospitality may also become presumptuous and aggressive in his attitude—as when a monk sends a visitor away again during the

[37] Joseph of Panepho 1.
[38] John the Cenobite; Macarius 16, 27, 41 (Ch. 4, pp. 108–9, 111).
[39] See Apollo 3 for an explicit statement of this.
[40] N 285.
[41] N 289.

night because he will not join with him in the *synaxis* (the visitor is too tired).[42] A monk will not receive the reward of his labour, an old man tells him, if he behaves like this.

Others knew both how to behave better, and what the real value to them of hospitality was. A brother asked forgiveness from an old man (whom he was visiting) for interfering with his regime.[43] 'It is my rule', he replied, 'to give you rest and to send you away in peace.' Orientation towards others, even in the solitary life, is necessary. Another old man—an anchorite who lives near a cenobium and practises many virtues (*πολιτεῖαι πολλαί*)—is visited by some brothers.[44] They too apologize for troubling him, but he comments that 'It is trouble for me when I do my own will'. It is possible to think that the reference to a cenobium here is significant and designed to draw attention to the fact that even a solitary has the same need to overcome his own will as a cenobite or a brother who lives in subjection to his abba. His contacts with others may be limited, but he must exploit what occasions he has to learn humility and overcome any feelings of hostility towards others from which he suffers. Hospitality is an ideal means for doing this. In another story, an old man rejoices at being made to break his fast: 'A fast has its reward, but someone who eats for the sake of charity fulfils two commandments, because he renounces his own will and fulfils the commandment [of charity].'[45]

In this section (in the story of Sisoes and Adelphius, in the charade of Joseph, and in the description of the anchorite mentioned in the last paragraph) we have begun to see how a life of responsiveness to other members of the community *could* be combined with a life which emphasized the value of penitence, asceticism, and solitude as well. Sayings on hospitality (more so than those on the *agape*) give clear reasons for preferring interaction with others to the solitude which may be imposed by a personal ascetic regime. Hospitality too takes its place in an accepted pattern of relationships within the semi-anchoritic monastic community. That the commandment of God was the final, essential reason for offering hospitality is illustrated again by a story about Moses, who received some brothers and cooked for them during

[42] N 473 (unpublished; see *Les Sentences . . . série des anonymes*, 157–8).

[43] N 283.

[44] N 284.

[45] N 288. The proper spirit in which hospitality should be offerred is summed up by Poemen (74), commenting on John Kolobos: 'He offered [a visitor] the charity of which the Apostle speaks: "Charity suffers long, and is kind"' (1 Cor. 13: 4).

a week of fasting in Scetis.[46] The priests were informed, but instead of rebuking him when he came to the church on Sunday they commended him, 'knowing the great virtue of Abba Moses', and said publicly that he had disobeyed the commandment of men, but fulfilled that of God.[47]

3. Solitude: The Role of the Cell

When Macarius and Sisoes the Theban fled from the church they fled to their cells—to a solitude in which a monk could, if he wished, defend himself from harmful contacts with others. In this section we shall examine the Desert Fathers' teaching on the importance of the cell in the monastic life.

It is important to remember at the outset that 'to sit in the cell' in one respect defines the normal existence of a monk; in a semi-anchoritic community, most monks spend most of their time working, praying, eating, and sleeping alone in their cells. The fact that many sayings emphasize the importance of sitting in the cell as the essential practice of a monk does not in itself say anything, positive or negative, about the attitude of the Desert Fathers to the conduct of relationships. To sit in your cell is normal, but it is not the whole of life; teaching, the *agape*, visits, the practice of hospitality, and other occasions for meeting are an accepted part of the routine of disciple and abba alike. Only some sayings on the cell, which portray it as in some sense a refuge, as the goal of flight from relationships, are important for the question of solitude *versus* interaction.

'Go and sit in your cell, and your cell will teach you everything.'[48] Moses' famous saying lays down that the normal practice of sitting in the cell has an educative function essential to the monastic life. But sitting in your cell is itself not easy; it is something which has to be learnt, and which some people never achieve properly, something which

[46] Moses 5.

[47] The 'commandment' here probably refers to Rom. 12: 13 and 1 Pet. 4: 9. Moses' great virtue or way of life (πολιτεία) could refer to his free hospitality, or his strict ascetic regime which, the priests knew, would not be broken without good reason. The 'commandment' also figures in Paphnutius 2. Here he accepts a drink of wine from a brigand, even though he did not readily drink wine, because he 'knew he wanted to obey the commandment of God, and wished to gain him'. Here too conversion results from the monk's renunciation of his own will.

[48] Moses 6.

requires 'tools' or perhaps 'capacity' (σκεῦος) as a rather opaque saying attributed to John Kolobos has it.[49]

Sitting in your cell is educative precisely because it is difficult. The cell is a place of combat against thoughts;[50] a place of compunction;[51] a place of refuge for a monk who fears the temptations that beset him in his relations with others or his involvement in things of the world.[52] But it is also a place of encounter with God: 'The cell of a monk is the furnace of Babylon, where the three children found the Son of God; and the pillar of cloud, from which God spoke to Moses.'[53] Endurance of the temptation to leave his cell proves a monk's capacity in the face of hardship and temptation itself. However reasonable such a temptation seems to be, the Desert Fathers emphasized, to succumb to it is not the answer. Thus a brother asked Arsenius what to do. 'My thoughts trouble me, saying, "You cannot fast or work; at least visit the sick, for this is charity."'[54] But Arsenius 'recognized the suggestion of the demons' and told the brother to 'go and eat, drink, and sleep, and do not work. But do not leave your cell.' He knew, the text concludes, 'that endurance of the cell puts a monk in order'. Other sayings affirm the view implied here, that the answer to temptation will be found in the cell or it will not be found at all. One brother, tempted to the point of giving up the monastic life, was told to 'go and sit in your cell, and offer your body as a pledge to the walls of your cell, and do not come out. Let your thought think what it likes, but do not let your body out of your cell.'[55] Another old man, more reassuringly, explained that if a tempted brother stayed in his cell his thoughts would come back to him—that is he would gain control of them.[56] It is no answer to straying

[49] Poemen 96; John Kolobos S 4 (Guy, *Recherches*, 24).

[50] John Kolobos 12.

[51] Silvanus 2, and of course Macarius 27, 41, already mentioned more than once.

[52] Isidore the Priest 1, 7 (Ch. 2, n. 216).

[53] N 206. The cell could also be seen as the place where a monk has time to acquire the knowledge of God: *On Thoughts*, 1 (cf. 3 for the dangers of a monk being driven out of his cell by the demons); or remembers God: John Kolobos 27. Fear of eternal punishment or hope of reward should enable a monk to stay in his cell: N 196 (Eth. Coll. 13.51).

[54] Arsenius 11; cf. the anonymous parallel in N 195. Sarmatas 4 makes a related point about resisting the thought of visiting the brothers, and N 394 (unpublished, see *Les Sentences ... série des anonymes*, 131) tells a brother to test his desire to visit the brothers to see whether a visit would be profitable and suggests a method of overcoming the desire if it is not. Cf. Evagrius, *Praktikos*, 12, 28.

[55] N 205.

[56] N 198.

thoughts to follow them where they lead.[57]

'Order' (*τάξις*) in Arsenius' saying suggests a particular level of achievement in the monastic life;[58] in this case the 'level' is a mere basic ability to resist temptation by staying in the cell and not trying to do anything more ambitious either in charity or in asceticism.[59] 'Sit in your cell, and do what you can without disturbance,' an old man told a brother worried about his lack of discipline, 'I believe that if you sit in your cell in the name of God and guard your conscience, you too will be found in the place of Abba Antony.'[60]

Thomas Merton and Simon Tugwell are therefore probably right to state that the Sayings portray the cell as a place of confrontation, a place for a monk to battle against himself and his thoughts as an essential preliminary to further progress in the monastic life.[61] Sitting in your cell is not portrayed as a special achievement, something to be aspired to only by the most advanced. It is precisely because it is so ordinary that it is so important, that it offers such a stark illustration of what temptation is like and of the fact that it must be resisted.

A disciple must be taught, of course, how to live in his cell. There are indications that a disciple could be prepared for the time when he would be ready to live alone by a period of training in the immediate

[57] Cf. Theodora 7: a brother decides to move on after suffering a 'multitude of temptations'. 'As he was putting on his sandals, he saw someone else putting his sandals on too, who said to him, "Are you leaving because of me? Behold, I will go before you wherever you go."' Also N 200: 'If temptation comes upon you in the place where you live, do not leave the place at the time of temptation, or wherever you go you will find what you fled.'

[58] Cf. N 168, 208 and Poemen 167: 'A man who guards his *τάξις* will not be troubled.'

[59] In the anonymous parallel the story continues with an account of how the brother struggles against hunger by working at his palm leaves, reading, and saying psalms, until he achieves his *τάξις* and defeats his thoughts. The continuation accords ill with Arsenius' approach, which was precisely not to suggest that the brother should undertake a particular ascetic discipline ('do not work' is excised from the anonymous text to avoid a clear contradiction). Cf. Paphnutius 5: 'Why sit here fruitlessly,' a brother asks himself, 'go to a cenobium, and bear fruit there.' Paphnutius tells him to sit in his cell: 'Say one prayer early, and one in the evening, and one at night. When you are hungry, eat; when you are thirsty, drink; when you are tired, sleep. Remain in the desert, and do not trust your thought.' Unconvinced, the brother asks someone else, who tells him to sit in his cell and not even to pray, and a third (Arsenius), who simply affirms what the others have said.

[60] N 202; see also Biare.

[61] Merton, 'The Spiritual Father', 281–3; also 'The Cell', in *Contemplation in a World of Action*, 252–9; Tugwell, *Ways of Imperfection*, 16 (referring to Paphnutius 5): 'Before you can truly pray, let alone achieve any more refined feats of spirituality or service, you have first of all got to make sure that you are really there. And the discipline of simply staying in your cell is intended to bring you face to face with yourself and with your real needs and capacities.'

company of an abba. A brother lived for many years with an abba, Heracleius said, before expressing a desire to live alone.[62] Antony, according to the *Lausiac History*, taught Paul to work and pray as a monk for several months before building him a separate cell, then left him with the significant comment, 'See, you have become a monk, stay here alone and gain experience of the demons.'[63] But it would be wrong to imagine that this form of training, and this progression from living with others to living alone, was an invariable norm. Many disciples no doubt spent long periods alone right from the beginning of their monastic careers. What was important was that they should not consider themselves independent of guidance.[64] Even when a brother left his abba to live alone, he would quite naturally remain under his supervision. The disciple in the story told by Heracleius is to return to his abba's cell on Saturdays, and in fact comes back early, unable to endure the temptations and the routine of life alone. He requires further instruction before returning to his cell.

These stories, both of which comment on the long distance of the disciple's new cell from that of his abba, do suggest a search for a deeper and more intense solitude than is necessarily implied by comments on the 'normal' practice of sitting in the cell.[65] Similarly, sayings of Antony and Sisoes indicate that a change of place, or the establishment of cells in a new area, took place in response to the desire for stillness (*ἡσυχάζειν*, *τὰ ἡσυχάζοντα*) when Nitria and Scetis were becoming crowded.[66] It is obvious that monastic settlements must have been formed and expanded in area in this way. Some sayings do even describe monks who have chosen, perhaps in response to the temptation of fornication, or in penitence for apostasy, a solitude so intense that their way of life becomes known to others only when a visitor is brought by divine

[62] Heracleius.

[63] *HL*, 22.9. See K. Ware, '"Separated from all and United to all": The Hermit Life in the Christian East', in A. M. Allchin (ed.), *Solitude and Communion: Papers on the Hermit Life* (Oxford, 1977), 33.

[64] See again Ch. 2, n. 39.

[65] This is emphasized by Ware, '"Separated from all"', esp. 34, on the preparation of monks in Nitria in order to live as solitaries in Kellia.

[66] Antony 34, Sisoes 28. Another text to portray withdrawal to deeper solitude is PJ VII: 24, which is not extant in Greek (*Les Sentences . . . troisieme recueil*, 77) and which may not even be an original part of the PJ text (Chadwick, *Western Asceticism*, 88, 348). But it is a rich source of observations on the difficulty of the solitary life, the importance of preparation for it, and the severity of the demonic temptation to leave the cell which may exploit even something good in itself, such as the desire to attend the eucharist.

guidance into the distant desert to see them.[67] But with the exception of this small group of sayings, texts on the search for solitude in the cell are still a long way from Cassian's picture of a trained cenobite setting out to live as a perfect solitary.

At first sight, a saying of Abba Joseph suggests something rather closer to Cassian's ideas. A brother asked him whether he should leave a cenobium in order to live alone.[68] In Joseph's view, there is only one reason for preferring one kind of life to another, and he replies, 'Live where your soul has rest and suffers no harm.' But this response does not imply that the brother should become a solitary in order to improve his life, for the brother goes on to tell Joseph that he has rest whether he is with others or not, and Joseph then tells him that in that case he should do whatever brings him most profit. In deciding this question of whether someone should live alone or with others, other abbas expressed a variety of preferences and no doubt, of responses to individual needs. An old man could offer a tempted monk the general advice to 'sit in your cell, and God will give you relief'.[69] On the other hand, a saying of Theodore suggests that when a solitary is in trouble his first resort should be to seek company: 'Humble your thought, submit, and be with others.'[70] The expression of a preference for one kind of life in these cases is not, any more than is Joseph's view, a statement that either solitude or communion is superior to the other, and there is no implication of bias either for or against the value of relationships in these remarks—in contrast, at first sight, to some of the apparently more isolationist sayings which were discussed at the beginning of Chapter 4.[71]

Philip Rousseau has again put forward the thesis that the views of the Desert Fathers underwent a chronological development. 'The literal privacy of the desert', he comments, 'gave place to privacy more fragile and intense within the group' during the course of the fourth century,

[67] N 132A-D. 132A refers to flight from fornication; 132B to apostasy. N 62 illustrates the sort of problems which could occur when such a total recluse visited a cenobium. Mark the Egyptian tells of another total recluse—though in his cell, rather than in the far desert. A. G. Elliott, *Roads to Paradise: Reading the Lives of the Early Saints* (Hanover, NH, 1987), includes a literary analysis of texts like these.

[68] Joseph of Panepho 8.

[69] N 147.

[70] Theodore of Pherme 2.

[71] Arsenius 44 is another apparently less sociable text: he praises those who 'are hesychasts and meet no one'. But is the isolation of even such a figure complete? Arsenius continues that a hesychast is able to 'satisfy all', which implies a measure of interaction, whereas someone who mixes freely is not.

and the value of the cell as a private resort came to be increasingly emphasized.[72] His main support for this is a comparison between a passage in the *Life of Antony* and its parallel in the *Apophthegmata*.[73] In the *Life* Antony tells some seculars that 'As fish die if they spend time on land, so monks who linger with you and spend time with you are harmed. So, as fish must hurry to the sea, we must hurry to the mountain.' In the saying this is quoted in the form, 'so monks who linger outside their cells or spend time with seculars lose the intensity of their *hesychia*. So, as fish must hurry to the sea, we must hurry to our cells.' Rousseau comments, 'In other words, the *Apophthegmata* have harnessed the reputation of Antony to a new emphasis on staying in one's cell.'[74]

The difference is striking, but does it mark a change from a 'private' to a 'group' mentality? In fact Antony was never an advocate of 'literal privacy'. The remark in the *Life* is one of several in praise of solitude which frame the work's extended description of his ministry to both monks and lay people.[75] It is made clear that his fear of praise and his yearning for contemplation drove him to live free from company when possible and to regret the disturbance caused by questioners and petitioners. But solitude is not of overwhelming importance in the *Life*, and Antony never neglects the responsibilities of his ministry. He is seen preeminently as one preserved by providence to minister and teach,[76] and it should be clear that the relationships in which this ministry involves him are an integral and central element of his monastic life, not something which he would rather reject.[77] Antony is therefore committed both to solitude and to interaction, not to an earlier, more isolated, form of monastic life which was superseded when numbers grew, wandering in the desert became less common, and communities

[72] Rousseau, *Ascetics, Authority, and the Church*, 45.

[73] *VA*, 85; Antony 10.

[74] Rousseau, *Ascetics, Authority, and the Church*, 45.

[75] *VA*, 49–50, 84–5. For an elaboration of these points about Antony, see Gould, 'Early Egyptian Monasticism and the Church', 3–4, and 'The *life of Antony* and the Origins of Christian Monasticism', 7–8.

[76] *VA*, 46.

[77] Cf. the introduction to *Athanasius: The Life of Antony and the Letter to Marcellinus*, trans. R. C. Gregg (New York, 1980), 9–10. I now feel that the statement that 'Antony remained at heart a lover of solitude'— G. E. Gould, 'Pachomios of Tabennesi and the Foundation of an Independent Monastic Community', in W. J. Sheils and D. Wood, (eds.) *Voluntary Religion* (SCH 23; Oxford, 1986), 19—does not adequately convey his attitude. But D. Baker, 'St. Antony and the Biblical Precedents for the Monastic Vocation', *Ampleforth Journal*, 76 (1971), 6–11, sees Antony as a much more solitary and less concerned figure.

became more stable.[78] The change in wording from the *Life* to the *Apophthegmata* may be due more to the removal of the saying from its specific context in the *Life* and its adjustment to apply to monks for whom 'the mountain' did not have the precise meaning it had for Antony,[79] than to any change in the outlook of the communities over time.

It is difficult to find any other evidence to support Rousseau's interpretation. He tries to illustrate the earlier 'literal privacy' phase with sayings of Macarius and Alonius, but both of these texts are in fact profoundly concerned with *attitudes* to others, and neither presupposes a strictly physical isolation.[80] The saying of Alonius is in any case undatable and cannot be used in a chronological argument. Finally, it is not clear how the alleged chronological development is to be related to the evidence of the function of the cell in the monastic life which has been outlined in this section. The cell played an important role in the routine of the monastic life and in the growth of monks in endurance and wisdom; but as noted at the outset, it did not, except in a very few cases such as those of Macarius and Sisoes, function as a means of enforcing 'privacy' at all, either in an earlier or a later phase of monastic development.[81] If Antony himself was able to combine, in his mountain retreat, the lives of solitude and of interaction, then there is no reason

[78] Rousseau, *Ascetics, Authority, and the Church*, 43–9, and 'The Desert Fathers, Antony, and Pachomius', 124, argue for a development in these terms. In the latter work he uses Arsenius 21, 25, Agathon 6, 11, Nisterus 1, and Poemen 26 to suggest a period of group wandering and separation before stable communities were formed after 'painful debate'; cf. *Ascetics, Authority, and the Church*, 46, for a similar use of the saying Eulogius the Priest. These interpretations do not seem to be correct.

[79] The Inner Mountain in *VA* is Antony's more distant solitary retreat; the Outer Mountain the community where he associates more freely with others: G. E. Gould, 'Moving on and Staying Put in the *Apophthegmata Patrum*', *SP* 22 (Leuven, 1989), 231–2.

[80] Macarius 36, Alonius 1; Rousseau, *Ascetics, Authority, and the Church*, 47. He then claims that 'The inner awareness of a later generation was quite different' (ibid.), but immediately adds that 'even the *Life of Antony* heralds the change', which surely suggests that the 'later' view always existed. Another strange comment occurs on p. 46: 'By the end of the fourth century, therefore, it was no longer enough even to sit in one's cell.' To prove this Rousseau cites Poemen 168, representing it as saying that sitting in the cell is 'superficial'. In fact Poemen's answer to the question 'How to live in the cell' is divided into two parts, *τὸ φανερόν*—the external practice of manual labour, fasting, silence, and meditation—and 'making hidden progress in the cell', which includes blaming yourself wherever you are, and persisting in regular and hidden prayers. There is nothing to suggest doubt about the practice itself.

[81] In Poemen 168 the ultimate concern of a saying on how to sit in the cell is with the conduct of relationships: 'The end of these things is to keep good company and avoid bad.'

to see anything in the Desert Fathers' teaching on the cell as serving anti-social purposes. They do not deny that it is possible for some to seek less, others more solitude; but they do not endorse the strict dichotomy between the solitary and communal lives of Cassian (which as we have in any case seen, Cassian himself is unable to maintain). Nothing precludes the view that the solitude of the cell and interaction with others through the *agape*, hospitality, and the other opportunities which were available for the pursuit of good relationships, were two aspects of a single, varied pattern of semi-anchoritic life.

4. Solitude: The Causes of Flight

It has been noted on more than one occasion that temptations arising from bad relationships may require flight, either into the cell, or in general from the situation in which temptation occurs.[82] The reasons for flight of this kind may be illustrated from a number of widely differing stories. Visitors from outside the monastic life do seem to have been a problem, particularly because of the 'problem of praise',[83] but also for other reasons. Arsenius once dissuaded Archbishop Theophilus from visiting him by threatening to leave the place: 'If you come I will admit you, but if I admit you, I admit everyone, and I will no longer live here.'[84] He refused, that is, to offer the archbishop special favours; but he also saw the disturbance to his monastic regime which a succession of visitors would cause as unacceptable. The same combination of motives may be illustrated by a story about Poemen, who prayed not to be given the grace (*χάρις*) of successful intercession with a magistrate on behalf of an imprisoned man of his own village, 'Otherwise they will not let me live in this place.'[85]

Without doubt also, there were monks who fled because they were offended by the behaviour of those around them. But it is significant

[82] e.g. John Kolobos 5, 6, Isidore 7 (Ch. 4, n. 33); Poemen 2 (Ch. 4, n 110); Isidore the Priest 1, 7 (above, n. 52).

[83] See Ch. 4, n. 120.

[84] Arsenius 8. For his rejection of involvement with seculars, cf. 7, 23, 28 (where the themes are disturbance and sexual temptation).

[85] Poemen 9; cf. 5 and 7 for similar attitudes. In different ways, many sayings teach that contacts with (especially favouritism towards) a monk's relatives should be avoided: Poemen 33, 186, N 233, 250, 286, 367, 404 (Evergetinos, 1.15.4.3.), 513–4 (Evergetinos, 1.15.4.4–5), Eth. Coll. 14.32. For further discussion, cf. Gould, 'Lay Christians, Bishops, and Clergy', and 'Moving on and Staying Put', 237 n. 35 (for N 250 and 367).

that these stories almost always end with a recognition of the need for reconciliation and the restoration of community life to harmony. Arsenius again provides an example, leaving his disciples because of the problem of disturbance (but by them or by lay visitors?); here however his action seems to be portrayed as a mistake—a cause of distress to his discples who do not know the reason for his departure—and the story ends with his return.[86] On the other hand, it was a profound feeling of his own unworthiness rather than a desire to avoid disturbance which led Theodore to refuse to exercise his ministry as a deacon and to flee to 'many places'—being brought back on each occasion.[87] Finally, he persuaded the brothers to allow him to settle the question by asking God to make known to him whether or not he was worthy:

> And he prayed to God, saying, 'If it is your will that I should stand in my place [as a deacon], assure me.' And a pillar of fire was shown to him, reaching from earth to heaven, and a voice said, 'If you can be like this pillar, go and be a deacon.' When he heard this he decided never to accept it; so when he went into the church the brothers prostrated themselves before him and said, 'If you do not want to be a deacon, at least take the chalice.' But he did not take it, saying, 'If you do not leave me alone I will withdraw from this place.' So they left him alone.

Here relationships within the community are restored, but only on a somewhat insecure basis: perhaps some of the brothers remained doubtful of Theodore's judgement or unsettled by the threat of his permanent departure.[88]

A more unambiguously successful example of reconciliation after flight is found in a story of Abba Motius, who founded two monasteries; in the second, 'by the action of the devil, there was a brother who hated and troubled him'.[89] Motius left the place and shut himself up as a

[86] Arsenius 32; cf. Gould, 'Moving on and Staying put', 236.

[87] Theodore of Pherme 25.

[88] Cf. Isaac of Kellia 1, where however his initial rejection of ordination gives way before signs of divine approval: 'It is God's will, and wherever I flee, I meet that.' Unwillingness to exercise priesthood is illustrated by Matoes 9: 'I trust God, that I will not be harshly judged because of my ordination, since I have not made the offering. Ordination is for those without reproach.' This motive for refusing ordination should be taken seriously and not seen as a cover for more sinister reasons such as a rejection of the importance of the priesthood and sacraments for monks. For this view, see H. Chadwick, *Priscillian of Avila: The Occult and the Charismatic in the Early Church* (Oxford, 1976), 14: 'reluctance of some to accept the call of ordination, which they seek to avoid on the ground that they are unworthy; i.e. an ascetic renunciation which rejects the pastoral office of the priesthood as "secular"'.

[89] Motius 2.

recluse in his own village. Some time later, the old men from the monastery brought the brother to Motius to try to effect a reconciliation. 'When he heard the name of the brother who has grieved him, the old man seized a hatchet with joy and broke down the door, and came out and ran to where the brother was, and prostrated himself before him, then greeted him.' And after three days of rejoicing with them, 'which he was not accustomed to do,' he returned to the community with them, both parties apparently having set aside the original cause of the problem. Poemen too once decided, along with one of his brothers, to leave their dwelling in Scetis, because their youngest brother was troubling them. But the youngest ran after them and pleaded for them all to stay together. 'The old man saw his lack of malice, and said to his brother, "Let us return, brother, for he does not want to do these things. It is the devil who does them to him."' And so the crisis in their relationship was defused.[90]

Another, more complex, reason for moving in the face of problems in relationships—here without the motif of reconciliation—is supplied by Nicon. Like Macarius, he is falsely accused of being responsible for a pregnancy and does penance for a time before the true culprit is found.[91] When the mistake is discovered, everyone comes to ask his forgiveness. 'As for forgiveness', he replies, 'you are forgiven. As for staying here, I will not stay any longer, for no one had the discernment to have compassion for me.'

All of these sayings concern the fears of a monk who flees for his own spiritual well-being in the face of misunderstanding or mistreatment by others. But in other sayings, the motives for flight from bad relationships are explored from a different angle, and with interesting results for this chapter's consideration of the general problem of solitude *versus* interaction. 'What shall I do,' a brother asked Matoes, 'for my tongue troubles me; when I am among men I cannot control it, but I condemn them for every good work and rebuke them.'[92] This is the problem of judgement in a severe form; the brother realizes that what he is doing is wrong, but feels he cannot prevent it. 'If you cannot control yourself,' Matoes replied, 'flee into solitude, for this is weakness.'

[90] Poemen 180. For Poemen's sometimes difficult relations with his brothers, cf. Anoub 1 (Isaiah, *Logos* 6, 2), Poemen 2, 3, 22, 108, and 173 (which have been discussed at various points), and N 448 (Evergetinos, 2.6.2.2): this reports another near breakdown in relations. Cf. P. Rousseau, 'Blood-Relationships among Early Eastern Ascetics', *JTS* n.s. 23 (1972), 141–3.

[91] Nicon; Macarius 1.

[92] Matoes 13.

And he added, with reference to himself, that it is the weak who must live in solitude, and the strong who can commune with others.

This approach to the purpose of solitude is very different from that apparently implied by sayings such as Alonius 1, or even the more balanced remarks of Joseph, quoted in the last section. Matoes is the clearest exponent of the view that flight into solitude is a response to weakness, to awareness of your own sin, rather than a search for rest and *hesychia*. But others than Matoes do take the same kind of view. Certain practices which separate a monk from others, whether physically or simply by the barrier of silence, may be regarded not as virtues but as symptoms of a weakness which drives them away from others. 'If you have attained silence, do not hold that you have achieved a virtue but say, "I am unworthy even to speak."'[93] Poemen's approach is particularly interesting. A brother told him that he had found a place which gave him complete rest from the brothers (*πᾶσαν ἀνάπαυσιν τῶν ἀδελφῶν*). Should he live there?[94] Poemen replied by directing the questioner's thoughts away from his own advantage, to consideration of the effects of his behaviour on others: 'Wherever you will not harm your brother—stay there.' A monk's attitude to the question of solitude or interaction should not, that is, be determined by his ideas about what he himself needs. If an attitude to himself is involved it is not the desire for rest or *hesychia* but a fear of his inability to avoid harming others.[95] Awareness of one's own sin is illustrated by another relevant saying. A brother who lived in solitude told two others who had become depressed by their failure to 'fulfil the commandment' in their ministry to others that 'He who is among men does not see his own sins because of the disturbance; but when he is still [*ἡσυχάσῃ*], especially in the desert, then he sees his failings.'[96] This saying does not imply that to choose a life

[93] N 321. See also N 573 (Evergetinos, 1.45.1.79): an old man comments that someone who lives in solitude (*ἡσυχάζων*) should not think he has achieved something great, but that he has been chased away from the crowd like a vicious dog.

[94] Poemen 159.

[95] PJ 15.63 (unpublished in Greek; translated from Greek in *Les Sentences ... série des anonymes*, 107, between N 305 and 306, at which point it occurs in a manuscript used by Regnault) takes a view of the value of solitude related to Poemen 159: if someone cannot bring himself to do good to those who harm him he must 'Flee, and choose silence'. Poemen 152 comments on the difficulty of living in a cenobium. N 67 is also interesting: an old man visits a gardener in the city to discover what it is that makes the gardener pleasing to God. As they are about to eat, the old man hears some people singing in the street, and asks the gardener if he is disturbed by them. 'I am never disturbed nor scandalized', he replies, '[I think] that they are all going to the Kingdom.' Confessing himself unable to reach this level of achievement, the old man withdraws to the desert.

[96] N 134.

of serving others is wrong; far from it—it teaches that your attitude to yourself must be corrected first.[97]

The sayings which have been examined in this section show that motives for flight as a response to bad relationships were mixed; but there are few hints that the values of community are rejected. Solitude could be seen not as an end in itself, but as a mere refuge from problems which it would have been better to have been able to overcome by learning to live properly with others in the first place. This view is carried to even greater lengths by another, highly revealing, story:

A brother was a hesychast in a cenobium, and often became angry. So he said to himself, 'I will withdraw into solitude, and because I have nothing to do with anyone, my passion will cease.' So he went out, and lived in a cave alone. One day however, when he had filled his water jug and put it on the ground, it suddenly fell over. He picked it up and filled it again, and again it fell over. He filled it and put it down for a third time, and again it fell over. He was enraged and took the jug and broke it. When he came to himself he realized that he had been deceived by a demon, so he said, 'Since I have withdrawn into solitude and yet have been overcome, I will go back to the cenobium, for everywhere struggle, endurance and the help of God are necessary.' So he got up and returned to his place.[98]

In this saying, solitude is not even a refuge from the temptations which are responsible for bad relationships. The brother has not overcome his passion by leaving others; it has remained with him to make him the sport of the demons. Significantly, the message of the text is not that the brother needs to try again to defeat his passions on his own before he can return to his community. He is more realistic and recognizes that his solitary episode was merely a mistaken attempt to find rest from

[97] Other sayings of Poemen make the point that attitude to yourself is more important than circumstances: 81 ('If you make yourself cheap you will have rest, wherever you live'); 84 ('If you are silent you will have rest in whatever place you live'); 95 ('If someone blames himself, he will endure anywhere'); and 168, on how to live in the cell but also advocating 'considering your own censure of yourself everywhere you go'. Cf. N 416 (unpublished; see *Les Sentences ... série des anonymes*, 139).

[98] N 201; cf. Evagrius, *Praktikos*, 22: when we are angry, the demons tempt us to withdraw into solitude, leaving the problem unresolved. Merton, 'The Spiritual Father', 278, comments that 'Retirement into solitude is of no use if the hermit is to live alone with aggressive and hostile fantasies'. In PJ 9.8 (not in the alphabetical–anonymous series, but see Evergetinos, 3.13.7.7, for the Greek text) a brother is told that his inability to live properly in his cell will be overcome if he ceases to be hostile to others. Theodore of Pherme 14, indicating a similar approach, emphasizes the correct motives for seeking solitude: 'Someone who has learnt the sweetness of his cell does not flee his neighbour as if he despises him.'

the struggle to master his anger. Seeking the help of God, he goes back to renew this struggle in the context of the community of brothers to which he properly belongs.

5. Exile and Silence

Abba Longinus asked Abba Lucius about three thoughts saying, 'I wish to go into exile [*ξενιτεῦσαι*].'

The old man said to him, 'If you do not control your tongue you will not be an exile, wherever you go. Control your tongue here, and you will be an exile.' He said to him, 'I wish to fast.' The old man answered, 'Isaiah the prophet said, "If you bend your neck as in a halter and a collar it will not be an acceptable fast." Rather, control your evil thoughts.' He said to him the third time, 'I wish to flee men.' The old man answered, 'If you do not live rightly with men first, you cannot live rightly alone.'[99]

Like the story of the brother and the water jug, this exchange is one of the most revealing discussions in the *Apophthegmata* on the subject of solitude and interaction. A monk's ability to achieve what he wants, Lucius explains, is dependent not on where he goes (or on ascetic practices like fasting) but on his ability to control his tongue and his passions. This saying states generally what the story of the brother and the water jug only implies in a particular case—that the passions which arise in community cannot be cured alone; that learning to live properly with others is essential, even for those who wish to exercise their right to choose a life of greater solitude.[100]

The saying is notable for the use of the concept of *ξενιτεία*, exile, in Longinus' question. Lucius does not accept the view that 'exile' implies a departure or flight from community life: literal exile, the move to another place, is not what matters; control of the tongue is. There are sayings in the *Apophthegmata* which support the literal views of exile which Lucius rejects—sayings which view wandering without care,

[99] Longinus 1. Isa. 58: 5.

[100] Cf. Gould, 'Moving on and Staying Put', 234–5, for further discussion of the significance of these sayings. Ammonas 4 is a related text, though it does not display Lucius' concern with the implications of moving for relationships. The three thoughts in this text are, 'To wander in the desert', 'to go abroad where no one knows me', and 'to enclose myself in my cell, and meet no one'. Ammonas tells him to ignore the thoughts, to sit in his cell, follow a moderate ascetic regime and 'hold the word of the publican always in your heart' (Luke 18:13).

freedom from attachment to one community or one place, as an ideal.[101] But on the other hand Lucius' idea of the meaning of exile is supported by several shorter texts. 'Exile', said Tithoes, 'is for a man to keep his mouth shut.'[102] Abba Isaiah too had heard an explanation of the meaning of exile, handed down to him by someone who asked Sisoes about it:

One of us asked him, 'What is exile, father?' He said, 'Be silent and in every situation say, "Who am I?" Wherever you dwell, do not get involved with anyone in any matter. This is exile.'[103]

A monk should consider himself and realize the importance of not mixing himself up in anything—dispute, judgement, and all of the things which make for bad relationships—which is not his business. This is in accord with Lucius' and Tithoes' view that an exile will cease to be so if he fails to control the use of his tongue.[104] For Poemen too being a stranger means being silent, and especially avoiding arrogant presumption about the value of your own words:

A brother asked Abba Poemen, 'How ought I to live in the place where I dwell?' The old man said to him, 'Have the mind of a stranger [*παροίκου*] in the place where you dwell, so as not to desire to parade your wisdom before you, and you will have rest.'[105]

What these few, but significant, sayings are, in effect, doing is mapping out a path by which such apparently isolationist, anti-communal ideas as 'exile' and 'silence' may be tranformed into essentially social, relational

[101] Bessarion 1, 12, Daniel 5, James 1, N 250, Eth. Coll. 13.4. The contrast between these and Lucius' view prompts Rousseau, *Ascetics, Authority, and the Church*, 43–4, 48–9, to argue that wandering was a phenomenon of the early years of desert monasticism, overtaken in time by an increasing emphasis on stability. Yet again, I do not think these arguments for a chronological development in the Desert Fathers' views are correct: 'Moving on and Staying Put', 237, esp. n. 35.

[102] Tithoes 2. Exile and silence are also linked by Andrew: 'These three things are proper to a monk: exile, poverty, and silent endurance'; also GSC 21.57 (*Les Sentences ... troisième recueil*, 108; also Pa 32.5, 1051C).

[103] Isaiah, *Logos* 6, 6Bb. Cf. Eth. Coll. 13.54.

[104] Arsenius 12 also advocates that an exile (in the straightforward sense of someone 'in a foreign land') should 'get involved in nothing, and he will have rest'. N 306 discusses the proper 'work of exile'. An exile, the old man says, leaves when he is driven away and comes back when he is called. In Joseph of Panepho 1 *ξενιζόμενοι* means simply 'travellers, visitors'.

[105] Poemen S 4 (Guy, *Recherches*, 30). Bessarion 10 also says that the way to live with others is to 'Be silent, and do not assess yourself.' That is, do not compare yourself with your companions, opening the way to judgement and its allied problems. Cf. Eth. Coll. 14.66—someone can be alone even in a crowd, provided he behaves as if he himself did not exist—and Syncletica 19.

ones. To keep silence, to live as an exile in the way defined by Sisoes and Poemen, is to avoid the difficulties of bad relationships without resorting to physical flight or literal exile. Community, dependent on good relations, can thus be maintained.

Silence, the answer to many difficult problems of relationships, is promoted in many sayings as something to be gained by effort and discipline. Agathon was said to have lived for three years with a stone in his mouth until he had learnt to be silent.[106] Arsenius said that he had often regretted speaking but never having been silent.[107] It is naturally preferable to be silent if you find no rest when you speak.[108] In Poemen's view if someone remembered the saying, 'By your words you will be justified, and by your words you will be condemned', he would choose to be silent.[109] But silence could also serve, in the same way as Lucius' exile, in an extended, non-literal way, as a virtue positively contributing to the possibility of good relationships within the community. Poemen again could say that someone who is apparently silent is really condemning others in his heart; by contrast, someone can be silent even if 'He talks from morning till night—that is, because he says nothing unprofitable.'[110] Poemen's own practice is consistent with this approach. A brother visits him during Lent, and tells him that he nearly did not come: 'I said, "Perhaps he will not admit me because it is Lent."'[111] 'We have not been taught to shut the wooden door,' Poemen replies, 'but the door of our tongue.' He thus teaches the necessity of silence and control of the tongue, but evidently silence does not impede his discussion about the brother's thoughts. True silence, the avoidance of anger, slander, judgement, and perhaps praise, does not prevent the conduct of good and necessary relationships.

6. Conclusion

The intention of this chapter has been to outline some of the ways in which the Desert Fathers discussed the question of 'solitude and

[106] Agathon 15. Carion 1 too shows silence gained by labour (though labour alone does not produce it in full measure).

[107] Arsenius 40.

[108] Nisteros 3.

[109] Poemen 42. Matt. 12: 37.

[110] Poemen 27; less developed, but implicitly similar views are expressed in Poemen 147 and N 237.

[111] Poemen 58.

interaction'—to what extent it is right to seek solitude rather than relationships with other people. In discussion of the *agape* and hospitality it was seen that these common elements of the monastic life were regarded as important, even though in some cases problematic occasions for interaction. The cell is seen as a place of private combat against thoughts, and spending long periods alone in it is a normal part of the monastic life. But only rarely, when the cell is viewed as a place of flight from inability to live properly with others, does it have a clear role in teaching on relationships. In discussing flight we have seen (in stories such as those of Arsenius and Archbishop Theophilus, or Poemen and his brothers) that a variety of criteria were applied to determine whether or not it was in order. Elsewhere, flight and solitude, though for some the goal of monastic training and an option to be chosen among the different available patterns of life, could be seen not as the aim of a perfect monk, but as something to be chosen for reasons—consciousness of his own inability to live properly with others—which reveal once again the concern of the Desert Fathers with the problems of bad relationships which were examined in Chapter 4. In the story of the brother and the water jug, and in the exchange between Longinus and Lucius, it has been observed that no one who had not learnt to overcome the passions of bad relationships could hope to live well even alone. It has also been suggested that the concepts of exile and even silence could be converted to serve as a shorthand for attitudes necessary as a condition of good relationships. None of these ideas suggests a clear-cut distinction between the life of the solitary and the more social figure. They reinforce the concern of the Desert Fathers with the value and proper conduct of relationships which was investigated in earlier chapters.

Nevertheless, this chapter must end on a cautionary note. Relationships remain difficult, however carefully they may be conducted. Isaiah again tells us that he was sitting with his abba, Abraham, when a brother came to ask Abraham how he should live with some brothers. 'Stay as if it was the first day of your coming,' said Abraham, 'guard your exile for the whole of your life, so as not to be free in speech [*παρρησιάζεσθαι*].'[112] He then told a story about his own master Agathon, who lived once with a brother (called Macarius) in the Thebaid. Agathon struggled to avoid being free in speech with the brother, treating him as a stranger.

[112] Isaiah, *Logos* 6, 5A (Agathon 1 is a shortened version).

Abba Macarius said to him, 'What is freedom of speech?' The old man answered, 'Freedom of speech is like a burning wind—when it blows, people flee from it, and it even destroys the fruit of the trees.' Abba Macarius said to him, 'Is freedom of speech so evil?' Abba Agathon answered, 'There is no passion stronger than freedom of speech, it is the origin of all evils. A hard worker must never be free in speech, even when he is alone in his own cell.'

The severity of Agathon's language amply witnesses to the Desert Fathers' awareness of the problems of personal relationships, and in particular the damage which sins of the tongue can do, both to the speaker and to those who hear.[113] Avoidance of these sins is a monk's first duty in all his relationships and should affect not only his outward behaviour, but (the end of Agathon's comment implies) his inward attitude and his conduct even when alone. Statements of principle like this, or the stories of Longinus and the brother and the water jug, have a good claim to be the most important thing which the Desert Fathers had to say about the dangers and the opportunities of the conduct of personal relationships.

[113] Agathon's attitude to *παρρησία* differs from that of Joseph of Panepho 1. See also Arsenius 38, Poemen 144, 184, Sisoes 5, for more positive uses of the word. In Pambo 14, N 592/53 (Evergetinos, 4.14.2.3) and N 622 (Evergetinos, 1.10.2.1), the term refers (positively) to confidence or freedom of speech before God.

6

Relationships and Prayer

1. Prayer and Hesychia

In the two previous chapters of this work the problem of the effect of relationships with others on a monk's own quest for rest and *hesychia* has been an important theme underlying some of the discussion. In Chapter 4 the suggestion has been put forward that despite sayings like Alonius 1 and Moses 7, Nilus 9 and Evagrius 2, *hesychia* and relationships may be compatible if it is only bad relationships involving anger, judgement, or praise which have an adverse effect on a monk's relationship with God; and in Chapter 5 it has been argued that a life of solitude (which allows scope for a relationship with God expressed in compunction and in prayer and ecstatic or visionary experiences) is compatible with the acceptance of a community life based on contacts with others through such means as the *agape* and the practice of hospitality. This is not to deny that the sayings referred to say what they do; but to claim that in the context of the Sayings as a whole they may be seen as only one, or as one-sided, viewpoints.[1] But the Desert Fathers' teaching on *hesychia* and prayer must nevertheless be examined in more detail.

The teaching of the *Apophthegmata* on prayer is not an easy subject to write about, for the text shows comparatively little sign of the overriding concern with forms of prayer and with the analysis of mystical experience characteristic, for instance, of some later Byzantine spiritual writings. The secondary literature on prayer in the *Apophthegmata* has, despite this handicap, concentrated on searching for teaching on con-

[1] See Ch. 4, Sect. 1, and nn. 58 and 107, and Ch. 5, nn. 27 and 38. It should again be noted that in Macarius 16, 27, 41, and Sisoes 37, or indeed in Alonius 1, no reason for the practice of solitude is given which would justify the view that these texts are essentially anti-social. Alonius certainly commends a single-minded devotion to God in labour (cf. Alonius 2, 3) and prayer, but does he exclude in principle that this *attitude* of devotion is compatible with an acceptance of good relationships?

tinual prayer and for signs of the use of short and often-repeated prayers such as, in particular, the Jesus prayer found, again, in later Greek works.[2] Our discussion in this concluding chapter will be concerned only to explore further the specific question of how, in the Desert Fathers' view, prayer and ecstatic experience fitted into a life which allowed for both solitude and interaction.

There are of course many sayings which refer to the importance of prayer in the monastic life or supply some explanation of its role, including some which stress the importance of continual prayer.

If God accuses us of carelessness in our prayers [εὐχαῖς] and waywardness in our psalmody we cannot be saved.[3]

When I was young and sat in my cell I set no limit to my office [σύναξεως]. Night and day were an office for me.[4]

These things are needed by everyone: to fear the judgement of God, to hate sin, to love virtue, and to pray [δέεσθαι] to God in everything.[5]

It is impossible to possess Jesus except through much labour, humility, and ceaseless prayer [προσευχῆς ἀπαύστου].[6]

These sayings are typical in their terminology and in their emphases. Other sayings follow their lead in stressing the importance of prayer and psalmody, the chief components of the *synaxis*, not only at set hours but at all times,[7] or in warning against lack of attention to the proper and regular praying of the *synaxis*.[8] Their inclusion of prayer in a short list of practices which make up the essence of the monastic life, or of virtue, is also typical; elsewhere a connection is forged between prayer

[2] Cf. K. Ware, '"Pray Without Ceasing": The Ideal of Continual Prayer in Eastern Monasticism', *ECR* 2 (1968–9), 253–61, and 'Silence in Prayer: The Meaning of *Hesychia*'. On formulaic and repeated prayers, cf. L. Regnault, 'La Prière continuelle "monologistos" dans la littérature apophtégmatique', *Irénikon*, 47 (1974), 467–93, reprinted in *Les Pères du désert à travers leurs Apophtegmes*, 113–39. On the Jesus prayer in Eastern monasticism, see K. Ware, 'The Origins of the Jesus Prayer: Diadochus, Gaza, Sinai', in C. Jones, G. Wainwright, E. Yarnold (eds.), *The Study of Spirituality* (London, 1986), 175–84; and for a discussion of its possible presence in the *Apophthegmata*, C. Wagenaar, 'Prière de Jésus et Sentences des Pères', *Collectanea Cisterciensia*, 46 (1984), 259–71.

[3] Theodore of Ennaton 3.

[4] Isidore 4.

[5] N 123.

[6] N 500 (Evergetinos, 4.5.2.56).

[7] Epiphanius 3; cf. N 104.

[8] See N 374 for an encouragement to struggle against the demons of boredom (ἀκηδία), discouragement (ὀλιγωρία), and complacency, especially at the time of the *synaxis*. On application to praying the *synaxis*, cf. N 395 (unpublished; see *Les Sentences ... série des anonymes*, 131) and N 435 (published as no. 398 in Nau's text).

and humility.[9] 'Do these things, and you can be saved,' said Benjamin, 'Rejoice always, pray continually [ἀδιαλείπτως], give thanks in everything.'[10]

One of the most articulate explanations of the importance of prayer in the monastic life is a saying of Agathon:

The brothers once asked him, 'Father, which virtue involves most labour among the different activities [πολιτείαις]?' He said to them, 'Forgive me, but I think there is no labour like praying to God. For always, when someone wants to pray, the enemies wish to stop him. For they know that nothing gets in their way except prayer to God. Whatever activity someone gets involved in, if he endures in it, he attains rest. But to pray requires combat to the last breath.'[11]

The difficulty of prayer is here pinpointed, and its role situated precisely in the combat against opposing forces in which a monk is directly engaged. 'How ought we to pray?' Macarius was asked.[12] 'There is no need to use a lot of words,' he replied, 'but stretch out your hands and say, "Lord, as you will and as you know, have mercy." And if the warfare is prolonged say, "Lord, help". He knows what is fitting, and has mercy on us.'

These comments, and other texts in which prayer as a cry for help or a confession of sin is prominent, show that for the Desert Fathers prayer is inevitably bound up with combat against the temptations which beset the monastic life.[13] A detailed intercession for one's needs is avoided; prayer, in Macarius' view, is an expression of surrender and trust in God in the face of a trial which could not otherwise be borne. 'I am sinking up to my neck in a mire and I weep before God saying,

[9] Tithoes 7, N 323 (cf. Ch. 4, n. 103, on the necessity of seeing yourself as inferior to others); N 323 ends with a call to continual prayer.

[10] Benjamin 4. 1 Thess. 5: 16–18.

[11] Agathon 9; cf. Theodora 3 for the temptation not to pray. Evagrius, *On Prayer*, 47, 48, 51, warns against the efforts of the demons to interfere with prayer. For prayer and psalmody as a weapon against the demons, see N 36; and against sin in general PJ 12.12 (Evergetinos, 4.8.10.14): 'To pray continually soon leads the mind to uprightness.'

[12] Macarius 19.

[13] Cf. the prayers for help or forgiveness quoted in Arsenius 3, Apollo 2, John Kolobos 13, Lucius 1, Sisoes 5, Sarah 1, N 16. These and others are cited by Regnault, 'La Prière continuelle', 472–3 (118–9 of the reprint) as examples of the short formulas and repeated prayers for which he is searching. Eth. Coll. 13.26, 42, 43, all contain the prayer 'Jesus, have mercy, Jesus, help me.' N 664 and 665 (labelled by Regnault J 696, 697; Evergetinos, 4.9.3.9–10, also PJ 12.4–5) are comments on (rather than examples of) the use of prayer in response to temptation, the latter stressing penitence: 'When an opposing thought enters your heart, do not try at that time to attain anything else in prayer, but sharpen the sword of tears against the warfare.' For short prayers, cf. Evagrius, *On Prayer*, 98.

"Have mercy on me." '[14] All these examples confirm Agathon's view that prayer is not easy; in his terms, it is not something by which a monk can easily expect to attain inner peace or rest, in the sense in which the other labours and practices of the monastic life may bring him rest in their own spheres.[15] As Antony too was aware, the 'great work [*ἐργασία*] of a man'—the work which requires most effort and is at the centre of the monastic life—'is to take his own guilt upon himself before God, and expect temptation to his last breath'.[16]

This aspect of the Desert Fathers' teaching on prayer has been stressed at the outset in order to indicate that their approach to the inner life of the monk, his relationship with God, is not always described in terms of the quest for *hesychia* and rest which has been referred to in connection with sayings like Alonius 1 and Evagrius 2. There is no reason to think that the teaching on prayer which has just been briefly described—the stress on attentive praying of the *synaxis*, the situation of prayer in a list of necessary virtues and practices of the monastic life, and the emphasis on short prayers of penitence and combat—in any way implies that a life of prayer and the proper conduct of relationships are incompatible in the way in which the more 'hesychastic' sayings noted might suggest. In fact prayer and the proper conduct of relationships are linked not only by sayings such as Tithoes 7 and N 323,[17] but also by a general comment on the necessity of a life oriented both to God in prayer and to our neighbour in good deeds,[18] and by several other points. To pray during a meeting with another person is an essential weapon for warding off slander.[19] Perhaps more significantly, since a

[14] Paul the Great 2.

[15] Again 'rest' (Ch. 4, n. 8) is an important goal, but its precise meaning remains elusive; Eth. Coll. has some sayings which see rest either as something obtainable in this life—given discernment (14.63), detachment from things (14.51), lack of concern for yourself (14.66), or other appropriate virtues (13.22, 14.4)—or as something properly reserved for heaven (13.51, 57).

[16] Antony 4. Agathon 21 shows however that the process of self-surrender in temptation can be seen as bringing rest: 'Go, cast your powerlessness before God and you will have rest'. Cf. Ch. 2, n. 59.

[17] Sisoes 13 (see again Ch. 4, n. 103), with its striking claim that 'It is no great thing' always to remember God, pursues the view of these texts further in the direction of concern with relationships. For 'remembering God', see John Kolobos 27, Macarius 36 (quoted below) and also N 377 (recommending continual awareness of the presence of God). For different views of the practice, see Regnault, 'La Prière continuelle', 484–6 (reprint, 130–2); I. Hausherr, *The Name of Jesus* (CSS 44; Kalamazoo, Mich., 1978), 158–65; and Ware, 'The Origins of the Jesus Prayer', 176–7.

[18] Poemen 160.

[19] N 502 (unpublished; see *Les Sentences ... série des anonymes*, 182).

monk's own prayer is emphatically a combat against demons, it must not, obviously, be allowed to act as a vehicle for the prosecution of bad human relationships. This is stated explicitly by Evagrius among many comments on the impermissibility of anger for one who wishes to pray.[20] In the *Apophthegmata* it is probably implied by a striking comment of Macarius: 'If we remember the wrongs done to us by men, we take away the power of remembering God. If we remember the evils of the demons, we shall be invulnerable.'[21] Despite the existence of 'hesychastic' sayings, the view is defensible that non-resistance to evil, avoidance of anger, and the pursuit of good relationships are essential constituents of a successful life of prayer.

With these very necessary reminders of the variegated nature of the Desert Fathers' teaching on prayer, spiritual combat, and relationships, we must however go on to discuss teaching on *hesychia* more fully. The view that contacts with others in general are a disturbance to a monk's inner life is expressed in a comment about John: 'When he came from the harvest, or from meeting the old men, he spent time in prayer, meditation and psalmody until his thoughts were re-established in the original order.'[22] The same strictness is perhaps implied by a saying on the need to purify the soul of alien things in order to pray.[23] John has lost something, a certain measure of achievement in the monastic life, through disturbance, and struggles to regain it by attention to the proper activities of the inner life.[24] His view is closely related to that of Evagrius 2 on the value of *hesychia* and the interference of relationships with it.[25]

But what then does *hesychia* mean, and is it in fact always incompatible with relationships? As indicated in Chapter 4, the word seems to imply

[20] Evagrius, *On Prayer*, 103 (cf. *Praktikos*, 23); that Evagrius regarded proper attitudes to others as essential in prayer, and indeed that he saw prayer for and with others as an essentially social activity, is amply illustrated by *On Prayer*, 13–14 (Nilus 1–2 in the *Apophthegmata*), 17, 20–2, 24, 26, 40, 42, 121–5.

[21] Macarius 36 (quoted by Evagrius, *Praktikos*, 93). Macarius' view may help to explain N 129: 'Is it good to adopt an attitude to one's neighbour?' The answer is, 'If you want to have an attitude, have it towards the passions.' On not using prayer to express anger against others, cf. Poemen 156 (Ch. 4, p. 119).

[22] John Kolobos 35 (a longer version adding an explanation for his conduct is found in PL, lxxiv. 365B–C; but this may be a secondary expansion); cf. Poemen 137 for disturbance or loss of rest caused by frivolous contacts with others. Poemen tells the brother to 'Be on guard inwardly, be on guard outwardly', that is, to pay attention both to the outward conduct of relationships and to his inward attitude to them. Cf. Ch. 2, n. 129.

[23] N 379.

[24] For meditation (on Scripture), see Achillas 5, Joseph of Panepho 7, and Hausherr, *The Name of Jesus*, 172–80.

[25] Cf. Antony 10 (Ch. 5, p. 155) for the same view.

one or both of two things, first, solitude considered in itself, and second, an inward disposition of freedom from disturbance.[26] These meanings, and other nuances, may be illustrated both from a number of sayings already referred to and from some new texts.[27] For our purposes here however, two texts are of special significance. In the first, *hesychia* clearly refers to an inward disposition of prayer or attention to God and of freedom from distraction, achieved through attendance at the eucharist. Isaac the Theban is described as 'possessing the *hesychia* of the holy offering':

When he came out of the church he used not to let anyone meet him, for he used to say that everything is good in its time. 'For there is a time for everything.' When the *synaxis* was dismissed, he used to behave as if pursued by fire, seeking to reach his cell. Often after the *synaxis* the brothers used to be given a biscuit and a cup of wine, but he used not to receive them, not rejecting the blessing of the brothers, but retaining the *hesychia* of the *synaxis*. It happened that he was ill, and when the brothers heard they went to see him. When they were sitting they asked him, 'Abba Isaac, why do you flee the brothers after the *synaxis*?' He said to them, 'I do not flee the brothers, but the evil action of the

[26] See Ch. 4, n. 12.

[27] Solitude (though not of course without some contacts with others): Arsenius 44, Poemen 90, N 224, 571, 573. In N 461 (Evergetinos, 4.5.2.36–8) the ruler of a cenobium withdraws (*ἡσυχάζειν*) from men for three weeks to pray; cf. Anoub 1. In N 538 (Evergetinos, 1.13.5.8) a hesychast is one who lives in solitude because of his awareness of the sins to which he is tempted by the world. In Antony 11 again the verb describes one who lives in the desert and is delivered from the warfare of 'hearing, speech, and sight' (but not from all warfare, so this does not necessarily contradict N 201). In Agathon 18 however the verb describes the inner calm which Agathon achieves through not judging. N 201 describes the brother as a 'hesychast in a cenobium' (cf. Eth. Coll. 14.4). Does this refer to his inner life, or mean simply that he lives in a separate cell but is dependent on the cenobium for his food etc.? I suspect the latter. In Arsenius 25 he claims that his *hesychia* (described as a possession of the 'heart') is disturbed by any outward sound or disturbance (cf. Poemen 155). Here clearly it is an inner disposition, but profoundly affected by outward circumstances—as in John Kolobos 25. In Antony 34 and Sisoes 28 the search for *hesychia* motivates deeper separation from others—relationships are in some way a disturbance. In N 622 (Evergetinos, 1.10.2.1) two brothers build separate cells and stay in them 'for the sake of *hesychia*'. Doulas 1 describes *hesychia* as a state which 'the enemy' tries to make us give up, and which with fasting is a powerful weapon against him. Here it may mean solitude, though it affects the inner life by training it for vigilance and warfare ('they make the interior eye keen'). Similarly in Theodora 3 it is something which 'the young' especially should cultivate in order to pray. In N 427 (Evergetinos, 2.28.7.5) *hesychia*, prayer, and fear of God are lost through jealousy of your companion's friendship with someone else. In Rufus 1 a brother asks what *hesychia* is and what is its value. It means, 'To sit in your cell with fear and knowledge of God, abstaining from remembrance of evil and from pride', and as such is the origin of all virtue. That is, *hesychia* could simply be a label for practices on which much stress was laid, namely living properly in the cell, and avoiding the effects of bad relationships with others.

demons. For if someone is holding a lamp, and stays standing in the open air, the lamp will be extinguished. Thus when we are enlightened by the holy offering, if we delay outside our cells our mind is darkened.' This was the way of life [*πολιτεία*] of the holy Abba Isaac.[28]

Isaac shares with Agathon the view that it is the aim of the demons to distract a monk from prayer—that prayer is, in effect, an extension of combat. But for him the maintenance of *hesychia* requires not merely vigilance against the demons but separation from the distraction of the *agape* and of contacts with others. As Moses said to Macarius, 'I wish to live in *hesychia* and the brothers will not let me.'[29] 'Abba Macarius said to him, "I see that you are kind by nature and cannot turn a brother away. If you wish to live in *hesychia*, go to the inner desert, to Petra, and live there in *hysychia*." He did this, and had rest.' Like Isaac, Moses chooses *hesychia* or rest and rejects the disturbance of relationships. But Moses himself was not renowned exclusively for his search for *hesychia*, but also for his kindness towards others and his willingness to receive them. This is shown not only by the saying about his hospitality during a week of fasting,[30] but also by the story of someone who visited him and Arsenius in turn, and found Moses welcoming and friendly, while Arsenius was silent and reserved, so that the brother found himself unable to speak freely [*μὴ εὑρὼν παρρησίαν*].[31] Here an old man prays to be told why it is that 'the one flees in your name, while the other is welcoming in your name'. He sees a vision of two boats, in one of which Arsenius is 'sailing with the Spirit of God in *hesychia*', while in the other he sees Moses with the angels of God, eating honey cakes.

Like some others this saying clearly expresses the view that *hesychia* is deliberately chosen as a way of life, and perhaps (in the old man's vision) suggests that it enjoys a reward different from or superior to that of other ways of life. But other sayings illustrate the view that several different ways of life were *equally* valuable. 'The saints resemble the trees of paradise—they bear different fruits but are watered by the same water. For the work [*ἐργασία*] of this saint and the work of that are different, but it is the same Spirit who works in all of them.'[32] Like

[28] Isaac the Theban 2. Eccles. 3: 1. *On Thoughts*, 2, is related.

[29] Macarius 22.

[30] Moses 5 (Ch. 5, pp. 149–50).

[31] Arsenius 38. In Eth. Coll. 14.65 Poemen, usually sociable, refuses to entertain some visitors in a friendly way: here his purpose is to convey a specific message.

[32] John Kolobos S 3 (Guy, *Recherches*, 24).

πολιτεία, which occurs in the story about Isaac, the term *ἐργασία* designates a particular way of life, or at least special activity, chosen by an individual.[33] Sayings of Poemen and Nisteros illustrate this most clearly. For Poemen to live in *hesychia*, to give thanks in illness, and to serve others in purity of thought may be described as 'one *ergasia*'.[34] For Nisteros hospitality, *hesychia*, and humility are equal activities all exemplified by different Old Testament figures. 'So whatever you see your soul desiring in accord with God, do that, and guard your heart.'[35]

Another story which illuminates ideas on different ways of life concerns Netras, who became bishop of Pharan.[36] He had followed a moderate ascetic regime in the desert, but when he became a bishop he started to be extremely severe on himself, commenting,

> In the desert there was *hesychia* and poverty, and I wished to look after my body in order not to be ill and have to look for something I did not have. Now in the world help is available. If I am ill here there is someone who will support me, and I will not cease to be a monk.

Netras' approach, based on his desire to be free of material cares and worry, is interesting as an example of how someone could change his way of life to cope with new circumstances and new responsibilities.[37] Again it is suggested that *hesychia*, whether meaning simply 'solitude' or something more akin to the attention and prayer of Isaac, is one of several ways of life.

There is thus certainly an element in the Desert Fathers' thought on *hesychia* which sees it and interaction as distinct ways of life, between which it is open to each to choose. One Abba Bane, known from the

[33] For *πολιτεία*, see Ch. 3, n. 61; also Poemen 68, N 284. 'Way of life' is usually a possible translation (as in Isaac the Theban 2 or in N 15), but sometimes seems too strong, hence the alternatives of 'virtue' or 'ascetic activity' which have been used. In Agathon 9 'activity' is clearly appropriate, as Agathon does not suggest that the different *πολιτεῖαι* of which prayer is one are exclusive of one another. For some comments on the term, see Hausherr, *The Name of Jesus*, 165–72. On *ἐργασία* as a special work, see also N 285. It too however may simply mean an activity or virtue, as in the case of Antony 4 and the 'interior activity' of Arsenius 9 and N 241.

[34] Poemen 29; cf. Ch. 2, n. 99, and Ch. 3, n. 10, for other sayings discussing different ways of life, esp. Pambo 2.

[35] Nisteros 2. John the Persian 4 uses Old Testament exemplars in a similar way, but here the point is that he possesses all the appropriate virtues.

[36] Netras.

[37] Apphy is a related text—though here the bishop was a very severe ascetic who tried to carry on with his asceticism among men and was unable to do so: 'In the desert there was no-one with you, and God supported you; now in the world, men support you.' Rousseau, *Ascetics, Authority, and the Church*, 64, is wrong to comment that Apphy and Netras became bishops 'with considerable misgivings'.

Coptic collection, gave up a life engaged in charity to others for that of a recluse, commenting that his previous activity was a 'profanation' compared with his life since his withdrawal.[38] This remark depressed some brothers who heard it because their own lives were not lived in seclusion—clearly they feared that Bane had condemned their life of interaction or service by his choice of life and his words; but Abba Abraham (who knew Bane) explained his behaviour differently: when he was charitable, he had not been able even to feed a whole village or town, but now, as a recluse, he was able to ask for abundance for the whole world, and to pray for the forgiveness of the sins of all.

These sayings—particularly those concerning Isaac, Arsenius and Moses, Netras, and Bane—all show that the question of solitude *versus* interaction was keenly debated by the Desert Fathers. This is a fact of significance which shows that the *hesychia* chosen by some was put to the test and justified—it was not taken for granted. Not all of these sayings imply that a life of *hesychia* is better than a life of interaction. In fact most of them go out of their way to avoid this suggestion, stressing the equal value of the two ways of life. Netras accepts that movement from one life to another is possible: with asceticism and freedom from care he will even be able to avoid losing what he has formerly gained. Even the story of Arsenius and Moses is not completely explicit in its evaluation of *hesychia* above concern for others.

But in any case, the fact that Moses was known both as a practitioner of hospitality and as a seeker after *hesychia* should warn us against thinking that these two ways of life were absolutely exclusive—as of course should the fact that even Arsenius' practice was far from consistently uninteractive.[39] Isaac's special way of life was recognized as requiring flight from contact in specific circumstances; but even he believed that there was a suitable time for everything and was willing to speak to the brothers when they visited him. Others teach more explicitly the possibility of praying when with others, even during the

[38] Ch 248–9.

[39] See Ch. 4, n. 19. Cassian, *Conferences*, 19.9, gives Moses as an example of someone who lived both the solitary and interactive lives to perfection. It is clear that the Sayings too are aware of the two aspects of his life; no purpose would be served by claiming that the various sayings refer to two different monks called Moses, for Macarius 22 itself proves that the same person could have a reputation both as a would-be hesychast and as one open to others. Moses 13 supports the tradition of his move to Petra and suggests that even there he offered hospitality. The idea that the various accounts of Moses should be divided between two monks of that name is rightly rejected by P. Devos, 'Saint Jean Cassien et saint Moïse l'Éthiopien', *Analecta Bollandiana*, 103 (1985), 61–74, esp. 70.

agape,[40] or criticize the search for a life of *hesychia*, in certain circumstances, as not being what the fathers recommended.[41] One of the most interesting sayings on prayer illustrates the successful union of continual prayer, manual labour, and concern for others into a single pattern of life.

When I spend the whole day working and praying I make about sixteen *numia*, and I put two of them by the door (the rest is for my food). Whoever takes the two coins prays for me while I am eating or sleeping, and so through the grace of God I attain continual prayer.[42]

Of these different comments on the relationship between prayer and interaction with others those about Moses ought probably to be regarded as the most significant. The two lives could be, as a matter of fact, combined. The semi-anchoritic life of Nitria and Scetis allowed each monk plenty of time for prayer, combat, and attention to the presence of God when alone in his cell for a day, a week, perhaps even on occasions a year at a time,[43] without preventing the importance of relationships in the monastic life from being recognized. Some sought a solitude deeper than was ordinarily available, or rejected contacts for the sake of *hesychia*; but both in the Sayings collectively and in individual units qualifications to teaching on *hesychia* are introduced: care was taken to show that other ways than the way of strict *hesychia* were valid; Moses was a master of both lives, open and kind to others despite his desire for *hesychia*; Arsenius protested his love for his companions;[44] Isaac was willing to explain the reasons for his conduct and denied that he was fleeing from the brothers. All these points illustrate the Desert Fathers' awareness of the need to defend the search for *hesychia* from

[40] Esaias 4: 'Be silent, brothers. I saw a brother eating with you and drinking as many cups as you, and his prayer was going up before God like fire.' Cf. N 85, for praying during the *agape*, and N 280, for praying while meeting others.

[41] N 413 (unpublished; see *Les Sentences ... série des anonymes*, 138).

[42] Lucius 1. The relationship between prayer and manual labour is referred to in various ways. In Antony 1 the importance of a regular routine of prayer and work is emphasized. In Apollo 2 we see someone who does not work but engages continually in penitential prayer. Paul the Barber 2 affirms that it is right to work at a trade during the day: 'The *hesychia* of the night is enough for us, if our minds are vigilant.' Abraham 3, John Kolobos 11, N 415 (unpublished; see *Les Sentences ... série des anonymes*, 139) illustrate or refer to prayer or contemplation (θεωρία) while working. *HL*, 20, suggests that Palladius believed in the value of a balanced regime of prayer, work, and contacts with others.

[43] Arsenius 17 may imply that for part of his life at least he would spend a whole year alone; cf. Sisoes 7.

[44] Arsenius 13.

the accusation that it implied a negative attitude towards others. It is the absence of qualifications like this which make Alonius 1 and Evagrius 2 seem so harsh and uncompromising in their choice of the hesychastic way. As has been noted already, it may be valid to apply the qualifications of the other sayings to these cases too.[45] But this is perhaps an undue attempt at harmonization; we should not deny in principle that the fervour of their desire for prayer and salvation led some to hold back from the corporate reality of monastic life. This too was a valid *ergasia*.

2. Ecstasy

Abba Lot came to Abba Joseph and said to him, 'Abba, as far as I can I offer my little *synaxis*, a little fasting, prayer, meditation, and *hesychia*; as far as I can I purify my thoughts. What more must I do?' The old man stood up and stretched out his hands to heaven, and his fingers became like ten flames of fire. And he said to him, 'If you want to, become entirely like fire.'[46]

Joseph is certain that the monastic life involves something that goes beyond the ordinary routine of asceticism and prayer—that the way is open for a monk who desires it to be caught up in a form of prayer that goes beyond the ordinary in its intensity, which in this saying is symbolized by the transformation of Joseph's praying hands into flame. 'I went once into his cell', said Abba Bessarion's disciple, 'and found him standing in prayer, his hands stretched out to heaven; he continued doing this for fourteen days.'[47] During his prayer Bessarion experiences a vision of the coming destruction of the pagan temples, which he feels compelled to relate to another old man whom he and his disciple visit for the purpose. It is convenient to use the word 'ecstasy', which occurs in a number of stories, to describe such intense or prolonged experiences of prayer or visions.[48] The metaphor of fire or flame which Joseph's story invokes is also found, with various different connotations, elsewhere. '"Our God is a consuming fire"', quoted Syncletica, 'so we

[45] Above, n. 1.

[46] Joseph of Panepho 7; cf. 6, and Sisoes 9.

[47] Bessarion 4. Two other sayings illustrating extended or intensive prayer may be noted: in Arsenius 30 he is said to pray with his hands outstretched for the whole of Saturday night (i.e. before attending the eucharist); in Xoius 2 he asks some drought-striken brothers on Sinai why they have not prayed for rain. They have. '"Then you certainly have not prayed with fervour; do you want to see that this is so?" Then he stretched out his hands to heaven in prayer, and immediately it began to rain.'

[48] Poemen 144, N 135, 211, 254, 622 (Evergetinos, 1.10.2.1); cf. *VA*, 82.

must kindle the divine fire in us with tears and labour.'[49] 'Is it not enough for you to have seen the fire', said Isaiah, turning an absent-minded failure to cook some lentils properly into a memorable saying: 'even this is a great comfort.'[50]

Some comments on ecstasy and visions must then be included in any discussion of the Desert Fathers' teaching on prayer. Though to some they may seem to lack reality compared with the practical nature of much of the Desert Fathers' teaching on relationships, they were taken seriously by the Desert Fathers themselves and remind us that they regarded the miraculous intervention of God in their lives as a normal and expected phenomenon.[51] As a part of the personal spiritual life of the monk, the desire and expectation of which Joseph encourages Lot to cultivate, ecstatic experiences may not, at first sight, be of any direct relevance to the conduct of relationships. The content of the vision received may of course be of profound value to those to whom the ecstatic monk communicates it; and we have seen already that visions both serve to warn about the future of the monastic community as a whole and form part of the resources which an abba uses in teaching.[52] But in addition to this, stories about visions, prayer, and experiences of ecstasy may also shed light, indirectly, on the quality of the relationships which exist among these involved in them. It is with this possibility in mind that this final section will ask what significance, if any, ideas on ecstatic prayer have for the Desert Fathers' understanding of relationships.

One of the simplest but most illuminating sayings for understanding the nature of ecstatic prayer and the attitude of the Desert Fathers' to it concerns Tithoes: 'Unless he quickly lowered his hands when he stood in prayer, his mind would be taken up. So if brothers were praying with him, he was careful to lower his hands quickly, so that his mind would not be seized and delay.'[53] Like the story of Bessarion this saying illustrates the extended and perhaps involuntary nature of the ecstasy which the Desert Fathers believed it was possible to enjoy.[54]

[49] Syncletica 1. Heb. 12: 29.

[50] Esaias 6; cf. Gould, 'A Note on the *Apophthegmata Patrum*', 137.

[51] Cf. Regnault, *La Vie quotidienne*, 223–37.

[52] See Ch. 1, p. 16; Ch. 2, pp. 42–4 and (for N 211) n. 117. Another interesting saying on visions is Olympius 1. Here a pagan priest tells a monk that those who have evil thoughts in their hearts do not see (*θεωρεῖν*) anything from God.

[53] Tithoes 1.

[54] In N 135, 211, 254, and 622 the visions recorded are all involuntary ecstatic seizures of the monk involved.

But Tithoes' attitude speaks for itself as an example of the concern of an abba for his relationships with others, even if we cannot easily probe exactly why he thought it was wrong to continue praying for long before them—perhaps it would be discouraging to those of lesser achievements, or would leave them feeling disturbed, worried about what was happening to their abba, or themselves unable to pray. Tithoes again was sitting with a brother by him, 'And he groaned without realising, for he was in ecstasy. So he made a prostration and said, "Forgive me, brother; I have not yet become a monk, because I groaned in front of you." '[55] Again, the activity of ecstatic prayer is bounded by the desire not to harm others.

'Abba Moses came once to draw water, and found Abba Zacharias praying by the well. And the Spirit of God was resting on him.'[56] Like the first saying about Tithoes, this text suggests that the prayer described is an experience of being taken up or of being overshadowed by divine power. Equally interesting is the fact that the divine favour enjoyed by one monk could be described as in some sense visible to another. Although not referring to prayer, another story illustrates this aspect of the Desert Fathers' teaching and shows what its significance could be:

One of the old men came into the cell of Abba John, and found him asleep. And an angel was standing by and fanning him. When he saw this he withdrew. When John got up he said to his disciple, 'Did anyone come while I was asleep?' He said 'Yes'—such and such an old man. Then Abba John knew that the old man was of his own stature, and had seen the angel.[57]

A variation on this pattern of behaviour and understanding is found in a story of Arsenius:

A brother came to the cell of Abba Arsenius in Scetis, and looking through the window, he saw the old man entirely like fire. (The brother was worthy to see this.) When he knocked the old man came out and saw that the brother was astonished. He said to him, 'Have you been knocking long? Did you see anything here?' He said 'No'. So he spoke to him and sent him away.[58]

[55] Tithoes 6. These two texts about Tithoes were probably transmitted together. John Kolobos 23 reports an incident similar to Tithoes 6, but contains no explicit reference to ecstasy.

[56] Zacharias 2. For the Holy Spirit as acquired by, indwelling, or accompanying a monk, see Cronius 1 (Isaiah, *Logos* 6, 3b), Longinus 5, Poemen 75, 136, N 241, Eth. Coll. 13.74. N 575 and N 592/39, sayings in which possession of the Holy Spirit depends on attitudes to others, were discussed in Ch. 4, nn. 106–7.

[57] John Kolobos 33.

[58] Arsenius 27. Another text involving someone being worthy to see someone else experiencing a vision is Ch 247.

In both of these cases, the accessibility of one person's ecstatic experience to another (not just the fact that one particular figure may have such experiences) is the significant point of the saying. John puts two and two together—the fact that a particular old man came, that he did not wake John but withdrew, not wishing to interrupt his experience—and concludes that here is someone who is his equal, who is himself worthy of the divine favour of seeing an angel. In the latter case the point of the discussion is more elusive; but the failure of Arsenius and the brother to discuss Arsenius' experience should not be seen as an indication that Arsenius regards the brother as an inferior (the *narrator* stresses his worthiness). Rather, Arsenius knows well enough that the brother has seen the event. What transpires is an example of a silent agreement, initiated by Arsenius with his worried questions but freely accepted by the brother, not to speak about what the brother has seen—a matter perhaps of humility or of the desire to avoid curiosity. It would not be an unjustified conclusion to say that both these stories witness to the promotion of good, understanding relationships between the different people involved.

Discussions and disclosures of the most personal experiences of prayer and contemplation are comparatively rare in the *Apophthegmata*,[59] and even where they occur a reluctance like that of Arsenius to speak of ecstatic or visionary experience is usual. In these other few cases however the discussion may be of significance in illustrating the quality of the relationship between an abba and his disciples which leads the visionary, however reluctantly, to relate what he has seen. Silvanus spoke of his vision of the judgement only when he was compelled to do so.[60] On another occasion when Silvanus was asked by his disciple (who had entered his cell several times during the day and seen him in ecstasy) to say what had been happening to him, he replied, 'I was ill today, my child.'[61] But his disciple does not accept this—'I will not let you go until you tell me what you saw'—and Silvanus confesses that he has been taken up into heaven and has seen the glory of God. A similar

[59] Cf. L. Regnault in his introduction to *Les Sentences des Pères du désert: Recueil de Pélage et Jean*, trans. J. Dion and G. Oury (Solesmes, 1966), 3: 'Tout le spirituel, de par sa nature même, échappe à nos investigations, et les Apophtegmes ne peuvent que nous laisser entrevoir les réalités de ce monde invisible dans lequel vivaient les Pères. Mais un éclair fugitif est parfois plus révélateur que des flots de lumière.' As an example of these 'flots de lumière' he cites Poemen 144.

[60] Silvanus 2.

[61] Silvanus 3: here, interestingly, the verb *ἡσυχάζειν* is used to mean simply 'to rest' or 'be at peace' after the end of his time in ecstasy, not to refer to the ecstasy itself.

story concerning Poemen was told by his disciple Isaac:

I saw him in ecstasy, and since I had great freedom of speech [παρρησίαν] with him, I made a prostration before him and besought him, saying, 'Tell me where you were'. Compelled to speak, he said, 'My thought was where the Holy Mary, the Theotokos, was standing and weeping by the cross of the Saviour. I wish I always wept like that.'[62]

In this case too, a story about the private experience of one old man serves to illustrate not only the high level at which he lives his own inner life (though he is aware, at the same time, of his inability to sustain the same quality of devotion at all times) but also his openness towards his disciple, who enjoys the privilege of hearing of such profound inward experiences. The 'compelled' of this text is applied to one who, unwilling to speak because of his personal humility, yet cannot avoid making known his own inner life to the disciple with whom he enjoys the closest of relationships—to the ultimate benefit, no doubt, of both.

These limited remarks on the teaching of the Desert Fathers on ecstatic prayer and on the physical transformations by which they sometimes represented it[63] have been made for a specific purpose. Throughout this work the aim has been to show that the Desert Fathers were profoundly concerned with the nature and the proper conduct of personal relationships. In this chapter it has been suggested that in some cases there was a tension between a life of prayer or *hesychia* and a life of interaction with others, but also that these two lives were not *absolutely* distinct nor of unequal value; that teaching on prayer almost always shows an awareness of its links with other virtues, and that it recognizes the importance of facing up to the accusation that the quest for a life of *hesychia* was anti-social. The sayings on ecstatic prayer which have been considered in this section help to reinforce this conclusion; they make it easier, perhaps, to believe that in the case of

[62] Poemen 144.

[63] Cf. Silvanus 12: 'One of the fathers said that someone once came to see Abba Silvanus, and when he saw his face and body shining like an angel, he fell on his face. He said that others too had this gift [χάρισμα]'; Pambo 12: 'As the face of Moses was glorified when he received the image of the glory of Adam, thus Abba Pambo's face shone like lightning, and he was like a king sitting on his throne' (cf. Pambo 1). In *VA*, 67, the author refers to Antony's remarkable physical presence, which meant that he could be recognized from among a group even by someone who had never seen him; the perfect state of his soul was reflected in his calm and radiant bodily disposition. In Arsenius 42 his disciple Daniel describes him physically in some detail, including the comment, 'His appearance was angelic, like that of Jacob.'

prayer too, the Desert Fathers were aware of the corporate, not simply personal, significance of their enterprise.

Ecstatic prayer is (in Joseph's view at least) the highest achievement of the monastic life; physical transformation is a *χάρισμα* given to great monks. These experiences are described with a sense of awe and fear, and with all due respect for a great monk's special receptivity to the visitation of God.[64] But they are not purely private; despite their strange quality, they do not remove the monks who receive them from the context of the ordinary life of their communities. Several stories of encounters with those in ecstatic prayer imply that it was also in some sense accessible and communicable to others, an occasion for recognition of their virtue or equality; that (in Tithoes' view) prayer must take explicit account of the presence and feeling of others; that the discussion of visionary experiences could be a proof of, and perhaps an occasion for the strengthening of, the relationship between an abba and his disciple. In all these ways, they help to show that, in prayer as in all else, the life of the Desert Fathers remained firmly rooted in the values and ideals of good relationships within the monastic community.

[64] e.g. the reverent account of Sisoes 14. As he lies dying he sees a vision of Antony, the prophets, the apostles, and finally Christ coming to him; here too there is a physical transformation: 'His face shone like the sun ... there was something like a flash of lightning, and the whole house was filled with a sweet odour.' A fitting final comment on Sisoes 14 and on many of the sayings on prayer and ecstasy which have been discussed in this chapter is found in K. Ware, 'Ways of Prayer and Contemplation I: Eastern', in B. McGinn, J. Meyendorff, and J. Leclercq (eds.), *Christian Spirituality: Origins to the Twelfth Century* (London, 1986), 395–6 (speaking in particular of Arsenius 27 and 30): 'Verbal "icons" are given of the human person at prayer, but usually there is no attempt to explain things in abstract argued terms ... There is a deliberate reticence here before the mystery of living prayer.'

CONCLUSION

The argument of this work has, as far as possible, been made clear in the preface and in the introductions and conclusions to the different chapters and sections. It has been intended to show that the teaching of the Egyptian Desert Fathers on the monastic life was profoundly concerned not only with such subjects as asceticism, prayer, and temptation, or with problems such as the place of monasticism in the wider Church and society, but also with the question of monastic community, or personal relationships within the monastic life.

Some will perhaps see this attempt to treat community as important to the Desert Fathers as an essentially apologetic attempt to gloss over their anti-social or individualist traits. It would certainly be wrong to deny that some Desert Fathers took more negative views about the value of relationships than others, or that the teaching of the *Apophthegmata* as a whole is marked by elements of contradiction which cannot in the end be reduced to harmony. In the first section of Chapter 4 this has been illustrated with reference to some sayings which, because of their emphasis on rest and stillness as goals of the monastic life, are pessimistic about the possibility of relationships with others. It was also pointed out, however, that in the general context of the *Apophthegmata* even these isolationist remarks may be seen as evidence, not of an absolute refusal of a sense of monastic community, but as reflections of an awareness of the problems of *bad* relationships (the Desert Fathers' views of which were elaborated in the rest of that chapter); and in Chapters 5 and 6 reasons have been given for believing that in the life of the majority of monks a balance between solitary and common life could be struck—for example through the practice of hospitality—even by those who were most concerned to emphasize the importance of prayer and *hesychia*. The case is intended to be cumulative—what is said about the corporate or social dimension of prayer and ecstatic experiences at the end of Chapter 6 would not of course establish that the Desert Fathers were as profoundly concerned with relationships as has been claimed, unless the evidence of earlier chapters had prepared the ground for this conclusion; in the light of these earlier chapters, texts on the social dimension of prayer fit into a broader pattern of concern with the shared experience of the monastic life.

The fact that personal relationships were the subject of such highly developed discussion is a more interesting discovery than, for example, the possibility that the views and practices of the community changed over time (a view which, in one particular form, I have criticized at a number of points) or that the attitudes of individuals differed widely, which they undoubtedly did. The complexity of the Desert Fathers' attitudes to personal relationships invalidates all simplistic attempts to see in the monastic movement a rejection of human contacts in the interests of a 'flight of the alone to the alone'—perhaps superseded, at a later date, by a rueful admission that community was an unavoidable necessity after all. Rather, the construction of a properly functioning monastic community, founded on good relations between individuals, must have been inherent in the goals of the Desert Fathers from the start. As Peter Brown writes,

> The overwhelming impression given by the literature of the early Egyptian ascetics, is that we are dealing with men who found themselves driven into the desert by a crisis in human relations. They came to analyze the tensions among their fellow men with anxious attention. They spoke about these with an authority and an insight that make *The Sayings of the Desert Fathers* the last and one of the greatest products of the Wisdom Literature of the ancient Near East.[1]

In this quotation, it is the fact that the Desert Fathers' concerns are seen as a response to the problems which they experienced in non-monastic society which is most distinctive of Brown's view. As has been noted in the course of this work,[2] Brown regards many of the Desert Fathers' positions on anger and related problems as a clear reflection of the frictions of Egyptian village life. The *Apophthegmata*, by showing what problems of relationships the Desert Fathers were particularly concerned to avoid, reveal which problems figured most largely in social tensions of the time. It has not been the purpose of this work to offer support to any particular thesis like this, which is in any case dependent less on gaining a complete understanding of the Desert Fathers' views on relationships than on capturing a sense of how particular points of their teaching, such as their emphasis on self-sufficiency through manual labour, would have struck (and appealed to) non-monastic contemporaries. Contemporaries, in Brown's reconstruction, were familiar

[1] *The Making of Late Antiquity*, 82.

[2] Ch. 4, n. 33.

with the attitudes of non-involvement and autarky considered desirable among independent small farmers of the time, and may be expected to have recognized and respected similar attitudes visible in the withdrawal of the monks from society.[3]

Some of Brown's arguments are open to criticism. The attitudes of the farmers he cites are not in any way ascetic, and the alleged links between them and the beliefs and practices of Christian anchorites may therefore appear tenuous; and it is difficult to know exactly how common the farmers' attitudes may have been. But Brown's observation is likely to be true at a general level; it is likely that the conditions of interpersonal conflict engendered by economic and social competition which the Desert Fathers left behind would have shaped to some extent the ideals of community which they embraced in the desert, even if there is very little evidence that any individual monk's initial act of renunciation of property and family to take up the monastic life was actually prompted by this rejection of socio-economic conflict.

What is important however is that this renunciation of society, this search for autarky and social 'death',[4] was not an individual quest like the self-determination of the small farmer. It did lead to the creation of a new community, a new social ideal, the ideal of the monastic centres of Nitria and Scetis which, loosely organized though they were compared with the cenobitic monasteries of Pachomius or later communities elsewhere, were far more than mere locations in which individuals lived mutually unrelated lives. In the relationships between their members and in the institution of the *agape* the communities possessed a means of cohering into an indentifiable group, the forum of an extended, community-wide discussion of the problems of the monastic life and the basis of a consensus on the relative importance of solitude and of relationships. In the teaching relationship the community possessed a means of renewing itself and of transmitting information about its history over the generations. In the *Apophthegmata*, first in oral and then in written form, the community bequeathed a corpus of memories and of insights which was to be the basis of the spiritual teaching of subsequent generations and new kinds of communities in Palestine and even (though this is not a subject which can be investigated here) in the West.

In Palestine, which current theories have indentified as the location

[3] Brown, *The Making of Late Antiquity*, 85–6.
[4] Ibid. 88–9.

in which the *Apophthegmata Patrum* emerged as a written document (or rather, originally, series of written documents), the fifth and sixth centuries saw a considerable flowering of monasticism centred on the region of Gaza and on the Judean desert.[5] The influence of the spirituality of the *Apophthegmata* on this process has yet to be studied in any detail, but its presence is illustrated by at least one source from the early sixth century, the sayings or *Dialogismoi* of Abba Zosimus.[6] Not only does this text quote from the Sayings at several points and refer explictly to the use of the '*Apophthegmata* of the holy old men' and to the delight of the 'blessed one' in reading them for the sake of virtue,[7] but Zosimus' own teaching shows marked signs of the influence of the *Apophthegmata*, particularly in his stress on avoiding praise and accepting blame for one's sins, and on obliterating any high estimate of oneself that would lead to a desire to retaliate when belittled or insulted by another.[8] Future work on other, more significant Palestinian sources than this small collection of reminiscences and sayings will no doubt reveal both the extent of the dependence of Palestinian monasticism on the *Apophthegmata*, and how this source interacted with others and with immediate concerns to produce the spirituality of the Palestinian movement.

But as has also been noted at an earlier point,[9] the *Apophthegmata* retain an importance which is not purely historical. One of the most important works of ancient Christian spirituality, they have also been prominent in modern enthusiasm for the ancient tradition and for a spirituality which is essentially practical in its goals. The *Apophthegmata* are the sayings of ascetics and desert-dwellers, and there is much which is alien to modern ideas in their teaching on demons, on sexuality, and even on relationships (for instance in their one-sided emphasis on the avoidance of anger, and on the obliteration of any concern for one's own feelings in situations of conflict); yet the Desert Fathers have proved their capacity to speak clearly even sixteen centuries after the

[5] Chitty, *The Desert a City*, 82–142; J.R. Binns, 'The Distinctiveness of Palestinian Monasticism, 450–550 A.D.', in J. Loades (ed.), *Monastic Studies: The Continuity of Tradition* (Bangor, 1990), 11–20.

[6] PG, lxxviii. 1680–1701; see Chitty, *The Desert a City*, 140.

[7] *Dialogismoi* 10 (1693C).

[8] *Dialogismoi* 5 (1685C–88B), quoting Moses 4; 7 (1692A), quoting Poemen 81. See also the quotation of N 343 (the story of the brother whose vegetables were rooted up by an old man as a test) in *Dialogismoi* 1 (1681B), though Zosimus sees this as a demonstration of the brother's detachment from possessions rather than of his endurance of ill-treatment as such.

[9] Ch. 1, n. 14.

hey-day of their communities. The reasons for this are not difficult to discern. The Desert Fathers placed no intellectual barriers in the way of understanding. They spoke to instruct and to warn, but also to encourage. They spoke with boldness about the harsh contours of an ascetic life of labour and endurance, but they spoke from experience, and whatever they may sometimes have said about laughter,[10] they spoke with a gentle humour formed by their intimate knowledge of many illuminating anecdotes about the great old men of the past.

The appeal of the Desert Fathers today confirms their effectiveness as teachers and communicators of the values of the monastic life. And the attractiveness of the *Apophthegmata* is a testimony to the Desert Fathers' wisdom in committing their message to the care of an oral and literary form which, alongside their teaching on the ideals of the monastic life, preserved so many finely drawn portraits of the individuals and of the incidents which made up the life of the community. It is this dual character of the *Apophthegmata*, as a text which is both the vehicle of an ideal and a means by which the historical life of the community is revealed in all its fulness, which makes the study of the text such an interesting enterprise. The defence of the theory of oral transmission of the *Apophthegmata* in the first chapter of this work, and the subsequent discussion, in which many narratives and stories have been analysed for their significance for the theme of personal relationships, are an indication of the importance which may be attributed to the historical as well as edificatory nature of the text. The character of the *Apophthegmata* as a witness to the reality of life in a monastic community is one of the factors which will ensure its continued popularity and fruitfulness as a resource for the study not only of the theme of community itself, but of many other aspects of early Christian spirituality as well.

[10] Ch. 5, nn. 19–20.

BIBLIOGRAPHY

TEXTS

Apophthegmata Patrum

Greek Alphabetical Series: PG, lxv. 72–440; additional material (S) ed. J.-C. Guy, *Recherches sur la tradition grecque des Apophthegmata Patrum* (Subsidia Hagiographica 36; Brussels, 1962, reprinted with additional comments, 1984), 19–36.

Greek Anonymous Series (N): N 1–392 ed. F. Nau, 'Histoires des solitaires égyptiens', *Revue d'orient chrétien*, 12 (1907), 48–68, 171–81, 393–404; 13 (1908), 47–57, 266–83; 14 (1909), 357–79; 17 (1912), 204–11, 294–301; 18 (1913), 137–46. N 132A-D (a small group falling between N 132 and N 133 in the manuscript) ed. separately by Nau in *Revue d'orient chrétien*, 10 (1905), 409–14. Unpublished material following N 392 available in translation in *Les Sentences des Pères du désert: Série des anonymes*, trans. L. Regnault (Solesmes, 1985). Some of the Greek texts not published by Nau are included in the eleventh-century anthology of Paul Evergetinos: *Εὐεργετινὸς ἤτοι συναγωγὴ τῶν θεοφθόγγων ῥημάτων καὶ διδασκαλιῶν τῶν θεοφόρων καὶ ἁγίων πατέρων* (4 vols.; Athens, 1957–66). The references are given in *Les Sentences … série des anonymes* (see Ch. 2, n. 12).

Greek Systematic Collection (GSC): unpublished; translation of material unique to this collection in *Les Sentences des Pères du désert*: *Troisième Recueil et tables*, trans. L. Regnault (Solesmes, 1976), 65–121.

Latin Systematic Collection (PJ): PL, lxxiii. 855–1022 as *Vitae Patrum*, bks. 5 and 6. For a list of variant readings, see O. Chadwick, *Western Asceticism* (London, 1958), 338–60.

Latin Collection of Paschasius of Dumium (Pa): received text: PL, lxxiii. 1025–62. Critical edition: *A Versão Latina por Pascásio de Dume dos Apophthegmata Patrum*, ed. J. G. Freire (2 vols.; Coimbra, 1971).

Collection of Abba Isaiah: *Les Cinq Recensions de l'Ascéticon syriaque d'Abba Isaïe, i. Introduction au problème isaïen. Versions des logoi I-XIII avec des parallèles grecs et latins*, ed. R. Draguet (CSCO 293; Scriptores Syri, 122; Louvain, 1968), *Logos* 6, pp. 27–81.

Coptic Collection (Ch): *Le Manuscrit de la version copte en dialecte sahidique des 'Apophthegmata Patrum'*, ed. M. Chaine (Bibliothèque des études coptes, 6; Cairo, 1960).

Ethiopic Collection (Eth. Coll.): *Collectio Monastica*, ed. V. Arras (CSCO 238–9; Series Ethiopici, 45–6; Louvain, 1963), vol. 238, 83–126 (text), vol. 239, 62–93 (Latin translation).

Other Sources

AMMON, *The Letter of Ammon*, in F. Halkin (ed.), *Sancti Pachomii Vitae Graecae*, (Subsidia Hagiographica, 19; Brussels, 1932), 97–121; also ed. J. E. Goehring, *The Letter of Ammon and Pachomian Monasticism* (Patristische Texte und Studien, 27; Berlin, 1986), 123–58.

ANTONY, *The Letters of Antony*, in *Lettres de S. Antoine: Version géorgienne et fragments coptes*, ed. G. Garitte (CSCO 148–9; Scriptores Iberici, 5 (text) and 6 (modern Latin translation); Louvain, 1955). Also in Latin in PG, xl. 977–1000, and in an English trans. based on other versions in *The Letters of Saint Antony the Great*, trans. D. J. Chitty (Oxford, 1975).

ATHANASIUS, *The Life of Antony* (*VA*), PG, xxvi. 835–976.

CASSIAN, JOHN, *Conferences*, in *Jean Cassien: Conférences*, ed. E. Pichery (3 vols.; Sources Chrétiennes, 42, 54, 64; Paris, 1955–9).

—— *Institutions*, in *Jean Cassien: Institutions Cénobitiques*, ed. J.-C. Guy (Sources Chrétiennes, 109; Paris, 1965).

EVAGRIUS of Pontus, *Praktikos*, in *Evagre le Pontique: Traité Pratique ou le Moine*, ed. A. and C. Guillaumont (2 vols.; Sources Chrétiennes, 170–71; Paris, 1971).

—— *On Prayer*, PG, lxxix. 1165–1200.

—— *On Evil Thoughts*, PG, lxxix. 1200–33.

—— *Outline of the Monastic Life*, PG, xl. 1252–64.

Historia Monachorum in Aegypto (*HM*), ed. A.-J. Festugière (Subsidia Hagiographica, 34; Brussels, 1961). Contains the text only: reissued with translation as Subsidia Hagiographica, 53 (Brussels, 1971).

HYPERECHIUS, *Sentences*, PG, lxxix. 1473–89.

JOHN RUFUS of Maiuma, *Plerophories*, ed. F. Nau (Patrologia Orientalis, 8: 1; Paris, 1912).

Life of Ephrem, PL, lxxiii. 321–4.

First Greek Life (G1) of Pachomius, in *Sancti Pachomii Vitae Graecae*, ed. F. Halkin (Subsidia Hagiographica, 19; Brussels, 1932), 1–97.

Sahidic Lives of Pachomius, in *Sancti Pachomii Vitae Sahidice scripta*, ed. L.

Th. Lefort (CSCO 99–100; Scriptores Coptici, 9–10; Louvain, 1933–4).

Life of Syncletica, PG, xxviii. 1487–1558.

PSEUDO-MACARIUS, *Homilies*, 51–7, in *Macarii Anecdota: Seven Unpublished Homilies of Macarius*, ed. G. L. Marriott, (Harvard Theological Studies, 5; Cambridge, Mass., 1918).

MOSCHUS, JOHN, *Pratum Spirituale*, PG, lxxxvii. 2851–3116.

On How to Live in the Cell and on Contemplation, ed. J.-C. Guy, 'Un Entretien monastique sur la contemplation', *Recherches de science religieuse*, 50 (1962), 230–41.

On Thoughts, ed. J.-C. Guy, 'Un Dialogue monastique inédit: *ΠΕΡΙ ΛΟΓΙΣΜΩΝ*', *RAM* 33 (1957), 171–88.

PALLADIUS, *The Lausiac History* (*HL*), in *The Lausiac History of Palladius*, ed. E. C. Butler (Texts and Studies, 6: 1–2; Cambridge, 1898, 1904).

SOZOMEN, *Ecclesiastical History*, in *Sozomenus Kirchengeschichte*, ed. J. Bidez (Die griechischen christlichen Schriftsteller, 50; Berlin, 1960). Also PG, lxvii. 853–1629.

ZOSIMUS, *Dialogismoi*, PG, lxxviii. 1680–1701.

MODERN WORKS

Note: this bibliography includes translations of early monastic writings which have been cited.

BAKER, D., 'St. Antony and the Biblical Precedents for the Monastic Vocation', *Ampleforth Journal*, 76 (1971), 6–11.

BELL, H. I., *Egypt from Alexander the Great to the Arab Conquest* (Oxford, 1948).

BINNS, J. R., 'The Distinctiveness of Palestinian Monasticism, 450–550 A.D.', in J. Loades (ed.), *Monastic Studies: The Continuity of Tradition* (Bangor, 1990), 11–20.

—— 'The Early Monasteries', *Medieval History*, 1: 2 (1991), 12–22.

BONDI, R. C., *To Love as God Loves: Conversations with the Early Church* (Philadelphia, 1987).

BOUSSET, W., *Apophthegmata: Studien zur Geschichte des ältesten Mönchtums* (Tübingen, 1923).

BROWN, P., 'The Rise and Function of the Holy Man in Late Antiquity', *Journal of Roman Studies*, 61 (1971), 80–101, reprinted in *Society and the Holy in Late Antiquity* (London, 1982), 103–52.

—— *Religion and Society in the Age of Saint Augustine* (London, 1972).

—— *The Making of Late Antiquity* (Cambridge, Mass., 1978).

BRÜNNER, H., 'Ptahotep bei den koptischen Mönchen', *Zeitschrift für Ägyptische Sprache*, 86 (1961), 145–7.

BUNGE, G., 'Evagre le Pontique et les deux Macaire', *Irénikon*, 56 (1983), 215–27, 323–60.

BURROWS, M. S., 'On the Visibility of God in the Holy Man: A Reconsideration of the Role of the Apa in the Pachomian *Vitae*', *Vigiliae Christianae*, 41 (1987), 11–33.

BURTON-CHRISTIE, D., '"Practice Makes Perfect": Interpretation of Scripture in the *Apophthegmata Patrum*', *SP* 20 (Leuven, 1989), 213–18.

BUTLER, E. C. (ed.), *The Lausiac History of Palladius* (Texts and Studies, 6: 1–2; Cambridge, 1898, 1904).

CHADWICK, H., *Priscillian of Avila: The Occult and the Charismatic in the Early Church* (Oxford, 1976).

CHADWICK, O., *Western Asceticism* (London, 1958).

CHITTY, D. J., *The Desert a City: An Introduction to the Study of Egyptian and Palestinian Monasticism under the Christian Empire* (Oxford, 1966).

——'Abba Isaiah', *JTS* n.s. 22 (1971), 47–72.

——'The Books of the Old Men', *ECR* 6 (1974), 15–21.

——(trans.), *The Letters of Saint Antony the Great* (Oxford, 1975).

DAUMAS, F., and GUILLAUMONT, A., *Kellia I: Kom 219: Fouilles exécutées en 1964 et 1965* (Cairo, 1969).

DEVOS, P., 'Saint Jean Cassien et saint Moïse l'Éthiopien', *Analecta Bollandiana*, 103 (1985), 61–74.

DIBELIUS, M., *From Tradition to Gospel* (London, 1934).

DODDS, E. R., *Pagan and Christian in an Age of Anxiety: Some Aspects of Religious Experience from Marcus Aurelius to Constantine* (Cambridge, 1965).

DÖRRIES, H., 'The Place of Confession in Ancient Monasticism', *SP* 5 (TU 80; Berlin, 1962), 284–311.

——'Die Bibel in ältesten Mönchtum', *Wort und Stunde I: Gesammelte Studien zur Kirchengeschichte des vierten Jahrhunderts* (Göttingen, 1966).

DONAHUE, C., 'The Ἀγάπη of the Hermits of Scete', *Studia Monastica*, 1 (1959), 97–114.

DRAGUET, R., 'Le Patérikon de l'Add. 22508 du British Museum', *Le Muséon*, 63 (1950), 25–46.

——'À la source de deux apophtegmes grecs (*PG* 65, Jean Colobos 24 et 32)', *Byzantion*, 32 (1962), 53–61.

ELLIOTT, A. G., *Roads to Paradise: Reading the Lives of the Early Saints* (Hanover, NH, 1987).

EVELYN-WHITE, H. G., *The History of the Monasteries of Nitria and Scetis*, vol. ii of *The Monasteries of the Wadi'n Natrun* (Metropolitan Museum of Art Egyptian Expedition Publications, 7; New York, 1932).

FREND, W. H. C., 'The Monks and the Survival of the East Roman Empire in the Fifth Century', *Past and Present*, no. 54 (1972), 3–24.

——'Town and Countryside in Early Christianity', in D. Baker (ed.), *The Church in Town and Countryside* (SCH 16; Oxford, 1979), 25–42.

——'Early Christianity and Society: A Jewish Legacy in the Pre-Constantinian Era', *Harvard Theological Review*, 76 (1983), 53–71.

FROST, P., 'Attitudes towards Blacks in the Early Christian Era', *Second Century*, 8 (1991), 1–11.

GOEHRING, J. E. (ed.), *The Letter of Ammon and Pachomian Monasticism* (Patristische Texte und Studien, 27; Berlin, 1986).

——'New Frontiers in Pachomian Studies', in B. A. Pearson and J. E. Goehring (eds.), *The Roots of Egyptian Christianity* (Philadelphia, 1986), 236–57.

——'The World Engaged: The Social and Economic World of Early Egyptian Monasticism', in J. E. Goehring, C. H. Hedrick, J. T. Sanders (eds.), with H. D. Betz, *Gnosticism and the Early Christian World: In Honor of James M. Robinson* (Sonoma, Calif., 1990), 134–44.

GORCE, D., 'Die Gastfreundlichkeit der altchristlichen Einsiedler und Mönche', *JAC* 15 (1972), 66–91.

GOULD, G. E., 'A Note on the *Apophthegmata Patrum*', *JTS* n.s. 37 (1986), 133–8.

——'Pachomios of Tabennesi and the Foundation of an Independent Monastic Community', in W. J. Sheils and D. Wood (eds.), *Voluntary Religion* (SCH 23; Oxford, 1986), 15–24.

——'Moving on and Staying Put in the *Apophthegmata Patrum*', *SP* 22 (Leuven, 1989), 231–7.

——'Early Egyptian Monasticism and the Church', in J. Loades (ed.), *Monastic Studies: The Continuity of Tradition* (Bangor, 1990), 1–10.

——'The *Life of Antony* and the Origins of Christian Monasticism in Fourth-Century Egypt', *Medieval History*, 1: 2 (1991), 3–11.

——'Lay Christians, Bishops, and Clergy in the *Apophthegmata Patrum*', forthcoming in *SP*.

——'Recent Work on Monastic Origins: A Consideration of the Questions Raised by Samuel Rubenson's *The Letters of St Antony*', forthcoming in *SP*.

GREGG, R. C. (trans.), *Athanasius: The Life of Antony and the Letter to Marcellinus* (New York, 1980).

GRIFFITHS, J. G., 'A Note on Monasticism and Nationalism in the Egypt of Athanasius', *SP* 16 (TU 129; Berlin, 1985), 24–8.

GUILLAUMONT, A., 'Le Problème des deux Macaires dans les *Apophthegmata Patrum*', *Irénikon*, 48 (1975), 41–59.

——'Histoire des moines aux Kellia', *Orientalia Lovanensia Periodica*, 8 (1977), 187–203.

GUY, J.-C., 'Remarques sur le texte des *Apophthegmata Patrum*', *Recherches de science religieuse*, 43 (1955), 252–8.

——'Note sur l'évolution du genre apophtégmatique', *RAM* 32 (1956), 63–8.

——'Les *Apophthegmata Patrum*', in G. Lemaître (ed.), *Théologie de la vie monastique: Études sur la tradition patristique* (Collection Théologie: Études publiées sous la direction de la faculté de théologie s. j. de Lyon-Fouvière, 49; Paris, 1961), 73–83.

——*Recherches sur la tradition grecque des Apophthegmata Patrum* (Subsidia Hagiographica, 36; Brussels, 1962; reprinted with additional comments, 1984).

——'Le Centre monastique de Scete dans la littérature du Ve siècle', *OCP* 30 (1964), 129–47.

——'Educational Innovation in the Desert Fathers', *ECR* 6 (1974), 44–51.

HALL, S. G., 'The Sects under Constantine', in W. J. Sheils and D. Wood (eds.), *Voluntary Religion* (SCH 23; Oxford, 1986), 1–14.

HAMILTON, A., 'Spiritual Direction in the Apophthegmata', *Colloquium*, 15 (1983), 31–8.

HAMMAN, A., 'Les Origines du monachisme chrétien au cours des deux premiers siècles', in C. Mayer (ed.), *Homo Spiritalis: Festgabe für Luc Verheijen, OSA zu seinem 70. Geburtstag* (Würzburg, 1987), 311–26.

HARDY, E. R., *Christian Egypt: Church and People* (New York, 1952).

HAUSHERR, I., *The Name of Jesus* (CSS 44; Kalamazoo, Mich., 1978) [a translation of *Noms du Christ et voies d'oraison* (OCA 157; Rome, 1960)].

——*Penthos: The Doctrine of Compunction in the Christian East* (CSS 53; Kalamazoo, Mich., 1982) [a translation of *Penthos: La Doctrine de la componction dans l'Orient Chrétien* (OCA 132; Rome, 1944)].

——*Spiritual Direction in the Early Christian East* (CSS 116; Kalamazoo, Mich., 1990) [a translation of *Direction spirituelle en orient autrefois* (OCA 144; Rome, 1955)].

HENRY, P., 'From Apostle to Abbot: The Legitimation of Spiritual Authority in the Early Church', *SP* 17 (Oxford, 1982), 491–505.

HEUSSI, K., *Der Ursprung des Mönchtums* (Tübingen, 1936).

HOLL, K., *Enthusiasmus und Bussgewalt beim griechischen Mönchtum* (Leipzig, 1898).

JONES, A., *Soul Making: The Desert Way of Spirituality* (London, 1986).

KAISER, M., 'Agathon und Amenemope', *Zeitschrift für Ägyptische Sprache*, 92 (1966), 102–5.

LAMPE, G. W. H. (ed.), *A Patristic Greek Lexicon* (Oxford, 1961).

LEECH, K., *True God: An Exploration in Spiritual Theology* (London, 1985).

LELOIR, L., 'La Bible et les Pères du Désert', *La Bible et les Pères, Colloque de Strasbourg (1er–3 Octobre 1969)* (Paris, 1971), 113–34.

——'Solitude et sollicitude: Le Moine loin et près du monde d'après les "Patérica" arméniens', *Irénikon*, 47 (1974), 307–24.

LIETZMANN, H., *The Era of the Church Fathers* (London, 1951).

LOUF, A., 'Spiritual Fatherhood in the Literature of the Desert', in J. R. Sommerfeldt (ed.), *Abba: Guides to Wholeness and Holiness East and West* (CSS 28; Kalamazoo, Mich., 1982), 37–63.

LUBHÉID, C., 'Antony and the Renunciation of Society', *Irish Theological Quarterly*, 52 (1986), 304–14.

MACKEAN, W. H., *Christian Monasticism in Egypt to the Close of the Fourth Century* (London, 1920).

MALONE, E. E., *The Monk and the Martyr* (Studies in Christian Antiquity, 12; Washington, DC, 1950).

MARKUS, R. A., *The End of Ancient Christianity* (Cambridge, 1990).

MEINARDUS, O. F. A., 'Historical Notes on the Lavra of Mar Saba', *ECR* 2 (1968–9), 392–401.

MERTON, T., 'The Cell', in *Contemplation in a World of Action* (London, 1971), 252–9.

—— 'The Spiritual Father in the Desert Tradition', in *Contemplation in a World of Action* (London, 1971), 269–93.

MURRAY, R., 'The Features of the Earliest Christian Asceticism', in P. N. Brooks (ed.), *Christian Spirituality: Essays in Honour of Gordon Rupp* (London, 1975), 65–77.

NAGEL, P., *Die Motivierung der Askese in der alten Kirche und der Ursprung des Mönchtums* (TU 95; Berlin, 1966).

—— 'Action-Parables in Earliest Christian Monasticism: An Examination of the *Apophthegmata Patrum*', *Hallel*, 5 (1977–8), 251–61.

O'NEILL, J. C., 'The Origins of Monasticism', in R. Williams (ed.), *The Making of Orthodoxy: Essays in Honour of Henry Chadwick* (Cambridge, 1989), 270–87.

PRICE, R. M. (trans.), *Theodoret of Cyrrhus: A History of the Monks of Syria* (CSS 88; Kalamazoo, Mich., 1985).

REGNAULT, L., 'The Beatitudes in the *Apophthegmata Patrum*', *ECR* 6 (1974), 22–43.

—— 'La Prière continuelle "monologistos" dans la littérature apophtégmatique', *Irénikon*, 47 (1974), 467–93, reprinted in *Les Pères du désert à travers leurs Apophtegmes* (Solesmes, 1987), 113–39.

—— 'Obéissance et liberté dans les Apophtegmes des Pères', *Studia Anselmiana*, 70 (Rome, 1977), 47–72, reprinted in *Les Pères du désert à travers leurs Apophtegmes* (Solesmes, 1987), 87–111.

—— 'Les Apophtegmes en Palestine aux Ve-VIe siècles', *Irénikon*, 54 (1981), 320–30, reprinted in *Les Pères du désert à travers leurs Apophtegmes* (Solesmes, 1987), 73–83.

—— 'Le Vrai Visage d'un Père du désert: Abba Jean Colobos', in E. Lucchesi and H. D. Saffrey (eds.), *Antiquité Païenne et Chrétienne: Memorial André-Jean Festugière* (Cahiers d'Orientalisme, 10; Geneva, 1984), 225–34, reprinted in *Les Pères du désert à travers leurs Apophtegmes* (Solesmes, 1987), 37–53.

—— 'Qui sont les Pères du désert?', *La Vie spirituelle*, 140 (1986), 183–97, reprinted in *Les Pères du désert à travers leurs Apophtegmes* (Solesmes, 1987), 19–36.

—— 'Aux origines des Apophtegmes', in *Les Pères du désert à travers leurs Apophtegmes* (Solesmes, 1987), 57–63.

—— 'La Transmission des Apophtegmes', in *Les Pères du désert à travers leurs Apophtegmes* (Solesmes, 1987), 65–72.

——'Aux origines des collections d'Apophtegmes', *SP* 18: 2 (Leuven, 1989), 61–74.

——*La Vie quotidienne des Pères du désert en Égypte au IVe siècle* (Paris, 1990).

——(trans.), *Les Sentences des Pères du désert: Nouveau Recueil* (Solesmes, 1970; 2nd edn. 1977).

——(trans.), *Les Sentences des Pères du désert: Troisième Recueil et tables* (Solesmes, 1976).

——(trans.), *Abba, dis-moi une parole* (Solesmes, 1984).

——(trans.), *Les Sentences des Pères du désert: Série des anonymes* (Solesmes, 1985).

——(ed.), with J. Dion and G. Oury (trans.), *Les Sentences des Pères du désert: Recueil de Pélage et Jean* (Solesmes, 1966).

RITTER, A. M., 'Statt einer Zusammenfassung: Die Theologie des Basileios im Kontext der Reichskirche am Beispiel seines Charismaverständnisses', in P. J. Fedwick (ed.), *Basil of Caesarea: Christian, Humanist, Ascetic* (2 vols.; Toronto, 1981), i. 411–36.

ROUSSEAU, P., 'Blood-Relationships among Early Eastern Ascetics', *JTS* n.s. 23 (1972), 135–44.

——'Cassian, Contemplation and the Cenobitic Life', *Journal of Ecclesiastical History*, 26 (1975), 113–26.

——*Ascetics, Authority, and the Church in the Age of Jerome and Cassian* (Oxford, 1978).

——*Pachomius: The Making of a Community in Fourth-Century Egypt* (Los Angeles, 1985).

——'The Desert Fathers, Antony and Pachomius', in C. Jones, G. Wainwright, and E. Yarnold (eds.), *The Study of Spirituality* (London, 1986), 119–30.

——'Christian Asceticism and the Early Monks', in I. Hazlett (ed.), *Early Christianity: Origins and Evolution to* A.D. *600. In Honour of W. H. C. Frend* (London, 1991), 112–22.

RUBENSON, S., *The Letters of St. Antony: Origenist Theology, Monastic Tradition and the Making of a Saint* (Bibliotheca Historico-Ecclesiastica Lundensis, 24; Lund, 1990).

SAUGET, J.-M., 'Une nouvelle collection éthiopienne d'*Apophthegmata Patrum*', *OCP* 31 (1965), 177–82.

——'Paul Evergetinos et la collection alphabético-anonyme des *Apophthegmata Patrum*', *OCP* 37 (1971), 223–35.

ŠPIDLÍK, T., *The Spirituality of the Christian East: A Systematic Handbook* (CSS 79; Kalamazoo, Mich., 1986) [a translation of *La Spiritualité de l'Orient chrétien: Manuel systématique* (OCA 206; Rome, 1978)].

STAROWIEYSKI, M., 'Remarques sur les sources de quelques Apophtegmes des Pères du désert', *SP* 18: 2 (Leuven, 1989), 293–8.

STEWART, C., 'Radical Honesty about the Self: The Practice of the Desert Fathers', *Sobornost*, 12 (1990), 25–39.

SUTHERLAND, D., 'Impassibility, Asceticism and the Vision of God', *Scottish Bulletin of Evangelical Theology*, 5 (1987), 197–210.

TUGWELL, S., *Ways of Imperfection: An Exploration of Christian Spirituality* (London, 1984).

VAN DER MEER, F., and MOHRMANN, C., *Atlas of the Early Christian World* (London, 1958).

VEILLEUX, A. (trans.), *Pachomian Koinonia* (3 vols.; CSS 45–7; Kalamazoo, Mich., 1980–2).

VON LILIENFELD, F., 'Anthropos Pneumatikos—Pater Pneumatophoros: neues Testament und *Apophthegmata Patrum*', *SP* 5 (TU 80; Berlin, 1962), 382–92, reprinted in *Spiritualität des frühen Wüstenmönchtums: Gesammelte Aufsätze 1962 bis 1971* (Erlangen, 1983), 1–13.

—— 'Jesus-Logion und Vaterspruch', in J. Irmscher (ed.), *Studia Byzantina* (Halle-Wittenberg, 1966), reprinted in *Spiritualität des frühen Wüstenmönchtums: Gesammelte Aufsätze 1962 bis 1971* (Erlangen, 1983), 14–29.

—— 'Paulus-Zitate und paulinische Gedanken in den *Apophthegmata Patrum*', *Studia Evangelica*, 5 (TU 103; Berlin, 1968), 286–95, reprinted in *Spiritualität des frühen Wüstenmönchtums: Gesammelte Aufsätze 1962 bis 1971* (Erlangen, 1983), 48–61.

—— 'Die Christliche Unterweisung der *Apophthegmata Patrum*', *Bulletin de la Société d'Archéologie Copte*, 20 (1971), 85–110, reprinted in *Spiritualität des frühen Wüstenmönchtums: Gesammelte Aufsätze 1962 bis 1971* (Erlangen, 1983), 86–113.

VÖÖBUS, A., *Literary Critical and Historical Studies in Ephrem the Syrian* (Papers of the Estonian Theological Society in Exile, 10; Stockholm, 1958).

WADDELL, H., *The Desert Fathers* (London, 1936).

WAGENAAR, C., 'Prière de Jésus et Sentences des Pères', *Collectanea Cisterciensia*, 46 (1984), 259–71.

WALTERS, C. C., *Monastic Archaeology in Egypt* (Warminster, 1974).

WARD, B., 'Spiritual Direction in the Desert Fathers', *The Way*, 24 (1984), 61–70.

—— (trans.), *The Wisdom of the Desert Fathers* (Oxford, 1975).

WARE, K., '"Pray Without Ceasing": The Ideal of Continual Prayer in Eastern Monasticism', *ECR* 2 (1968–9), 253–61.

—— 'Silence in Prayer: The Meaning of *Hesychia*', in M. B. Pennington (ed.), *One Yet Two: Monastic Tradition East and West* (CSS 29; Kalamazoo, Mich., 1976), 22–47.

—— '"Separated from all and United to all": The Hermit Life in the Christian East', in A. M. Allchin (ed.), *Solitude and Communion: Papers on the Hermit Life* (Oxford, 1977), 30–47.

—— 'The Spiritual Father in Orthodox Christianity', in J. Garvey (ed.), *Modern Spirituality: an Anthology* (London, 1986), 39–58.

—— 'The Origins of the Jesus Prayer: Diadochus, Gaza, Sinai', in C. Jones,

G. Wainwright, E. Yarnold (eds.), *The Study of Spirituality* (London, 1986), 175–84.

——'Ways of Prayer and Contemplation I: Eastern', in B. McGinn, J. Meyendorff, and J. Leclercq (eds.), *Christian Spirituality: Origins to the Twelfth Century* (London, 1986), 395–414.

WILLIAMS, R. D., *The Wound of Knowledge: Christian Spirituality from the New Testament to St John of the Cross* (London, 1979).

WILMART, A., 'Le Recueil Latin des *Apophthegmata Patrum*', *Revue Bénédictine*, 34 (1922), 185–98.

WISSE, F., 'Gnosticism and Early Monasticism in Egypt', in B. Aland (ed.), *Gnosis: Festschrift für Hans Jonas* (Göttingen, 1978), 431–40.

YOUNG, F. M., *From Nicaea to Chalcedon: A Guide to the Literature and its Background* (London, 1983).

INDEX

Names which occur only in the *Apophthegmata Patrum* are not indexed. Names of modern scholars are indexed only where there is a discussion of their views.